THE F.A. PREMIER LEAGUE

OFFICIAL PREMIER LEAGUE YEARBOOK 1992–93

THE F.A. PREMIER LEAGUE

OFFICIAL PREMIER LEAGUE YEARBOOK 1992–93

STANLEY PAUL
LONDON

Stanley Paul & Co Ltd

An imprint of Random House (UK) Ltd
20 Vauxhall Bridge Road, London SW1V 2SA

Random House Australia (Pty) Ltd
20 Alfred Street, Milsons Point, Sydney 2061

Random House New Zealand Ltd
18 Poland Road, Glenfield, Auckland 10

Random House South Africa (Pty) Ltd
PO Box 337, Bergvlei 2012, South Africa

First published 1992

**morrismen
productions**

Set in Frutiger and Concorde
Design/make up by Roger Walker

Printed and bound in Great Britain
by Scotprint Ltd, Musselburgh

A catalogue record for this book is available upon request
from the British Library

ISBN 0 09 177184 6

The Premier League and the publishers would like to thank
Action Images and Allsport for allowing the use of
copyright photographs

The players are listed under their current clubs at the time
of going to press (July 1992). Further transfers are therefore
not recorded

Frontispiece:
Eric Cantona scores for Leeds against Chelsea

CONTENTS

THE F.A. PREMIER LEAGUE

INTRODUCTION

Sir John Quinton
Chairman, The F.A. Premier League

Evolution or revolution? However it is seen, the prime purpose of the newly formed FA Premier League is to entertain. It has taken time, much attention to detail and forward-planning – and the support of an army of people, principally the member clubs – to set the stage for the new League and an exciting new era of English football.

The goal of the Premier League is excellence, both off the field where high priority is being given to ensuring the best possible facilities to bring our stadia into line with the best in the world; and on the field where we are striving for playing standards which will match anything in Europe, both at club and international level. By generating additional income the Premier League aims to help all of the clubs to implement the Taylor Report, and also to retain our best players in the face of increasing challenges from Europe.

The structure of The F.A. Premier League is based on one club, one vote. Management responsibility is delegated by the twenty-two club chairmen and representatives to an executive management team comprising myself and the chief executive, Rick Parry.

For the next three seasons, the Premier League will consist of twenty-two clubs with the usual promotion and relegation pattern of three up and three down at the end of the first two seasons. At the end of season 1994-95 there will be four clubs relegated to The Football League and two promoted, resulting in a Premier League of twenty clubs. This will bring English football into line with France, Germany, Spain and other major European countries. From season 1995–96, we will revert to three clubs up and three clubs down until further notice.

Interest in the game has not been so great for the past two decades. The future looks bright and we must go forward and build the Premier League together.

The image of English football both on and off the field has been much improved in recent seasons, and with the creation of the Premier League I for one believe that the prospects for the game have never been better.

The Premier League brings exciting new possibilities to the game, with greater commercial opportunities to help provide the funding which can enhance English football at all levels.

There is considerable expectation that by establishing an 'elite', the football authorities and leading clubs will have the chance to promote excellence in quality of play and sportsmanship, and to provide improved facilities for those who pay to watch the game.

With the new financial rewards available there are many people who hope that the money will not simply be used to fuel the transfer markets, but will instead be reinvested in the game at every level.

Fans' loyalty deserves the reward of safe, comfortable and affordable facilities, as well as success on the field. The tragedies of recent years – Heysel, Hillsborough and Bradford – cannot, will not, be forgotten. It is our duty to ensure that the game is played in this country in stadia which meet the highest criteria of safety and comfort.

Equally, continuing success relies on the nurturing of new talent, and some of the commercial rewards in the new age of football should support a framework which both encourages and sustains the players of tomorrow.

With the creation of the Premier League, the English game has an ideal opportunity to achieve these goals.

I wish the Premier League well, for nobody wants to see attractive, successful English football more than I.

Rt Hon David Mellor, QC, MP
Secretary of State for National Heritage
July 1992

Premier League Officers

Chairman: Sir John Quinton
Chief Executive: Rick Parry
Secretary: Mike Foster
Assistant Secretary: Adrian Cook

I have to confess that when I first heard about the possible formation of a premier league based on a whole new set of ideas, I was tempted to get a little bit excited!

After all my years in management I had come to the view that the system in this country was in need of a radical overhaul. Major changes were needed to revitalise the game and take it into the twenty-first century. As chairman of the League Managers' Association, I'd had many discussions with managers from all levels of football, which only served to harden that view.

With publication of the Blueprint, fact eventually replaced rumour. As you would expect there were areas with which one could argue. However, the notion that quality at all levels was to be the basis for any future changes, was seen as manna from heaven by anyone who claimed to have the best interests of the game at heart.

A great deal of idealism that encompassed many of those early proposals has evaporated but, nevertheless, we are about to embark on a new era, and the spirit of change is blowing through the game.

'Quality and quantity' – say them quickly and they sound nearly the same whereas, in fact, they are a million miles apart. I earnestly hope that whenever and whatever policy matters are discussed, the interested parties have the wisdom and courage to put aside personal differences and vested interests and cast their vote for football. The Premier League is the flagship for football in this country – we have to ensure its captaincy and its course are beyond question.

Howard Wilkinson
Manager
Leeds United AFC
July 1992

TIMETABLE THAT MADE HISTORY

by Rick Parry

There cannot have been a more momentous year in the history of football. After one hundred years of Football League control, the Football Association in April 1991 announced the formation of a new Premier League with the expressed intention of benefiting the future of the game and the England team.

The giant steps forward taken in those twelve months may be forgotten or underestimated, so here for the record is the timetable of events.

APRIL 1991: The Football Association called all the First Division clubs together in secret to outline the concept of the new Football Association Premier League. The plan was presented by Graham Kelly, the chief executive, and Charles Hughes, the director of coaching. At that stage I was a consultant to the FA.

Within days the plan went before the FA Council and the idea in principle was given their blessing.

MAY 1991: The first formal meeting between all the clubs and the FA took place on 12 May with the aim of establishing the clubs' approval of the new League. The FA were pressing for a reduction to an 18-club League but the clubs saw 20 as a compromise.

JUNE 1991: I chaired the first meeting of the First Division clubs. The meeting lasted just three hours but more constitutional changes were agreed than in the previous century of English football. This gathering in London was the cornerstone, the foundation, of the Premier League.

A skeleton constitution was drawn up which remained in tact during the next twelve months of debate and controversy. It was a simple one club, one vote system with a two-thirds majority needed for a proposal to succeed. There was to be an independent chairman and a chief executive. Gone were the days of management committees or any committees at all. This League was not to be dominated by self-interest.

There was also immediate agreement on the distribution of television income, which eleven months later, was to outstrip all expectations. Half the money is split equally, 25 per cent is distributed in facility fees and the remaining 25 per cent on a ladder basis – the higher a club finishes in the League the more money it receives.

The clubs also decided that they would offer their resignations to the Football League *en bloc* and become the pioneers in the new era for the sport.

JULY 1991: The Football League began a High Court action to try to prevent the breakaway and the formation of the Premier League. For a month the game was entangled in legal battles and no progress could be made.

At the Premier League we tried hard to persuade the Football League not to take the litigation route, but they were determined and consequently lost the costly case.

As expected Justice Rose announced to the High Court that the FA, despite the League's pro-tests, did have the powers, as the highest body in the land, to create and run any competition it wished.

AUGUST 1991: The League announced they were to contest the court decision with an appeal. On the very eve of the new season the League became unmanageable after the First Division represent-atives were told they were no longer able to serve on the Manage-ment Committee. The Management Committee collapsed in chaos after a meeting at the Gosforth Park Hotel, outside Newcastle, and the League announced they would call in an administrator to allow day-to-day business to continue.

Later that day, 13 August – a Friday – I delivered the notice to quit of all 22 First Division clubs, giving the mandatory three-year notice. The League kicked off on 14 August.

SEPTEMBER 1991: Negotiations with the remaining League clubs continued until agreement on criteria for grounds and promotion and relegation as well as financial conditions was reached on 23 September at a League EGM. In return the League dropped the need for the Premier League clubs to give three years' notice to quit and agreed that the new competition could begin within a year.

It had always been the intention of the Premier League to negotiate rather than dictate to the other clubs in the Football League because we felt that there was scope for a vibrant, repackaged new League. This has been born out by the television and sponsorship deals the League has negotiated. No one wanted to dump the Football League and leave it without a viable future. It was always the Premier League's desire to ensure that the Football League was no worse off in the new footballing world. The Premier League needs a strong Football League existing alongside.

OCTOBER 1991: Down to work! Task forces and working parties were set up to handle the vast amount of preparation that was needed for the new League. They covered commercial aspects, rules, players and, importantly, the relationship with the FA. On 10 October I was asked to take on the role of chief executive until May 1992.

DECEMBER 1991: Sir John Quinton, a respected figure not only in the City but also in football, was asked by the clubs, at their meeting in Nottingham, to be the independent chairman.

FEBRUARY 1992: The FA Council finally gave its backing to the new League. It was agreed that the Premier League would be a limited company outside the FA rather than a committee of the FA.

The matter had been deferred, disappointingly, at the Council's January meeting but now, having studied the aims, objectives and structure of the new League, they gave it their approval – another historic moment in a year of change.

Every club had a single share in the new Premier League but the FA would have a special share that gave them the power of veto which prevented changes in the League's direction that were contrary to the FA's objectives.

MARCH 1992: When one problem was solved another, inevitably, reared its head. The Professional Footballers' Association were demanding a greater voice in the running of the League as well as a greater share of the television revenue.

There had been open threats of strike action since before Christmas but we were always confident that a negotiated settlement was possible with the PFA.

By the end of March the matter had been nailed down to a question of money. Within the confines of the new League, the PFA had their voice and other important issues such as pensions were guaranteed. What had not been agreed was the money aspect. Talks took place in Manchester and London in an attempt to break the deadlock while the PFA sent out strike ballot papers.

APRIL 1992: A solution to the PFA crisis was found in a formula that gave the players' union a greater slice of the television cake. The subsequent deal, agreed one month later with BSkyB and the BBC, will generate £2.5 million for the players, compared with the £500,000 they received in the 1991–92 season.

The ballot results backed strike action but fortunately at the eleventh hour, a negotiated peace was possible to prevent what would have been the first strike in British football history.

MAY 1992: Another momentous month for the Premier League. We negotiated the biggest television deal in British sporting history with BSkyB and the BBC. It was worth a staggering £304 million and involved the screening of up to 60 live matches a season on BSkyB with the return of the popular BBC 'Match of the Day' programme on Saturday nights.

After months of negotiations we felt that we had achieved a television deal that was visionary rather than mercenary, and that television was at last entering into a partnership with football rather than taking it over.

The deal was signed on 18 May and although ITV appealed to the High Court on 26 May claiming that the deal should be nullified because of an alleged 'breach of confidentiality', the judge overwhelmingly ruled in favour of the Premier League's right to sign a deal with BSkyB and the BBC.

In June 1992, Rick Parry accepted a three-year contract as Premier League chief executive.

PREMIER LEAGUE FIXTURES FOR SEASON 1992-93

Saturday, 15 August, 1992
Arsenal v Norwich City
Chelsea v Oldham Athletic
Coventry City v Middlesbrough
Crystal Palace v Blackburn Rovers
Everton v Sheffield Wednesday
Ipswich Town v Aston Villa
Leeds United v Wimbledon
Sheffield United v Manchester United
Southampton v Tottenham Hotspur

Sunday, 16 August, 1992
Nottingham Forest v Liverpool

Monday, 17 August, 1992
Manchester City v Queen's Park Rangers

Tuesday, 18 August, 1992
Blackburn Rovers v Arsenal
Wimbledon v Ipswich Town

Wednesday, 19 August, 1992
Aston Villa v Leeds United
Liverpool v Sheffield United
Manchester United v Everton
Middlesbrough v Manchester City
Norwich City v Chelsea
Oldham Athletic v Crystal Palace
Queen's Park Rangers v Southampton
Sheffield Wednesday v Nottingham Forest
Tottenham Hotspur v Coventry City

Saturday, 22 August, 1992
Aston Villa v Southampton
Blackburn Rovers v Manchester City
Manchester United v Ipswich Town
Middlesbrough v Leeds United
Norwich City v Everton
Oldham Athletic v Nottingham Forest
Queen's Park Rangers v Sheffield United
Sheffield Wednesday v Chelsea
Tottenham Hotspur v Crystal Palace
Wimbledon v Coventry City

Sunday, 23 August, 1992
Liverpool v Arsenal

Monday, 24 August, 1992
Southampton v Manchester United

Tuesday, 25 August, 1992
Crystal Palace v Sheffield Wednesday
Everton v Aston Villa
Ipswich Town v Liverpool
Leeds United v Tottenham Hotspur
Sheffield United v Wimbledon

Wednesday, 26 August, 1992
Arsenal v Oldham Athletic
Chelsea v Blackburn Rovers
Coventry City v Queen's Park Rangers
Manchester City v Norwich City

Saturday, 29 August, 1992
Arsenal v Sheffield Wednesday
Chelsea v Queen's Park Rangers
Coventry City v Blackburn Rovers
Crystal Palace v Norwich City
Everton v Wimbledon
Leeds United v Liverpool
Manchester City v Oldham Athletic
Nottingham Forest v Manchester United
Sheffield United v Aston Villa
Southampton v Middlesbrough

Sunday, 30 August, 1992
Ipswich Town v Tottenham Hotspur

Monday, 31 August, 1992
Norwich City v Nottingham Forest

Tuesday, 1 September, 1992
Liverpool v Southampton
Middlesbrough v Ipswich Town
Oldham Athletic v Leeds United
Wimbledon v Manchester City

Wednesday, 2 September, 1992
Aston Villa v Chelsea
Manchester United v Crystal Palace
Queen's Park Rangers v Arsenal
Sheffield Wednesday v Coventry City
Tottenham Hotspur v Sheffield United

Saturday, 5 September, 1992
Aston Villa v Crystal Palace
Blackburn Rovers v Nottingham Forest
Liverpool v Chelsea
Norwich City v Southampton
Oldham Athletic v Coventry City
Queen's Park Rangers v Ipswich Town
Sheffield Wednesday v Manchester City
Tottenham Hotspur v Everton
Wimbledon v Arsenal

Sunday, 6 September, 1992
Manchester United v Leeds United

Monday, 7 September, 1992
Middlesbrough v Sheffield United

Saturday, 12 September, 1992
Arsenal v Blackburn Rovers
Chelsea v Norwich City
Crystal Palace v Oldham Athletic
Everton v Manchester United
Ipswich Town v Wimbledon
Manchester City v Middlesbrough
Nottingham Forest v Sheffield Wednesday
Sheffield United v Liverpool
Southampton v Queen's Park Rangers

Sunday, 13 September, 1992
Leeds United v Aston Villa

Monday, 14 September, 1992
Coventry City v Tottenham Hotspur

Tuesday, 15 September, 1992
Blackburn Rovers v Everton

Saturday, 19 September, 1992
Aston Villa v Liverpool
Everton v Crystal Palace
Norwich City v Sheffield Wednesday
Nottingham Forest v Coventry City
Oldham Athletic v Ipswich Town
Queen's Park Rangers v Middlesbrough
Sheffield United v Arsenal
Southampton v Leeds United
Tottenham Hotspur v Manchester United
Wimbledon v Blackburn Rovers

Sunday, 20 September, 1992
Manchester City v Chelsea

Saturday, 26 September, 1992
Blackburn Rovers v Oldham Athletic
Chelsea v Nottingham Forest
Coventry City v Norwich City
Crystal Palace v Southampton
Ipswich Town v Sheffield United
Leeds United v Everton
Liverpool v Wimbledon
Manchester United v Queen's Park Rangers
Middlesbrough v Aston Villa

Sunday, 27 September, 1992
Sheffield Wednesday v Tottenham Hotspur

Monday, 28 September, 1992
Arsenal v Manchester City

Saturday, 3 October, 1992
Arsenal v Chelsea
Blackburn Rovers v Norwich City

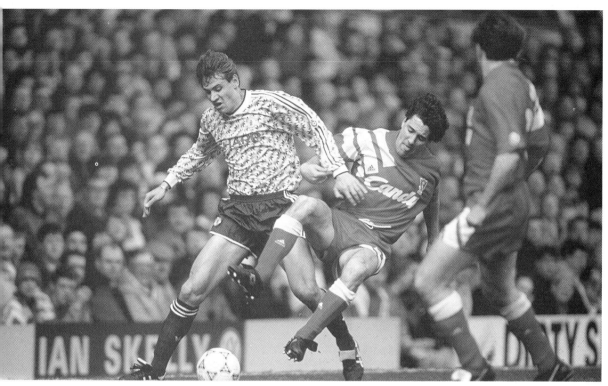

Manchester United's Andrei Kanchelskis tries to shake off Dean Saunders of Liverpool

Coventry City v Crystal Palace
Ipswich Town v Leeds United
Liverpool v Sheffield Wednesday
Manchester City v Nottingham Forest
Middlesbrough v Manchester United
Queen's Park Rangers v Tottenham Hotspur
Sheffield United v Southampton
Wimbledon v Aston Villa

Sunday, 4 October, 1992
Oldham Athletic v Everton

Saturday, 17 October, 1992
Chelsea v Ipswich Town
Crystal Palace v Manchester City
Everton v Coventry City
Leeds United v Sheffield United
Norwich City v Queen's Park Rangers
Nottingham Forest v Arsenal
Sheffield Wednesday v Oldham Athletic
Southampton v Wimbledon
Tottenham Hotspur v Middlesbrough

Sunday, 18 October, 1992
Manchester United v Liverpool

Monday, 19 October, 1992
Aston Villa v Blackburn Rovers

Wednesday, 21 October, 1992
Nottingham Forest v Middlesborough

Saturday, 24 October, 1992
Arsenal v Everton
Blackburn Rovers v Manchester United
Coventry City v Chelsea
Ipswich Town v Crystal Palace
Liverpool v Norwich City
Manchester City v Southampton
Middlesbrough v Sheffield Wednesday
Oldham Athletic v Aston Villa
Queen's Park Rangers v Leeds United
Sheffield United v Nottingham Forest

Sunday, 25 October, 1992
Wimbledon v Tottenham Hotspur

Saturday, 31 October, 1992
Chelsea v Sheffield United
Everton v Manchester City
Leeds United v Coventry City
Manchester United v Wimbledon
Norwich City v Middlesbrough
Nottingham Forest v Ipswich Town
Sheffield Wednesday v Blackburn Rovers
Southampton v Oldham Athletic
Tottenham Hotspur v Liverpool

Sunday, 1 November, 1992
Aston Villa v Queen's Park Rangers

Monday, 2 November, 1992
Crystal Palace v Arsenal

Saturday, 7 November, 1992
Arsenal v Coventry City
Aston Villa v Manchester United
Blackburn Rovers v Tottenham Hotspur
Chelsea v Crystal Palace
Ipswich Town v Southampton
Liverpool v Middlesbrough
Manchester City v Leeds United
Nottingham Forest v Everton
Oldham Athletic v Norwich City
Wimbledon v Queen's Park Rangers

Sunday, 8 November, 1992
Sheffield United v Sheffield Wednesday

Saturday, 21 November, 1992
Coventry City v Manchester City
Crystal Palace v Nottingham Forest
Everton v Chelsea
Leeds United v Arsenal
Manchester United v Oldham Athletic
Middlesbrough v Wimbledon
Norwich City v Sheffield United
Sheffield Wednesday v Ipswich Town
Southampton v Blackburn Rovers
Tottenham Hotspur v Aston Villa

Monday, 23 November, 1992
Queen's Park Rangers v Liverpool

Saturday, 28 November, 1992
Arsenal v Manchester United
Aston Villa v Norwich City
Blackburn Rovers v Queen's Park Rangers
Chelsea v Leeds United
Ipswich Town v Everton
Liverpool v Crystal Palace
Manchester City v Tottenham Hotspur
Nottingham Forest v Southampton
Oldham Athletic v Middlesbrough
Sheffield United v Coventry City
Wimbledon v Sheffield Wednesday

Saturday, 5 December, 1992
Coventry City v Ipswich Town
Crystal Palace v Sheffield United
Leeds United v Nottingham Forest
Manchester United v Manchester City
Middlesbrough v Blackburn Rovers
Norwich City v Wimbledon
Queen's Park Rangers v Oldham Athletic
Sheffield Wednesday v Aston Villa
Southampton v Arsenal
Tottenham Hotspur v Chelsea

Monday 7 December, 1992
Everton v Liverpool

Saturday, 12 December, 1992
Aston Villa v Nottingham Forest
Ipswich Town v Manchester City
Leeds United v Sheffield Wednesday
Liverpool v Blackburn Rovers
Manchester United v Norwich City
Middlesbrough v Chelsea
Queen's Park Rangers v Crystal Palace
Sheffield United v Everton
Southampton v Coventry City
Tottenham Hotspur v Arsenal
Wimbledon v Oldham Athletic

Saturday, 19 December, 1992
Arsenal v Middlesbrough
Blackburn Rovers v Sheffield United
Chelsea v Manchester United
Coventry City v Liverpool
Crystal Palace v Leeds United
Everton v Southampton
Manchester City v Aston Villa
Oldham Athletic v Tottenham Hotspur
Sheffield Wednesday v Queen's Park Rangers

Sunday, 20 December, 1992
Nottingham Forest v Wimbledon

Monday, 21 December, 1992
Norwich City v Ipswich Town

Saturday, 26 December, 1992
Arsenal v Ipswich Town
Blackburn Rovers v Leeds United

Chelsea v Southampton
Coventry City v Aston Villa
Crystal Palace v Wimbledon
Everton v Middlesbrough
Manchester City v Sheffield United
Norwich City v Tottenham Hotspur
Nottingham Forest v Queen's Park Rangers
Oldham Athletic v Liverpool
Sheffield Wednesday v Manchester United

Monday, 28 December, 1992
Aston Villa v Arsenal
Ipswich Town v Blackburn Rovers
Leeds United v Norwich City
Liverpool v Manchester City
Manchester United v Coventry City
Middlesbrough v Crystal Palace
Queen's Park Rangers v Everton
Southampton v Sheffield Wednesday
Tottenham Hotspur v Nottingham Forest
Wimbledon v Chelsea

Tuesday, 29 December, 1992
Sheffield United v Oldham Athletic

Saturday, 9 January, 1993
Arsenal v Sheffield United
Blackburn Rovers v Wimbledon
Chelsea v Manchester City
Coventry City v Nottingham Forest
Crystal Palace v Everton
Ipswich Town v Oldham Athletic
Leeds United v Southampton
Liverpool v Aston Villa
Manchester United v Tottenham Hotspur
Middlesbrough v Queen's Park Rangers
Sheffield Wednesday v Norwich City

Saturday, 16 January, 1993
Aston Villa v Middlesbrough
Everton v Leeds United
Manchester City v Arsenal
Norwich City v Coventry City
Nottingham Forest v Chelsea
Oldham Athletic v Blackburn Rovers
Queen's Park Rangers v Manchester United
Sheffield United v Ipswich Town
Southampton v Crystal Palace
Tottenham Hotspur v Sheffield Wednesday
Wimbledon v Liverpool

Tuesday, 26 January, 1993
Blackburn Rovers v Coventry City
Middlesbrough v Southampton
Oldham Athletic v Manchester City
Tottenham Hotspur v Ipswich Town
Wimbledon v Everton

Wednesday, 27 January, 1993
Aston Villa v Sheffield United
Liverpool v Leeds United

Manchester United v Nottingham Forest
Norwich City v Crystal Palace
Queen's Park Rangers v Chelsea
Sheffield Wednesday v Arsenal

Saturday, 30 January, 1993
Arsenal v Liverpool
Chelsea v Sheffield Wednesday
Coventry City v Wimbledon
Crystal Palace v Tottenham Hotspur
Everton v Norwich City
Ipswich Town v Manchester United
Leeds United v Middlesbrough
Manchester City v Blackburn Rovers
Nottingham Forest v Oldham Athletic
Sheffield United v Queen's Park Rangers
Southampton v Aston Villa

Saturday, 6 February, 1993
Aston Villa v Ipswich Town
Blackburn Rovers v Crystal Palace
Liverpool v Nottingham Forest
Manchester United v Sheffield United
Middlesbrough v Coventry City
Norwich City v Arsenal
Oldham Athletic v Chelsea
Queen's Park Rangers v Manchester City
Sheffield Wednesday v Everton
Tottenham Hotspur v Southampton
Wimbledon v Leeds United

Tuesday, 9 February, 1993
Arsenal v Wimbledon
Crystal Palace v Aston Villa
Ipswich Town v Queen's Park Rangers
Leeds United v Manchester United
Sheffield United v Middlesbrough

Wednesday, 10 February, 1993
Chelsea v Liverpool
Coventry City v Oldham Athletic
Everton v Tottenham Hotspur
Manchester City v Sheffield Wednesday
Nottingham Forest v Blackburn Rovers
Southampton v Norwich City

Saturday, 13 February, 1993
Arsenal v Queen's Park Rangers
Chelsea v Aston Villa
Coventry City v Sheffield Wednesday
Crystal Palace v Manchester United
Everton v Blackburn Rovers
Ipswich Town v Middlesbrough
Leeds United v Oldham Athletic
Manchester City v Wimbledon
Nottingham Forest v Norwich City
Sheffield United v Tottenham Hotspur
Southampton v Liverpool

Saturday, 20 February, 1993
Aston Villa v Everton
Blackburn Rovers v Chelsea
Liverpool v Ipswich Town
Manchester United v Southampton
Middlesbrough v Nottingham Forest
Norwich City v Manchester City
Oldham Athletic v Arsenal
Queen's Park Rangers v Coventry City
Sheffield Wednesday v Crystal Palace
Tottenham Hotspur v Leeds United
Wimbledon v Sheffield United

Saturday, 27 February, 1993
Aston Villa v Wimbledon
Chelsea v Arsenal
Crystal Palace v Coventry City
Everton v Oldham Athletic
Leeds United v Ipswich Town
Manchester United v Middlesbrough
Norwich City v Blackburn Rovers
Nottingham Forest v Manchester City
Sheffield Wednesday v Liverpool
Southampton v Sheffield United
Tottenham Hotspur v Queen's Park Rangers

Saturday, 6 March, 1993
Arsenal v Nottingham Forest
Blackburn Rovers v Aston Villa
Coventry City v Everton
Ipswich Town v Chelsea
Liverpool v Manchester United
Manchester City v Crystal Palace
Middlesbrough v Tottenham Hotspur
Oldham Athletic v Sheffield Wednesday
Queen's Park Rangers v Norwich City
Wimbledon v Southampton

Sunday, 7 March, 1993
Sheffield United v Leeds United

Tuesday, 9 March, 1993
Arsenal v Leeds United
Blackburn Rovers v Southampton
Ipswich Town v Sheffield Wednesday
Oldham Athletic v Manchester United
Wimbledon v Middlesbrough

Wednesday, 10 March, 1993
Aston Villa v Tottenham Hotspur
Chelsea v Everton
Liverpool v Queen's Park Rangers
Manchester City v Coventry City
Nottingham Forest v Crystal Palace
Sheffield United v Norwich City

Saturday, 13 March, 1993
Coventry City v Arsenal
Crystal Palace v Chelsea
Everton v Nottingham Forest

Leeds United v Manchester City
Manchester United v Aston Villa
Middlesbrough v Liverpool
Norwich City v Oldham Athletic
Queen's Park Rangers v Wimbledon
Southampton v Ipswich Town
Tottenham Hotspur v Blackburn Rovers

Sunday, 14 March, 1993
Sheffield Wednesday v Sheffield United

Saturday, 20 March, 1993
Arsenal v Southampton
Aston Villa v Sheffield Wednesday
Blackburn Rovers v Middlesbrough
Chelsea v Tottenham Hotspur
Ipswich Town v Coventry City
Liverpool v Everton
Manchester City v Manchester United
Nottingham Forest v Leeds United
Oldham Athletic v Queen's Park Rangers
Sheffield United v Crystal Palace
Wimbledon v Norwich City

Tuesday, 23 March, 1993
Crystal Palace v Liverpool
Leeds United v Chelsea
Middlesbrough v Oldham Athletic
Tottenham Hotspur v Manchester City

Wednesday, 24 March, 1993
Coventry City v Sheffield United
Everton v Ipswich Town
Manchester United v Arsenal
Norwich City v Aston Villa
Queen's Park Rangers v Blackburn Rovers
Sheffield Wednesday v Wimbledon
Southampton v Nottingham Forest

Saturday, 3 April, 1993
Arsenal v Tottenham Hotspur
Blackburn Rovers v Liverpool
Chelsea v Middlesbrough
Coventry City v Southampton
Crystal Palace v Queen's Park Rangers
Everton v Sheffield United
Manchester City v Ipswich Town
Norwich City v Manchester United
Nottingham Forest v Aston Villa
Oldham Athletic v Wimbledon
Sheffield Wednesday v Leeds United

Friday, 9 April, 1993
Tottenham Hotspur v Norwich City

Saturday, 10 April, 1993
Aston Villa v Coventry City
Ipswich Town v Arsenal
Leeds United v Blackburn Rovers
Liverpool v Oldham Athletic

Manchester United v Sheffield Wednesday
Middlesbrough v Everton
Queen's Park Rangers v Nottingham Forest
Sheffield United v Manchester City
Southampton v Chelsea
Wimbledon v Crystal Palace

Monday, 12 April, 1993
Arsenal v Aston Villa
Blackburn Rovers v Ipswich Town
Chelsea v Wimbledon
Coventry City v Manchester United
Crystal Palace v Middlesbrough
Everton v Queen's Park Rangers
Manchester City v Liverpool
Nottingham Forest v Tottenham Hotspur
Oldham Athletic v Sheffield United
Sheffield Wednesday v Southampton

Wednesday, 14 April, 1993
Norwich City v Leeds United

Saturday, 17 April, 1993
Aston Villa v Manchester City
Ipswich Town v Norwich City
Leeds United v Crystal Palace
Liverpool v Coventry City
Manchester United v Chelsea
Middlesbrough v Arsenal
Queen's Park Rangers v Sheffield Wednesday
Sheffield United v Blackburn Rovers
Southampton v Everton
Tottenham Hotspur v Oldham Athletic
Wimbledon v Nottingham Forest

Saturday, 1 May, 1993
Aston Villa v Oldham Athletic
Chelsea v Coventry City
Crystal Palace v Ipswich Town
Everton v Arsenal
Leeds United v Queen's Park Rangers
Manchester United v Blackburn Rovers
Norwich City v Liverpool
Nottingham Forest v Sheffield United
Sheffield Wednesday v Middlesbrough
Southampton v Manchester City
Tottenham Hotspur v Wimbledon

Saturday, 8 May, 1993
Arsenal v Crystal Palace
Blackburn Rovers v Sheffield Wednesday
Coventry City v Leeds United
Ipswich Town v Nottingham Forest
Liverpool v Tottenham Hotspur
Manchester City v Everton
Middlesbrough v Norwich City
Oldham Athletic v Southampton
Queen's Park Rangers v Aston Villa
Sheffield United v Chelsea
Wimbledon v Manchester United

Arsenal

(The Gunners)

Founded 1886

Arsenal Stadium,
Avenell Road, Highbury N5 1BU

Telephone numbers
Ground: 071-226 0304
Clubcall: 0898-202020
Ticket details: 071-354 5404
Club shop: 071-354 8397
Commercial/marketing:
071-359 0808
Sports hall: 071-226 2150
Club fax: 071-226 0329

*A*rsenal, founded in 1886 by Woolwich munitions workers at the Royal Arsenal, had to wait until the 1930s to claim the first of their ten Championships and five triumphs in 11 Wembley FA Cup finals. This rise to eminence followed a period of trauma. Elected to Division Two in 1893 and promoted in 1904, they spent nine modest years in Division One until relegation in 1913 coincided with a crisis from which they were rescued by the autocratic Sir Henry Norris, who moved the club to Highbury.

Yet, although it was Norris who negotiated a unique promotion to an enlarged Division One in 1919 (Arsenal had finished only sixth in Division Two in 1915), the real turning point was Herbert Chapman's arrival as manager in 1925. Chapman led them to their first FA Cup success in 1930 and their first League title in 1931; and though he died in 1934 midway through a third successful Championship campaign, his influence was evident as Arsenal concluded the pre-war phase with another Cup triumph (1936) and two more titles (1935 and 1938).

Tom Whittaker's early post-war side clinched two titles (1948 and 1953) and one FA Cup victory (1950) in two finals, but lean years followed until, a year after a Fairs Cup success in 1970, Arsenal, under Bertie Mee, achieved the League and Cup double so elusive to the legendary Chapman. Defeated in the League Cup final in 1968 and the FA Cup final in 1972 (on both occasions by Leeds), Arsenal slumped to 17th in Division One in 1976, but triumphed at Wembley in 1979, playing in the second of three successive FA Cup finals, and reached the European Cup Winners' Cup final in 1980.

George Graham, returning to Highbury as manager in 1986, has revived Arsenal's fortunes in six years which have seen them win the Championship twice (1989 and 1991) and reach the League Cup final twice, winning in 1987 and losing in 1988. In addition, they have finished outside the top four only once, as well as reaching the last eight in the FA Cup three times and once (1991) going to the semi-final.

RECORDS

Biggest wins
League: 12–0 v Loughborough Town, Division Two, March 1900
9–1 v Grimsby Town, Division One, Jan 1931
FA Cup: 11–1 v Darwen, 3rd round, Jan 1932
Record defeat:
0–8 v Loughborough Town, Division Two, Dec 1896
Most appearances: David O'Leary, 705, League and Cup, 1975–92
Most goals (aggregate): Cliff Bastin, 182, League and Cup, 1929–39 (+70 in wartime)

Most goals in a season: Ted Drake, 43, League and Cup, 1934–35
Most capped players:
Past – Kenny Sansom, 77 (86), England
Present – David O'Leary, 66, Republic of Ireland
Other leading internationals:
England: Eddie Hapgood 30; Cliff Bastin 21; Tony Adams 19; George Eastham 19
Scotland: Charlie Nicholas 13 (20)
Wales: Jack Kelsey 41
Northern Ireland: Terry Neill 44 (59); Pat Jennings 42 (119)

GILLESPIE ROAD NORTH BANK

WEST STAND HIGHBURY HILL

110 YDS

71 YDS

EAST STAND AVENELL ROAD

CLOCK END

Finsbury Park

HORNSEY ROAD

SEVEN SISTERS ROAD

LORDSHIP PARK MANOR RD

GREEN LANES

ALBION ROAD

STOKE NEWINGTON ROAD

ARSENAL F.C.

HIGHBURY PK

DRAYTON PK

HOLLOWAY ROAD

Holloway Road

CALEDONIAN ROAD

LIVERPOOL ROAD

ST PAUL'S RD

BALLS POND RD

KINGSLAND ROAD

ESSEX ROAD

UPPER ST

NEW NORTH RD

YORK WAY

Ground capacity (1992–93): 30,000
Number of seats: 17,500 (North Stand redevelopment in progress)
Ground capacity (10 years ago): 55,000
Record attendance: 73,295 v Sunderland, Division One, 9 March, 1935

Directions to ground
By car: **From north**, exit M1 at Junction 2 following City signs. After Holloway Road station (6 miles) take third left into Drayton Park Road, turn right into Avenell Road.
From south, from London Bridge to Bank of England then Angel. Right at lights to Highbury roundabout into Holloway Road then into Drayton Park Road (then as north).
From west, A501 London inner ring road, turn left at Angel to Highbury roundabout (then as south).
By tube: Arsenal (Piccadilly Line)
By train: Finsbury Park Station, Drayton Park Station

Paul Merson

THE F.A. PREMIER LEAGUE

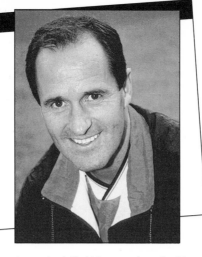

George Graham

Date of birth: 30 Nov, 1944
Birthplace: Bargeddie
Date of appointment: May 1986
Previous club: Millwall

Managerial honours:
Millwall: Football League Trophy winners 1983
Arsenal: League champions 1989, 1991; Littlewoods Cup winners 1987, runners-up 1988

PEN PIX

TONY ADAMS (defender): England international who captained Arsenal to their 1989 and 1991 Championships. Joined the club as a trainee and made his debut as a 17-year-old in November 1983. Born Romford 10.10.66.

STEVE BOULD (defender): Central defender signed from Stoke City for £390,000 in the summer of 1988. England B international who joined Stoke from school and had a loan spell at Torquay. Born Stoke 16.11.62.

KEVIN CAMPBELL (forward): Youth team top scorer in 1987 and 1988 who made his League debut in May 1988. England Under-21 international, who has had loan spells at Leyton Orient and Leicester. He scored 13 goals last season. Born London 4.2.70.

JIMMY CARTER (forward): Made his Arsenal debut at Nottingham Forest in December 1991 following £500,000 move from Liverpool in October. Spent less than 12 months at Anfield after £800,000 move from Millwall. The winger played at Crystal Palace and QPR before joining Millwall. Born London 9.11.65.

PAUL DAVIS (midfielder): A former trainee who made his debut in a north London derby with Tottenham on Easter Monday, 1980. England Under-21 and B international, who soon established himself in the Arsenal midfield but made only 17 appearances last season. Born London 9.12.61.

LEE DIXON (defender): After several years in the lower Divisions, the England right-back joined Arsenal from Stoke for £350,000 in January 1988. The club's penalty-taker, he began his career at Burnley and also played for Chester City and Bury. Born Manchester 17.3.64.

PERRY GROVES (forward): Joined Colchester from school where he established himself as a right-winger. Became George Graham's first signing, for £65,000, in September 1986. Born Bow 19.4.65.

NEIL HEANEY (forward): A winger, who joined the club as a trainee four years ago. A member of the club's 1988 FA Youth Cup-winning side who made his Arsenal senior debut as a substitute at Sheffield United in April 1992, having already played three League games while on loan to Hartlepool. Born Middlesbrough 3.11.71.

DAVID HILLIER (midfielder): Captain of the Arsenal side that won the FA Youth Cup in 1988. Versatile England Under-21 player who forced his way into the side for the second half of 1990–91 season. Born Blackheath 18.12.69.

JOHN JENSEN (midfielder): Danish international who scored the first goal in Denmark's 2–0 defeat of Germany in the 1992 European Championship final. Started at Brondby, had a brief spell with SV Hamburg in the Bundesliga, before returning to Brondby. Joined Arsenal for £1.1 million in July 1992. Born Copenhagen 3.5.65.

ANDERS LIMPAR (forward): Now playing League football in his fourth different country having signed from Italian side Cremonese for £1 million after the 1990 World Cup. His first major club was Orgryte, Sweden, and he then joined Young Boys Berne in Switzerland. Born Sweden 24.9.65.

ANDY LINIGHAN (defender): Central defender signed from Norwich for a tribunal-set fee of £1.25 million in July 1990. Started his career with Hartlepool and played for Leeds,

Ian Wright

Oldham and then Norwich. Born Hartlepool 18.6.62.

PAL LYDERSEN (defender): Signed for £500,000 in September 1991 from the Start club of Norway, but had to wait two months for his work permit to come through. Made his debut in March and played a further six times. Born Norway 10.9.65.

PAUL MERSON (forward): England international who was the PFA Young Player of the Year in 1989. Joined the club as a trainee, making his League debut in November 1986. Also had a spell on loan at Brentford. Born Northolt 20.3.68.

ALLAN MILLER (goalkeeper): Joined the club from the FA School of Excellence and was the first Lilleshall graduate to win England Under-21 honours. On loan at Plymouth during the 1988–89 season but has yet to play for Arsenal. Born Epping 29.3.70.

STEPHEN MORROW (defender): Northern Ireland international who played for Irish side Bangor while still at school. Joined the club as a trainee and following a loan spell at Reading, made his Arsenal debut in April. Born Kilclenny 2.7.70.

DAVID O'LEARY (defender): Has made more than 700 appearances for Arsenal, including 547 in League, having made his debut in August 1975. Republic of Ireland international brought up in Dublin, who joined the club from school. Played in three successive FA Cup finals (1978, 1979, 1980). Born London 2.5.58.

RAY PARLOUR (midfielder): Joined the club three years ago and made his full debut at Liverpool in January 1992. Played a further five first-team matches and scored at Wimbledon in March. Born Romford 7.3.73.

COLIN PATES (defender): Signed from Charlton in January 1990 for £350,000. Began his career at Chelsea where he won a Second Division title medal in 1984 before moving across London in 1988. Had a loan spell with Brighton. Born Carshalton 10.8.61.

DAVID ROCASTLE (midfielder):

ARSENAL: 10–YEAR RECORD

	Div	P	W	D	L	F	A	Pts	Pos	FA Cup	Lge Cup
1982–83	1	42	16	10	16	58	56	58	10	SF	SF
1983–84	1	42	18	9	15	74	60	63	6	3	4
1984–85	1	42	19	9	14	61	49	66	7	4	3
1985–86	1	42	20	9	13	49	47	69	7	5	5
1986–87	1	42	20	10	12	58	35	70	4	QF	W
1987–88	1	40	18	12	10	58	39	66	6	QF	F
1988–89	1	38	22	10	6	73	36	76	1	3	3
1989–90	1	38	18	8	12	54	38	62	4	4	4
1990–91	1	38	24	13	1	74	18	83*	1	SF	4
1991–92	1	42	19	15	8	81	46	72	4	3	3

* 2 pts deducted for disciplinary reasons

Leading League scorers in last 10 seasons

		League hat-tricks
1982–83	Woodcock 14	Talbot (1), Woodcock (1)
1983–84	Woodcock 21	Meade (1), Woodcock (1 x 5)
1984–85	Allinson 10, Talbot 10, Woodcock 10	—
1985–86	Woodcock 11	—
1986–87	Hayes 19	—
1987–88	Smith 11	Smith (1)
1988–89	Smith 23	Smith (1)
1989–90	Smith 10	—
1990–91	Smith 23	Smith (1)
1991–92	Wright 24	Merson (1), Wright (1 x 4, 2 x 3)

England international who joined the club from school. He made his debut against Newcastle in September 1985. Back to full fitness last season after two years of injuries. Born Lewisham 2.5.67.

DAVID SEAMAN (goalkeeper): England international who has not missed an Arsenal game since his £1.3 million transfer from QPR in May 1990. Was given a free transfer by first club Leeds, won England Under-21 honours while at Peterborough, and went on to play for Birmingham. Born Rotherham 19.9.63.

ALAN SMITH (forward): Seventeen goals last season for the England striker who began his career with non-League Alvechurch. Teamed up with Gary Lineker at Leicester and joined Arsenal in an £850,000 deal in

March 1987. Born Bromsgrove 21.11.62.

NIGEL WINTERBURN (defender): England left-back who started his career with Birmingham. Given a free transfer to Oxford before moving on to Wimbledon, where he made his League debut, and signed for Arsenal for £350,000 in May 1987. Born Coventry 11.12.63.

IAN WRIGHT (forward): Top-scorer last season with 26 goals, following £2.5 million transfer in September from Crystal Palace. England international who spent six full seasons at Palace after signing from non-League Greenwich Borough. Born Woolwich 3.11.63.

Aston Villa
(The Villans)
Founded 1874

Villa Park, Trinity Road,
Birmingham B6 6HE

Telephone numbers:
Ground: 021-327 2299
Clubcall: 0898 121148
Ticket details: 021-327 5353
Credit card sales: 021-327 7373
Club shop: 021-327 2800
Supporters' club: 021-327 3293
Club fax: 021-322 2107
Commercial department:
021-327 5399
Lottery office: 021-328 3322
Travel club: 021-328 2246

Aston Villa, founded in 1874 and original members of the Football League in 1888, have spent only 12 seasons outside the top grade in 104 years, boasting seven First Division titles and seven FA Cup successes – including, in 1897, a League and Cup double. Yet the bulk of Villa's peaks loom in the distant past, although they were Champions in 1981 and European Cup winners in 1982; and, having been the first winners of the League Cup in 1961, they won the trophy again in 1975 and 1977 after losing in the finals of 1963 and 1971. That title triumph of 1981 was their first since 1910, while their only FA Cup success since 1920 came as long ago as 1957. In 1990 Graham Taylor led them into second place in Division One and to the FA Cup quarter-finals, but the ultimate prizes remained elusive.

Villa first won the FA Cup a year before the League's formation and, between 1892 and 1905, won the First Division five times and triumphed in three of four FA Cup finals. They were champions again in 1910, and lifted the Cup in 1913 and 1920, but had to wait 37 years before claiming another major honour. Meanwhile relegation came, in 1936, for the first time in 48 years and, returning in 1938, Villa endured a long modest run. They lost their top-grade status briefly in 1959 and then again for eight years from 1967, falling into Division Three before climbing again.

Six years after their title success under Ron Saunders in 1981, Villa were again relegated, but Taylor promptly led them back, and within two seasons they had reached second spot; but his successor, Dr Jozef Venglos, could not prevent a slide to 17th in 1991. Last season, when Ron Atkinson moved in, they finished seventh.

RECORDS

Biggest wins:
League: 12–2 v Accrington Stanley, Division One, March 1892
11–1 v Charlton Athletic, Division Two, Nov 1959
FA Cup: 13–0 v Wednesbury Old Athletic, 1st round, Oct 1886
Record defeats:
1–8 v Blackburn Rovers, FA Cup, 3rd round, Feb 1889
0–7 v Blackburn Rovers, Division One, Oct 1889; v WBA, Division One, Oct 1935; v Manchester United, Division One, Oct 1964
Most appearances: Charlie Aitken, 656, League and Cup, 1961–76
Most goals (aggregate): Billy Walker, 244, League and Cup, 1919–34; Harry Hampton, 242, League and Cup, 1904–20

Most goals in a season: Pongo Waring, 49, Division One, 1930–31
Most capped players:
Past – Peter McParland, 33 (34), Northern Ireland
Present – Paul McGrath, 24 (55), Republic of Ireland
Other leading internationals:
England: David Platt, 22 (32); Billy Walker, 18; Charlie Athersmith, 12
Scotland: George Cummings, 6 (9); Andy Gray, 6 (20)
Wales: Vic Crowe, 16
Northern Ireland: Chris Nicholl, 12 (51)
Republic of Ireland: Con Martin, 24 (30)

THE MANAGER

Ron Atkinson

Date of birth: 18 March, 1939
Birthplace: Liverpool
Date of appointment: July 1991
Previous clubs: Kettering Town, Cambridge United, West Bromwich Albion, Manchester United, Atletico Madrid, Sheffield Wednesday

Managerial honours:
Cambridge United: Promotion to Division Two 1978; promotion to Division Three 1977
Manchester United: FA Cup winners 1983, 1985; Milk Cup finalists 1983
Sheffield Wednesday: Promotion to Division One 1991; Rumbelows Cup winners 1991

Tony Daley

Aston Villa

THE F.A. PREMIER LEAGUE

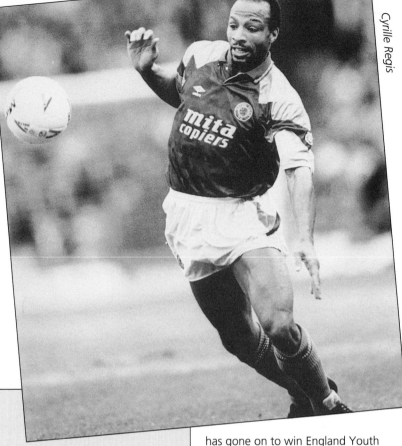

Cyrille Regis

DALIAN ATKINSON (forward): Signed by Ron Atkinson while at Sheffield Wednesday. Gained England B recognition at Hillsborough before joining Real Sociedad. Moved to Villa Park for £1.6 million in July 1991. Born Shrewsbury 21.3.68.

EARL BARRETT (defender): England international who joined Villa for £1.7 million from Oldham in February. A regular in the side to the end of the season. Joined Oldham in 1987 from Manchester City, spent time on loan to Chester City. Born Rochdale 28.4.67.

STEFAN BEINLICH (midfielder): Joined with Matthias Breitkreutz from Bergmann Borsig in a £250,000 deal last October. Three appearances as substitute last season. Born Berlin, Germany, 13.1.72.

MARK BLAKE (midfielder): Signed professional forms in July 1989 and

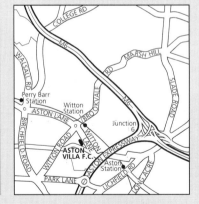

Ground capacity: 40,312
Number of seats: 21,102
Ground capacity (10 years ago): 48,000
Record attendance: 76,588 v Derby County, FA Cup, 6th round, 2 March, 1946

Directions to ground
By car: **From all directions**, leave M6 at Junction 6. Follow signs for Birmingham NE, take fourth exit at roundabout to A38 (M) and after half-a-mile turn right into Aston Hall Road.
By train: From city centre to Witton or Aston stations.
By bus: From city centre Nos 7 & 11

has gone on to win England Youth and Under-21 honours. Has been on loan to Wolves. Scored his first goal for Villa last season. Born Nottingham 16.12.70.

MARK BOSNICH (goalkeeper): Australian goalkeeper who joined Villa on a free from Sydney side Croatia in February 1992. He had previously played three League matches for Manchester United but he could not get a work permit. His one appearance for Villa came at Luton in April. Born Fairfield, Australia, 13.1.72.

MATTHIAS BREITKREUTZ (midfielder): German player, signed with Stefan Beinlich for a combined £250,000 from Bergmann Borsig last October. Made eight League appearances for Villa. Born Crivitz, Germany, 12.5.71.

NEIL COX (defender): After only 25 first-team games at Scunthorpe was transferred to Villa for £400,000 in February 1991. Made his debut for Villa in March 1992 and went on to play seven League games. Born Scunthorpe 8.10.71.

TONY DALEY (forward): England international winger, joined the club as an apprentice and made his senior debut in April 1985. Struggled over the last three seasons with a series of injuries. Born Birmingham 18.10.67.

UGO EHIOGU (defender): Joined Villa from West Brom for £20,000 in August 1991. Just two appearances for West Brom and made ten for Villa in his first season. Born London 3.11.72.

STEPHEN FROGGATT (forward): Former Villa trainee who shone on his handful of appearances last season. Scored his only goal for the club against Swindon in the FA Cup 5th round. Born Lincoln 9.3.73.

DARIUSZ KUBICKI (defender): Right-back who quickly established himself in the Villa side after transfer in July 1991. A Polish international who signed from Legia Warsaw for £200,000. Born Warsaw, Poland, 6.6.63.

PAUL McGRATH (defender): Republic of Ireland international who joined the club from Manchester United for £400,000 in July 1989. Started his career with League of Ireland club St Patrick's Athletic. Born Ealing 4.12.59.

GARRY PARKER (midfielder): Ever-present since his £650,000 move from Nottingham Forest in November 1991. Began his career with Luton, joining Forest from Hull in March 1988. England Youth, Under-21 and B international. Born Oxford 7.9.65.

CYRILLE REGIS (forward): Eleven goals last season after joining on a free from Coventry the previous summer. Began his career with West Brom after being spotted at non-league Hayes. Joined Coventry for £250,000 in October 1984. Born Mariapousoula, French Guyana, 9.2.58.

KEVIN RICHARDSON (midfielder): Started his career at Everton as an apprentice in 1980. Joined Watford in 1986. Moved to Arsenal for £200,000 and then Real Sociedad before joining Villa for £450,000 in August 1991. Ever-present last season. Born

Newcastle 4.12.62.

LES SEALEY (goalkeeper): Signed on a free as cover for Nigel Spink and kept his place for four months last season. An FA Cup and European Cup Winners' Cup winner with Manchester United previously with Coventry, Luton and Plymouth (loan). Born Bethnal Green 29.9.57.

BRYAN SMALL (defender): Former Villa trainee who has just completed his first season as a professional, making 13 appearances. Born Birmingham 15.11.71.

NIGEL SPINK (goalkeeper): Villa's longest-serving player, who came on as a substitute in the 1982 European Cup final win over Bayern Munich. England international who signed from non-League Chelmsford for £4,000 in January 1977. Born Chelmsford 8.8.58.

STEVE STAUNTON (defender): Republic of Ireland international signed for £1.1 million from Liverpool in summer 1991. Joined Liverpool from Dundalk and made his senior debut while on loan at Bradford. Born Drogheda 19.1.69.

SHAUN TEALE (defender): A £300,000 signing from Bournemouth in July 1991. Central defender who joined Bournemouth in January 1989 following spells with non-League Southport, Northwich Victoria and Weymouth. Ever-present last season. Born Southport 10.3.64.

DWIGHT YORKE (forward): Top-scorer last season with 17 goals. Spotted by Villa while the club was on tour of Trinidad & Tobago during the summer of 1989, he signed for the club in December 1989 for £120,000. Born Tobago 3.11.71.

ASTON VILLA: 10–YEAR RECORD

	Div	P	W	D	L	F	A	Pts	Pos	FA Cup	Lge Cup
1982–83	1	42	21	5	16	102	50	68	6	QF	2
1983–84	1	42	17	9	16	59	61	60	10	3	SF
1984–85	1	42	15	11	16	60	60	56	10	3	3
1985–86	1	42	10	14	18	51	67	44	16	4	SF
1986–87	1	42	8	12	22	45	79	36	22 (R)	3	4
1987–88	2	44	22	12	10	68	41	78	2 (P)	4	4
1988–89	1	38	9	13	16	45	56	40	17	4	QF
1989–90	1	38	21	7	10	57	38	70	2	QF	3
1990–91	1	38	9	14	15	46	58	41	17	3	QF
1991–92	1	42	17	9	16	48	44	60	7	QF	2

Leading League scorers in last 10 seasons		*League hat-tricks*
1982–83	Shaw 17	—
1983–84	Withe 16	—
1984–85	Rideout 14	Rideout (1)
1985–86	Stainrod 10, Walters 10	—
1986–87	Evans 6, Stainrod 6, Thompson 6	—
1987–88	Aspinall 11, Thompson 11	Walters (1)
1988–89	McInally 14	—
1989–90	Platt 19	—
1990–91	Platt 19	Platt (1)
1991–92	Yorke 11	—

Blackburn Rovers

(Blue and Whites)

Founded 1875

Ewood Park,
Blackburn BB2 4JF

Telephone numbers:
Ground: 0254 55432
Clubcall: 0898 121179
Ticket details: 0254 55432
Club shop: 0254 55432
Supporters' club: 0254 55432
Club fax: 0254 671042

Blackburn Rovers, numbered among football's most famous old names and founder members of the Football League, figure in the new Premier League following one of the most remarkable seasons in their 117-year history. Their return to the top for the first time since 1966 lacked neither drama nor irony as they climbed via the play-offs, after hopes of automatic promotion had faded with an unexpected, dismal late run of one win in 13 games. Pipped in three play-offs in the previous four years, Rovers only just scraped in this time, and their belated return to winning ways finally ensured a dividend on benefactor Jack Walker's huge investment, which included recruiting Kenny Dalglish as manager in October.

Thus an eventful chapter was added to a club history in which most of the glory had been concentrated in the early years – the time when Rovers led the northern challenge during the birth and rise of the professional game in the 1880s. Founded in 1875, Rovers won the FA Cup five times in six finals between 1882 and 1891, including three successive triumphs. They have won the Cup only once since then, in 1928, and last reached a final in 1960, while in the League they have been Champions only twice, in 1912 and 1914. Modern times have been lean, and since their first relegation in 1936 ended a 44-year run in Division One, they have spent just ten seasons in the top grade.

Their 34 seasons in Division Two span five spells, of which the latest was the longest, and since they were last in the top grade, they have also spent five years in Division Three. They climbed from there in 1980, but thereafter seemed set for perennial Second Division status. Bobby Saxton took them close to promotion in 1985, before Don Mackay endured failure in three successive play-offs. Then, when a lean season was followed by a poor start to 1991–92, Dalglish arrived to answer Mr Walker's call for a big push for Premier status – and the goal was reached in a nail-biting finale as dramatic as anything in Ewood Park's 100-plus years.

RECORDS

Biggest wins:
League: 9–0 v Middlesbrough, Division Two, Nov 1954
FA Cup: 11–0 v Rossendale, 1st round, Oct 1884
Record defeat:
0–8 v Arsenal, Division One, Feb 1933
Most appearances: Derek Fazackerley, 667, League and Cup, 1970–86
Most goals (aggregate): Simon Garner, 197, League and Cup, 1978–92

Most goals in a season: Ted Harper, 45, League and Cup, 1925–26
Most capped players:
Past – Bob Crompton, 41, England
Present – Kevin Moran, 18 (62), Republic of Ireland
Other leading internationals:
England: Bryan Douglas, 36; Ron Clayton, 35; Keith Newton, 19 (27)
Scotland: John Hutton. 3 (10)
Wales: Mike England 20 (44)
Northern Ireland: Noel Brotherston, 27
Republic of Ireland: Mick McGrath 18 (22)

Blackburn Rovers

THE MANAGER

Kenny Dalglish

Date of birth: 4 March, 1951
Birthplace: Glasgow
Date of appointment: October 1991
Previous club: Liverpool

Managerial honours:
Liverpool: FA Cup winners 1986, 1989, finalists 1988; League Champions 1986, 1988, 1990; Screen Sports Super Cup winners 1986; Littlewoods Cup finalists 1987
Blackburn Rovers: Promotion to Division One 1992

PEN-PIX

STEVE AGNEW (midfielder): £700,000 signing from Barnsley, his only other club, in June 1991. Played in first four games of last season, was then injured and unable to regain his place. Born Shipley 9.11.65.

MARK ATKINS (defender): Former Scunthorpe player who cost Blackburn £45,000 in June 1988. Missed just three games in Blackburn's promotion-winning season of 1991–92. Born Doncaster 14.8.68.

RICHARD BROWN (defender): Signed from non-League Kettering Town two seasons ago and played in 27 League games in the 1991–92 season, although he missed the play-offs. Started with Sheffield Wednesday and has been to Maidstone on loan. Born Nottingham 13.1.67.

GORDON COWANS (midfielder): England international signed from Aston Villa in November 1991 for £200,000. With Villa won League Championship, European Cup and League Cup. Had a spell in Italy with Bari. Born Durham 27.10.58.

MATT DICKINS (goalkeeper): Signed on transfer deadline day last season from Lincoln City for £250,000 and made one appearance for his new club. Other clubs are Sheffield United and Leyton Orient (loan). Born Sheffield 3.9.70.

SIMON GARNER (forward): Blackburn's all-time record scorer with 197 goals since signing in July 1978 from non-League Boston United. Five goals in 30 appearances last season. Born Boston, Lincolnshire, 23.11.59.

COLIN HENDRY (defender): Scottish player in second spell at Ewood Park, having been signed from Manchester City for £750,000 in November 1991. Versatile player who began at Dundee before move to Blackburn. Born Keith 7.12.65.

KEITH HILL (defender): Joined Blackburn as an apprentice and signed professional forms in May 1987. Made 36 appearances last season, although he did not participate in play-offs. Born Bolton 17.5.69.

STEVE LIVINGSTONE (forward): Signed from first club Coventry for £450,000 in January 1991. Struggled to gain a first-team place last season, making only 11 appearances and scoring once. Born Middlesbrough 8.9.69.

LEE MAKEL (midfielder): Highly skilful teenager signed from Newcastle in June 1992. A former Newcastle trainee who made just 12 League appearances for the north-east club. Born Sunderland 11.1.73.

DAVID MAY (defender): Joined Rovers as a trainee and turned professional in June 1988. Struggled to maintain a first-team place last season, making 15 appearances in total. Born Oldham 24.6.70.

THE F.A. PREMIER LEAGUE

Ground capacity: 19,947
Number of seats: 7,417
Ground capacity (10 years ago): 25,000
Record attendance: 61,783 v Bolton Wanderers, FA Cup, 6th round, 2 March, 1929

Directions to ground

By car: **From north, south and west**, exit M6 at Junction 31, or take A666, follow signs for Blackburn then for Bolton Road; after one-and-a-half miles turn left into Kidder St.
From east, use A679 or A667 and follow signs for Bolton Road (then as above).
By train: Blackburn station – one-and-a-half miles from ground.
By bus: Town bus station to Darwen route, stops 2 minutes walk from ground, various numbers.

CHRIS PRICE (defender): Former Aston Villa full-back in his second spell at the club having signed in February 1992 for £150,000. Began at Hereford before move to Ewood Park in July 1986. Played 15 games for Blackburn last season. Born Hereford 30.3.60.

NICKY REID (midfielder): England Under-21 player signed on a free transfer from Manchester City in July 1987. Made 26 appearances last season, scoring once. Born Ormston 30.10.60.

LEE RICHARDSON (midfielder): Started career at Halifax before £150,000 move took him to Watford in February 1989. Valued at £250,000 in exchange deal in August 1990. Made 29 appearances in all last season. Born Halifax 12.3.69.

BOBBY MIMMS (goalkeeper): Another in his second spell with the club (he was on loan at Ewood Park in January 1988) following £250,000 signing from Spurs in December 1990. England Under-21 international who has also played for Halifax, Rotherham and Everton and has had loan spells with Notts County, Sunderland, Manchester City and Aberdeen. Born York 12.10.63.

KEVIN MORAN (defender): Experienced Republic of Ireland international signed on a free transfer in January 1990 from Sporting Gijon, Spain. Won FA Cup twice with first club Manchester United, in 1985 and 1987. Club captain. Born Dublin 29.4.56.

MIKE NEWELL (forward): England B striker who became club's record signing following £1.1 million move from Everton in November 1991. Other clubs are Crewe, Liverpool, Leicester, Luton and Wigan Athletic. Scored the penalty that won play-off final. Born Liverpool 27.1.65.

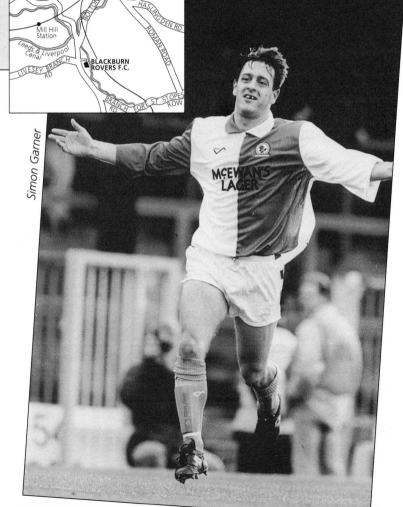

Simon Garner

BLACKBURN ROVERS: 10–YEAR RECORD

	Div	P	W	D	L	F	A	Pts	Pos	FA Cup	Lge Cup
1982–83	2	42	15	12	15	58	58	57	11	3	2
1983–84	2	42	17	16	9	57	46	67	6	5	2
1984–85	2	42	21	10	11	66	41	73	5	5	2
1985–86	2	42	12	13	17	53	62	49	19	4	2
1986–87	2	42	15	10	17	45	55	55	12	3	2
1987–88	2	44	21	14	9	68	52	77	5	3	2
1988–89	2	46	22	11	13	74	59	77	5	5	3
1989–90	2	46	19	17	10	74	59	74	5	3	2
1990–91	2	46	14	10	22	51	66	52	19	3	3
1991–92	2	46	21	11	14	70	53	74	6 (P)	4	1

Leading League scorers in last 10 seasons		*League hat-tricks*
1982–83	Garner 22	—
1983–84	Garner 19	Garner (1 x 5, 1 x 3)
1984–85	Thompson 15	Quinn (1)
1985–86	Garner 12	Patterson (1)
1986–87	Barker 11	Garner (1 x 4)
1987–88	Garner 14	—
1988–89	Garner 20	Garner (2)
1989–90	Garner 18	Garner (1)
1990–91	Stapleton 10	Stapleton (1)
1991–92	Speedie 23	Speedie (2)

STUART RIPLEY (forward): Joined Rovers from Middlesbrough for £1.3 million in July 1992. Former Boro apprentice who was one of the longest-serving players on the club's playing staff, having made his debut in February 1985. England Under-21 international. Born Middlesbrough 20.11.67.

TIM SHERWOOD (midfielder): Another Dalglish signing – £500,000 from Norwich in February 1992. The England Under-21 international started with local club Watford. Made 11 appearances for Blackburn last season. Born St Albans 6.2.69.

DAVID SPEEDIE (forward): Experienced Scottish international signed from Liverpool in August 1991 for £450,000 and was club's top scorer last season with 26 goals. Other clubs are Chelsea, Coventry, Darlington and Barnsley. Born Glenrothes 20.2.60.

ROY WEGERLE (forward): Made his USA debut against Eire in May 1992. The former Chelsea, Luton and QPR striker, who has also been on loan to Swindon, cost Blackburn £1 million

in March 1992. Two goals in 12 games for Blackburn last season. Born Johannesburg, South Africa, 19.3.64.

JASON WILCOX (forward): Joined Rovers as a trainee and signed professional forms in June 1989. Made 39 appearances in all competitions last season and scored four times. Born Bolton 15.7.71.

ALAN WRIGHT (defender): Highly rated player who was Dalglish's first signing, costing £500,000 from Blackpool. England Youth international who is now a member of the Under-21 squad. Born Ashton-under-Lyne 28.9.71.

Tim Sherwood

Chelsea

(The Blues)

Founded 1905

Stamford Bridge, Fulham Road,
London SW6 1HS

Telephone numbers
Ground: 071-385 5545
Clubcall: 0898 121159
Ticket details: 0898 121011
Club shop: 071-381 4569
Supporters' club: 071-385 5545
Club fax: 071-381 4831

Chelsea spent 57 of their 76 seasons in the Football League in Division One. Between 1930 and 1975 they passed only one year outside the top grade, and although they dropped into Division Two three times after the mid-1970s, only one of the last eight years has been spent there.

Yet Chelsea's history has often been unspectacular. Founded in 1905, they had to wait until their Jubilee year, 1955, to claim their only Championship; while the promise of a treble in 1965 faded when, defeated in the FA Cup semi-final and finishing third in Division One, Tommy Docherty's side finally won only the League Cup. At last, in 1970, having reached a final (1967), two semi-finals and two quarter-finals in a five-year run of near-misses, they won the FA Cup for the only time – in a replay at Old Trafford, where they had lost their first final in 1915. Fairs Cup semi-finalists in 1966, Chelsea won the European Cup Winners' Cup in 1971.

Goal average or goal difference has often featured in Chelsea's fate. It brought relegation in 1924 and 1975, put them into the ill-fated play-offs when they went down in 1988, and cost them promotion in 1980. But it spared them relegation in 1951, saw them pip Sunderland to promotion in 1963, and sealed the Second Division title in 1984.

Life is seldom dull at Chelsea. Promoted twice, relegated once and FA Cup finalists all in their first ten years, they beat the drop in 1915 only because Division One was enlarged, and they had some close calls in the years just before that 1955 Championship under Ted Drake.

After their early 1970s peak under Dave Sexton, Chelsea fell twice in the later years of the decade, slipping to 18th in Division Two in 1983 before finishing top in 1984; and, after another fall in 1988, they promptly bounced back as Champions a year later. Ian Porterfield, coach to that 1989 promotion side, returned to Stamford Bridge as manager in 1991, and they finished 14th in his first season.

RECORDS

Biggest wins:
League: 9–2 v Glossop NE, Division Two, Sept 1906
7–1 v Leeds United, Division One, March 1935; v WBA, Division One, Dec 1960
FA Cup: 9–1 v Worksop Town, 1st round, Jan 1908
European Cup Winners' Cup: 13–0 v Jeunesse Hautcharage, 1st round, 2nd leg, Sept 1971
Record defeat: 1–8 v Wolverhampton Wanderers, Division One, Sept 1953
Most appearances: Ron Harris, 803, League and Cup, 1962–80

Most goals (aggregate): Bobby Tambling, 202, League and Cup, 1958–70
Most goals in a season: Jimmy Greaves, 43, League and Cup, 1960–61
Most capped players:
Past – Ray Wilkins, 24 (84), England
Present – Andy Townsend 14 (31), Republic of Ireland
Other leading internationals:
England: Vic Woodley, 19; Jimmy Greaves, 15 (57); Roy Bentley, 12
Scotland: Eddie McCreadie, 23
Wales: Mickey Thomas, 9 (51)
Northern Ireland: Kevin Wilson, 22 (27)
Republic of Ireland: Paddy Mulligan, 11 (50)

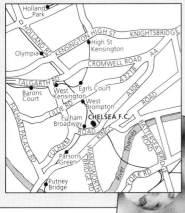

FULHAM ROAD   THE SHED

114 YDS

75 YDS

EAST STAND

WEST STAND

NORTH TERRACE

Ground capacity: 36,965
Number of seats: 20,040
Ground capacity (10 years ago): 45,000
Record attendance: 82,905 v Arsenal, Division
One, 12 Oct, 1935

Directions to ground

By car: **From north and east**, follow central
London signs from A1/M1 to Hyde Park Corner,
then the Guildford (A3) signs to Knightsbridge
(A4); after one mile turn left into Fulham Road.
From south, take A13 or A24, then A219. Cross
Putney Bridge and follow West End signs (A304)
to join A308 into Fulham Road.
From west, take M4 then A4 to central London,
then follow signs for Westminster (A3220). After
three-quarters-of-a-mile turn right at crossroads
into Fulham Road.
By bus: No 14 stops outside Stamford Bridge;
Nos 91, 295 and 28 stop outside Fulham
Broadway station; Nos 22 and
11 stop in King's Road (parallel
to Fulham Road).
By tube: Fulham Broadway
(District Line)

Andy Myers

THE F.A. PREMIER LEAGUE

Ian Porterfield

Date of birth: 11 Feb, 1947
Birthplace: Dunfermline
Date of appointment: June 1991
Previous clubs: Rotherham United, Sheffield United, Aberdeen, Reading

Managerial honours:
Rotherham United: Division Three Champions 1981
Sheffield United: Division Four Champions 1982; promotion to Division Two 1984

Celtic in February 1992, with Tom Boyd going to Parkhead. A Republic of Ireland international, formerly with Gillingham, Millwall and Aston Villa. Born St Paul's Cray 1.9.62.

STEVE CLARKE (defender): Scottish international with over 150 appearances for the club. Signed from St Mirren in January 1987 for £422,000. Previously with Beith Juniors. Born Saltcoats 29.8.63.

ALAN DICKENS (midfielder): Joined from West Ham in June 1989, for a tribunal-set £635,000 fee and scored

PEN-PIX

JOE ALLON (forward): Signed from Hartlepool United in August 1991 for a tribunal-set fee of £200,000 plus a further £100,000 after 25 games. Began his career at Newcastle United, before joining Swansea. Born Gateshead 12.11.66.

DARREN BARNARD (midfielder): Attacking winger signed from non-League Wokingham. Used largely in the reserves, but made his first-team debut at the end of last season. Born Rinteln 30.11.71.

DAVE BEASANT (goalkeeper): Former England international signed from Newcastle United in January 1989, for £725,000. An FA Cup winner with his first club, Wimbledon. Born Willesden 20.3.59.

CRAIG BURLEY (midfielder): A Scotland Under-21 international, he is also their most capped youth player. A nephew of former Ipswich player George, he signed from school. Born Ayr 24.9.71.

TONY CASCARINO (forward): Scored on his debut after signing in an exchange deal from

Graeme Le Saux

on his debut. A former England Under-21 international. Born Plaistow 3.9.64.

PAUL ELLIOTT (defender): England Youth and B international, signed from Celtic for £1.4 million in July 1991. Formerly with Charlton, Luton, Aston Villa and Pisa (Italy). Chelsea's Player of the Year 1991-92. Born London 18.3.64.

GARETH HALL (defender): Welsh international full-back, who joined the club as an apprentice in June 1985, signing as a professional the following April. Born Croydon 20.3.69.

KEVIN HITCHCOCK (goalkeeper): A £250,000 signing from Mansfield Town in March 1988, who started with Nottingham Forest and has been on loan to Northampton. Kept Beasant out of team for part of last season. Born Custom House 5.10.62.

ERLAND JOHNSEN (defender): Norwegian international signed from German club Bayern Munich, in November 1989, for £306,000. Limited first-team appearances last season. Born Fredrikstad, Norway, 5.4.67.

VINNIE JONES (midfielder): Formerly with Wealdstone, Wimbledon, Leeds and Sheffield United, he signed for £575,000 in August 1991. An FA Cup winner with Wimbledon. Born Watford 5.1.65.

DAVID LEE (defender/midfielder): Joined the club as a trainee in July 1986 and is an England Under-21 international. Spent part of last season on loan at Reading and Plymouth. Born Bristol 26.11.69.

GRAEME LE SAUX (midfielder): Left-sided England Under-21 and B international. Made his first-team debut in May 1989 at Portsmouth. Born Jersey 17.10.68.

DAMIEN MATTHEW (midfielder): An England Under-21 international, he signed professional forms in June 1989. Had a foot injury for most of last season. Born Islington 23.9.70.

KENNETH MONKOU (defender): Dutch B international signed from Feyenoord in March 1989 for £100,000. A former male model and

		Div	P	W	D	L	F	A	Pts	Pos	FA Cup	Lge Cup
1982–83		2	42	11	14	17	51	61	47	18	4	3
1983–84		2	42	25	13	4	90	40	88	1(P)	3	3
1984–85		1	42	18	12	12	63	48	66	6	4	SF
1985–86		1	42	20	11	11	57	56	71	6	4	QF
1986–87		1	42	13	13	16	53	64	52	14	4	3
1987–88		1	40	9	15	16	50	68	42	18(R)	4	2
1988–89		2	46	29	12	5	96	50	99	1(P)	3	2
1989–90		1	38	16	12	10	58	50	60	5	4	2
1990–91		1	38	13	10	15	58	69	49	11	3	SF
1991–92		1	42	13	14	15	50	60	63	14	QF	2

Leading League scorers in last 10 seasons   *League hat-tricks*

1982–83	Fillery 9	—
1983–84	Dixon 28	Canoville (1), Dixon (1)
1984–85	Dixon 24	Davies (1), Dixon (1)
1985–86	Dixon 14, Speedie 14	—
1986–87	Dixon 10	—
1987–88	Durie 12	—
1988–89	Dixon 25	Durie (1 x 5), Dixon (1 x 4)
1989–90	Dixon 20	Dixon (1)
1990–91	Durie 12	—
1991–92	Wise 10	—

the club's Player of the Year for 1989–90. Born Surinam 29.11.64.

ANDY MYERS (midfielder): A graduate of the FA School of Excellence, he deputised at left-back at the end of last season. Young Player of the Year in 1990–91. Born Isleworth 3.11.73.

IAN PEARCE (defender/forward): Made his Chelsea debut as a 17-year-old, in May 1991, after signing from school. A tall, commanding player in defence or attack. Born Bury St Edmunds 7.5.74.

FRANK SINCLAIR (defender): Has been with the club since he was ten. Banned for nine games last season, after being sent off while on loan at WBA, before returning to Chelsea first team. Born Lambeth 3.12.71.

GRAHAM STUART (forward): Another graduate of the FA School of Excellence and an England Under-21 international. A regular first-team player last season. Born Tooting 24.10.70.

ANDY TOWNSEND (midfielder): Republic of Ireland international and the club's captain. Formerly with Weymouth and Southampton, he signed from Norwich in July 1990 for £1.2 million. Born London 23.7.63.

DENNIS WISE (midfielder): Signed from Wimbledon in July 1990 for a club record £1.6 million. Formerly an apprentice with Southampton, he is an England international. Born Kensington 15.12.66.

Coventry City

(Sky Blues)

Founded 1883

Highfield Road Stadium,
King Richard Street,
Coventry CV2 4FW

Telephone numbers:
Ground: 0203 223535
Clubcall: 0898 121166
Ticket details: 0203 225545
Club shop: 0203 257707
Club fax: 0203 630318

Coventry, founded as Singer's FC by cycle factory workers in 1883, did not attain Football League status until 1919, when they joined the enlarged Second Division, and by the time they finally reached Division One in 1967, they had achieved the distinction of having figured in all six grades of the League. In their first six years they had languished near the foot of Division Two before relegation took them into the Third Division (North) for a year until the switch to the Southern Section. Under Harry Storer's influence they enjoyed a peak spell in the 1930s, winning promotion in 1936 and twice going close to Division One.

After falling again in 1952, though, they were among the founders of the new Fourth Division in 1958, and two years after prompt promotion in 1959, Jimmy Hill arrived to guide them from the Third to the First in a memorable six-year spell, when Coventry were the talk of football – as much for their approach off the field as on it. The Second Division title followed three years after they lifted the Third Division crown in 1964.

Coventry have remained in the top grade for 25 years, an unbroken sequence bettered by only three other clubs. However, they have frequently flirted with relegation, narrowly escaping seven times (including last season), and have finished in the top seven on only three occasions, while finishing in the bottom half in 18 seasons. They were sixth in 1970 and seventh in 1989, but the highlight of their recent history was the FA Cup triumph of 1987, when they beat Spurs in extra time in the Wembley final. On that Cup run they beat Manchester United – a sweet and symbolic victory in that they had lost to the Old Trafford side in a famous tie in 1963 when City were in Division Three.

Last season Coventry passed 1,000 games in Division One, but failed to score in half their matches and, not finding the net in 12 of their final 18 fixtures (only three were won), they survived to reach the Premier League only because Luton lost on the last day of an era in football.

THE MANAGER

Bobby Gould

Date of birth: 12 June, 1946
Birthplace: Coventry
Date of appointment: May 1992
Previous clubs: Coventry City, Bristol Rovers, Wimbledon, West Bromwich Albion

Managerial honours:
Wimbledon: FA Cup winners 1988

RECORDS

Biggest wins:
League: 9–0 v Bristol City, Division Three (S), April 1934
6–1 v Sunderland, Division One, April 1982
FA Cup: 7–0 v Scunthorpe United, 1st round, Nov 1934
Record defeat: 2–10 v Norwich City, Division Three (S), March 1930
Most appearances: George Curtis, 538, League and Cup, 1956–70
Most goals (aggregate): Clarrie Bourton, 180, League and Cup, 1931–37
Most goals in a season: Clarrie Bourton, 50, League and Cup, 1931–32

Most capped players:
Past – Dave Clements, 21 (48), Northern Ireland
Present – Kevin Gallacher, 8 (12), Scotland
Other leading internationals:
England: Reg Matthews, 5; Danny Thomas, 2; Cyrille Regis, 1 (5)
Scotland: Tommy Hutchison, 17
Wales: Ronnie Rees, 21 (39); Terry Yorath, 20 (59)
Northern Ireland: Willie Humphries, 10 (14)
Republic of Ireland: Jimmy Holmes, 17 (30)

Brian Borrows

PEN-PIX

PETER ATHERTON (defender): Signed from Wigan in August 1991 for £400,000. Made his Wigan debut as a 17-year-old and is now building a successful central defensive partnership with Andy Pearce. Born Orrell 6.4.70.

PHIL BABB (midfielder): Versatile player who signed for £500,000 from Bradford City in July 1992. Began his career as an apprentice at Millwall before a free transfer to Bradford in August 1990. Born Lambeth 30.11.70.

PETER BILLING (defender): Played only one game for Everton before joining Crewe, where he played in their 1988–89 promotion-winning season before moving to Coventry for £120,000 in June 1989. Born Liverpool 24.10.64.

THE F.A. PREMIER LEAGUE

MARTYN BOOTY (defender): Signed from a trainee and made his League debut in a 1–0 defeat by Chelsea last November. Made three League appearances last season. Born Kirby Muxloe 30.5.71.

BRIAN BORROWS (defender): Right-back who played 27 League games for Everton before moving to Bolton. Was signed for £80,000 during the summer of 1985. Injury seven days before the 1987 FA Cup final cost him a Wembley place. Born Liverpool 20.12.60.

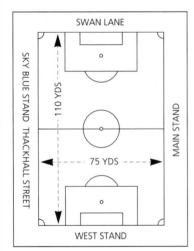

KEVIN DRINKELL (forward): Spent nine years with home-town club Grimsby Town before spells at Norwich (where he was top-scorer for three consecutive seasons) and Glasgow Rangers. Joined Coventry from Rangers in October 1989 for £800,000. Born Grimsby 18.6.60.

PAUL EDWARDS (defender): Was bought from Crewe for £300,000 in March 1990. Attacking left-back who played non-League football until the age of 24. Crewe paid Altrincham £2,000 for him in 1988. Born Birkenhead 25.12.63.

SEAN FLYNN (midfielder): Following in the footsteps of Andy Pearce, he was signed from Halesowen Town in November 1991. A right-sided midfielder, he scored on his League debut in a 3–0 win at Sheffield United on Boxing Day 1991. Born Birmingham 13.3.68.

KEVIN GALLACHER (forward): The club's top-scorer last season with ten goals in all competitions. Cost a club record fee of £900,000 from Dundee United in January 1990. A crowd favourite who is also a Scottish international. Born Clydebank 23.11.66.

JONATHAN GOULD (goalkeeper): Son of Coventry boss Bobby Gould who spent one-and-a-half seasons at Halifax before moving to West Brom to team up with his dad. Bobby then moved to Coventry and his 6ft 1in son followed in July for a small fee. Born London 18.7.68.

CHRIS GREENMAN (defender): Joined the club straight from school and made his League debut in a 2–1 defeat against Crystal Palace last October. Born Bristol 22.12.68.

MICHAEL GYNN (midfielder): Former Peterborough player who was signed by Coventry in August 1983 for £60,000 and has been a consistent performer ever since. Injury restricted his appearances last season. Born Peterborough 19.8.61.

LEE HURST (midfielder): Joined the club as an apprentice and broke into the side during the 1989–90 season. Has made 12 League appearances for the club. Born Nuneaton 21.9.70.

LLOYD McGRATH (midfielder): Former club junior who is one of only three survivors from the Coventry side which beat Tottenham 3–2 in the 1987 FA Cup final. Former England Youth international. Born Birmingham 24.2.65.

PETER NDLOVU (forward): Zimbabwe international who impressed the club during the 1990 summer tour of the African country. His first seven appearances last season were as substitute. Born Bulawayo, Zimbabwe, 25.2.73.

STEVE OGRIZOVIC (goalkeeper): Started at Chesterfield and had spells at Liverpool and Shrewsbury from where Coventry signed him for £72,500 in June 1984. Has played cricket for Shropshire in the Minor Counties League. Born Mansfield 12.9.57.

ANDY PEARCE (defender): Like team-mate Flynn, he was brought from non-League Halesowen Town. Joined in July 1990 and has made 47 League

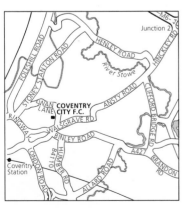

Ground capacity: 25,311
Number of seats: 17,661
Ground capacity (10 years ago): 20,000
Record attendance: 51,455 v Wolverhampton Wanderers, Division Two, 29 April, 1967

Directions to ground

By car: **From north, west and south**, at M6 motorway junction, take the A4600 and follow signs for city centre; follow this road for approximately 3 miles and just under the railway bridge, turn right at the traffic lights into Swan Lane; Highfield Road Stadium is on the left.

From east and south, take M45 motorway then A45; pass the Peugeot Talbot plant and at next roundabout, take the third exit A423, then in approximately 1 mile at the next roundabout follow B4110 signposted Stoke; follow this road across all traffic lights to T-junction, then turn left into Walsgrove Road and immediately right into Swan Lane.

By train: To Coventry Station. Take either No 17 or 27 bus to Gosford Green.

COVENTRY CITY: 10–YEAR RECORD

	Div	P	W	D	L	F	A	Pts	Pos	FA Cup	Lge Cup
1982–83	1	42	13	9	20	48	59	48	19	4	3
1983–84	1	42	13	11	18	57	77	50	19	4	3
1984–85	1	42	15	5	22	47	64	50	18	4	2
1985–86	1	42	11	10	21	48	71	43	17	3	3
1986–87	1	42	17	12	13	50	45	63	10	W	4
1987–88	1	40	13	14	13	46	53	53	10	4	3
1988–89	1	38	14	13	11	47	42	55	7	3	3
1989–90	1	38	14	7	17	39	59	49	12	3	SF
1990–91	1	38	11	11	16	42	49	44	16	4	QF
1991–92	1	42	11	11	20	35	44	44	19	3	4

Leading League scorers in last 10 seasons		*League hat-tricks*
1982–83	Whitton 12	Melrose (1)
1983–84	Gibson 17	Gibson (1)
1984–85	Gibson 15	—
1985–86	Gibson 11	—
1986–87	Regis 12	—
1987–88	Regis 10	—
1988–89	Speedie 14	Speedie (2)
1989–90	Speedie 8	—
1990–91	Gallacher 11	—
1991–92	Gallacher 8	—

Stewart Robson

just one season in League football. Began with Cradley Town before joining Swansea for £10,000 in August 1991. Won the Rumbelows Sprint Challenge at Wembley in April 1992, collecting £10,000. Born Birmingham 11.5.68.

RAY WOODS (forward): Was signed after two impressive displays for Wigan against Coventry in an FA Cup tie during the 1990–91 season. Started his career at Tranmere. Born Birkenhead 7.6.65.

appearances since. Born Bradford 20.4.66.

STEWART ROBSON (midfielder): Experienced player who was signed on a free transfer in 1992 after an injury-plagued four-year spell at West Ham. Former England Under-21 captain who began his career at Arsenal. Born Billericay 6.11.64.

ROBERT ROSARIO (forward): A 6ft 4in former England Under-21 international who spent eight years with his first club, Norwich, with a loan spell at Wolves, he joined Coventry in a £600,000 transfer in March 1991. Born Hammersmith 4.3.66.

KENNY SANSOM (defender): Former Crystal Palace and Arsenal full-back who won 86 England caps between 1979–88. He also played for Newcastle and QPR, moving to Coventry in a £100,000 deal in March 1991. Born Camberwell 26.9.58.

DAVID SMITH (midfielder): Former apprentice and England Under-21 international winger who made his club debut against Manchester United in February 1988. Born Gloucester 29.3.68.

JOHN WILLIAMS (forward): Cost £250,000 from Swansea in July after

Crystal Palace

(The Eagles)

Founded 1905

Selhurst Park,
London SE25 6PU

Telephone numbers
Ground: 081-653 4462
Club call: 0898 400333
Match information:
0898 400334
Box office: 081-771 8841
Club shop: 081-653 5584
Club fax: 081-771 5311

Crystal Palace, founded in 1905, were admitted to the Football League in 1920 and celebrated by emerging a year later as first Champions of the new Third Division; but they had to wait another 48 years to reach Division One, and it is only since Steve Coppell led them up via the play-offs in 1989 that they have consolidated their top-grade status.

Arriving in Division Two in 1921, they remained there four years before spending nearly four decades in the lower Divisions, and though they narrowly missed promotion in 1929, 1931 and 1939, they endured bleak days in the 1950s and ended up in the new Fourth Division in 1958. The 1960s were brighter. Arthur Rowe's side went up in 1961, Dick Graham's team reached Division Two in 1964, and Bert Head led them into Division One for the first time in 1969. But, after three dramatic escapes in successive seasons, relegation caught them in 1973 – and again in 1974, when they slid into Division Three.

They returned to Division Two in 1977, thanks to a last-day win at Wrexham, and Terry Venables' side were Second Division Champions in 1979; but a mere six wins in 1981 saw them plummet down again. Steve Coppell's arrival proved a turning point, but Palace were pipped to the play-offs in 1987 and 1988 before taking that route back to the top in 1989. The first season back is remembered with pain because of a record 0–9 defeat at Liverpool in September 1989, but also with pride because Palace reached their first ever FA Cup final, losing 0–1 to Manchester United in a replay after a 3–3 draw. The following season, 1990-91, Palace finished third in the table, the highest position in their history, and though they slipped to tenth in 1992, they had proved their credentials, a feature of their recent record being a big improvement in their away form.

RECORDS

Biggest wins:
League: 9–0 v Barrow, Division Four, Oct 1959
5–1 v Sheffield United, Division One, Dec 1971
FA Cup: 7–0 v Luton Town, 3rd round replay, Jan 1929
League Cup: 8–0 v Southend United, 2nd round, 1st leg, Sept 1990
Record defeat: 0–9 v Liverpool, Division One, Sept 1989
Most appearances: Jim Cannon, 657, League and Cup, 1972–88

Most goals (aggregate): Peter Simpson, 165, League and Cup, 1929–35
Most goals in a season: Peter Simpson, 54, League and Cup, 1930–31
Most capped players:
Past – Peter Nicholas, 14 (73), Wales. Paddy Mulligan, 14 (50), Republic of Ireland.
Present – Geoff Thomas, 9, England
Other leading internationals:
England: Kenny Sansom, 9 (86); Peter Taylor, 4
Northern Ireland: Bob McCracken, 4

THE MANAGER

Steve Coppell

Date of birth: 9 July, 1955
Birthplace: Liverpool
Date of appointment: June 1984
Managerial honours:
Crystal Palace: Promotion to Division One 1989; FA Cup finalists 1990; Zenith Data Systems Cup winners 1991

Andy Thorn

THE F.A. PREMIER LEAGUE

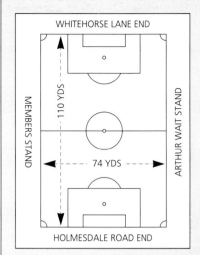

WHITEHORSE LANE END

110 YDS

74 YDS

MEMBERS STAND

ARTHUR WAIT STAND

HOLMESDALE ROAD END

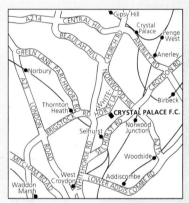

Ground capacity: 30,312
Number of seats: 15,712
Ground capacity (10 years ago): 38,500
Record attendance: 51,482 v Burnley, Division Two, May 5, 1979

Directions to ground

By car: **From north**, M1/A1 to North Circular (A406) to Chiswick; take South Circular (A205) to Wandsworth, A3 to A214 and follow signs to Streatham to A23; turn left on to B273 (1 mile), follow to end and turn left into High Street and into Whitehorse Lane. **From east**, A232 (Croydon Road) to Shirley and join A215 (Norwood Road) for two-and-a-quarter miles, then turn left into Whitehorse Lane. **From south**, A23 and follow signs for Crystal Palace (B266) through Thornton Heath into Whitehorse Lane. **From west**, M4 to Chiswick (then as north).
By train: (BR) Selhurst, Thornton Heath, Norwood Junction
By bus: No 68 to Whitehorse Lane, Nos 50 or 250 to Thornton Heath High St.

DEAN GORDON (defender): Former apprentice who made League debut against Tottenham in December 1991. Finished season with six League and Cup appearances. Born Thornton Heath 10.2.73.

JOHN HUMPHREY (defender): A £425,000 signing from former Selhurst Park tenants Charlton in June 1990. Previously with Wolves. Missed only a handful of appearances in his first two seasons with Palace. Born Paddington 31.1.61.

NIGEL MARTYN (goalkeeper): Made England debut against CIS in April 1992 and travelled to Sweden as understudy to Chris Woods for the European Championship finals. Became Britain's first £1 million goalkeeper when signed from Bristol Rovers in November 1989. Born St Austell 11.8.66.

STUART MASSEY (midfielder): Signed from Sutton United in July 1992 for a 'five-figure sum'. Began

PEN-PIX

ANDY BARNES (forward): Made League debut at QPR in final match of 1991–92 season. Cost £100,000 from non-League Sutton United in September 1991, but out for seven months with badly damaged ligaments. Born Croydon 31.3.67.

MARK BRIGHT (forward): Top-scorer with 22 goals and ever-present last season. A bargain £75,000 buy from Leicester City in November 1986. Previously with Port Vale. Scored more than 100 goals for Palace. Born Stoke 6.2.62.

CHRIS COLEMAN (defender): Scored on debut for Wales against Austria in April 1992. Scored four goals as emergency striker for Palace at end of last season. Signed from Swansea for £275,000 in June 1991. Born Swansea 10.6.70.

STAN COLLYMORE (forward): Signed from non-League Stafford Rangers for £100,000 in December 1990. Previously with Wolves and Walsall. Yet to establish regular place. Born Stone 22.1.71.

Eddie McGoldrick

career with Chipstead, also played for Carshalton and Walton & Hersham. Born Crawley 17.11.64.

EDDIE McGOLDRICK (midfielder): Republic of Ireland international – made debut against Switzerland in March 1992. Cost £200,000 from Northampton in January 1989. Born London 30.4.65.

JAMIE MORALEE (forward): Made League debut against Coventry City in February 1992 and finished season with six appearances. Prolific goalscorer at reserve and youth levels. Born Streatham 2.12.71.

PAUL MORTIMER (midfielder): A £500,000 buy in October 1991 from Aston Villa where he made only 14 appearances, just three months after leaving Charlton for a similar fee. Previously with Fulham. Born Kensington 8.5.68.

MARTYN O'CONNOR (midfielder): Cost £30,000 from Beazer Homes League Premier Division champions Bromsgrove Rovers in May 1992. Born Walsall 10.12.67.

SIMON OSBORN (midfielder): Former Youth team captain at Palace. Made full League debut at Liverpool in April 1991 and became a regular last season. However, he missed final two months with a broken shoulder. Born New Addington 19.1.72.

SIMON RODGER (midfielder): Signed from non-League Bognor Regis for a nominal fee, he made a breakthrough last season and established a regular place. Born Shoreham, Sussex 3.10.71.

JOHN SALAKO (forward): England international who needed special donor surgery in the United States after a serious knee ligament injury ended his season in October 1991. Made England debut against Australia in June 1991. A former YTS player. Born Nigeria 11.2.69.

RICHARD SHAW (defender): Suffered injury problems last season and made only ten appearances. The former apprentice had been a regular in defence. Born Brentford 11.9.68.

LEE SINNOTT (defender): Former England Under-21 international signed from Bradford City for

	Div	P	W	D	L	F	A	Pts	Pos	FA Cup	Lge Cup
1982–83	2	42	12	12	18	43	52	48	15	5	3
1983–84	2	42	12	11	19	42	52	47	18	4	1
1984–85	2	42	12	12	18	46	65	48	15	3	2
1985–86	2	42	19	9	14	57	52	66	5	3	2
1986–87	2	42	19	5	18	51	53	62	6	4	3
1987–88	2	44	22	9	13	86	59	75	6	3	3
1988–89	2	46	23	9	11	71	49	81	3 (P)	3	3
1989–90	1	38	13	9	16	42	66	48	15	F	3
1990–91	1	38	20	9	9	50	41	69	3	3	3
1991–92	1	42	14	15	13	53	61	57	10	3	3

Leading League scorers in last 10 seasons   *League hat-tricks*

1982–83	Mabbutt 10	—
1983–84	Evans 7	—
1984–85	Aylott 8	—
1985–86	Gray 10	—
1986–87	Wright 9	—
1987–88	Bright 25	Wright (1)
1988–89	Wright 24	Bright (1), Wright (1)
1989–90	Bright 12	—
1990–91	Wright 15	Wright (1)
1991–92	Bright 17	—

£300,000 in July 1991. Played left-back in absence of Richard Shaw. Previous clubs are Walsall and Watford. Born Pelsall 12.7.65.

GARETH SOUTHGATE (midfielder): Former apprentice who made League debut at Liverpool in April 1991. Played right-back and in centre of defence before settling in midfield last season. Born Watford 3.9.70.

GEOFF THOMAS (midfielder): Club captain and England midfielder. Omitted from European Championship squad despite not being on losing side in nine internationals under Graham Taylor. Began his career with Rochdale and cost £50,000 from Crewe in May 1987. Born Manchester 5.8.64.

ANDY THORN (defender): A former England Under-21 international he

was a member of Wimbledon's victorious FA Cup-winning side against Liverpool in 1988. Spent a year at Newcastle before a £650,000 move to Palace in November 1989. Born Carshalton 12.11.66.

DAVID WHYTE (forward): Given a chance after the departure of Ian Wright to Arsenal last season. Signed from same local side as Wright, Greenwich Borough, and had loan spell with Charlton at end of season. Born Greenwich 20.4.71.

ERIC YOUNG (defender): Made international debut for Wales against Costa Rica in May 1990 at 30. Was Andy Thorn's partner in defence with Wimbledon in 1988 FA Cup final and joined Palace for £850,000 two years later. Previously with Brighton. Born Singapore 25.3.60.

Everton
(The Toffees)
Founded 1878

Goodison Park,
Liverpool L4 4EL

Telephone numbers
Ground: 051-521 2020
Clubcall: 0898 121199
Ticket details (Box office):
051-523 6666
Ticket information: 0898 121599
Club shop: 051-521 2020
Supporters' club: 051-525 2207
Dial-a-seat: 051-521 1231
Lottery office: 051-525 4891
Club fax: 051-525 9666

*E*verton, who celebrated 100 years at Goodison Park in August 1992, were founded in 1878 by cricketers from St Domingo's Church and became original members of the Football League in 1888. Since then they have spent only four seasons outside the top grade – 1930-31 and from 1951 to 1954. They have been First Division Champions nine times (the last in 1987), runners-up on seven occasions and have won four of 11 FA Cup finals, their latest triumph, in 1984, ultimately leading to the European Cup Winners' Cup in 1985. In the same year they again reached the FA Cup final and were also League Champions.

In the 1980s, Everton appeared in six Wembley finals (including the Simod Cup), playing four in three years – in 1984 they reached the League Cup final for a second time. They lost this in a Maine Road replay to Liverpool, who were to beat them in the FA Cup final in 1986 (also pipping them to the title) and 1989. The intense Merseyside rivalry dates back to 1892, when Everton quit Anfield to relocate across Stanley Park at Goodison, by which time they had already won their first Championship (1891), although they finished runners-up six times before repeating the feat in 1915.

The Toffees also played in two finals (1893 and 1897) before finally winning the FA Cup in 1906, and when they next won it, in their first Wembley appearance in 1933, it concluded a remarkable five-year phase during which they were also Champions twice (1928 and 1932), suffered relegation (1930), and won the Second Division title (1931). Champions again in 1939, Everton ended a long, lean spell in 1963 with their sixth title, lifted the FA Cup in 1966 with a 3–2 triumph after trailing 0–2 to Sheffield Wednesday and, following defeat at Wembley in 1968, took the Championship again in 1970. This was to be their last major honour until 1984, although they were League Cup finalists in 1977. After gaining four trophies between 1984 and 1987, Everton have found the prizes elusive, and last season finished in their lowest position since 1981.

THE MANAGER

Howard Kendall

Date of birth: 22 May, 1946
Birthplace: Ryton-on-Tyne, Co. Durham
Date of appointment: Nov 1990
Previous clubs: Blackburn Rovers, Everton, Athletico Bilbao, Manchester City

Managerial honours:
Everton: League Champions 1985, 1987; FA Cup winners 1984, finalists 1985, 1986; Milk Cup finalists 1984; Zenith Data Systems Cup finalists 1991; European Cup Winners' Cup winners 1985

RECORDS

Biggest wins:
League: 9–1 v Manchester City, Division One, Sept 1906; v Plymouth Argyle, Division Two, Dec 1930
FA Cup: 11–2 v Derby County, 1st round, Jan 1890
Record defeat: 4–10 v Tottenham Hotspur, Division One, Oct 1958
Most appearances: Brian Labone, 530, League and Cup, 1959–72; Ted Sagar, 466, League and Cup, 1929–53
Most goals (aggregate): Bill 'Dixie' Dean, 377, League and Cup, 1925–37
Most goals in a season: Bill 'Dixie' Dean, 63, (including record 60 in Division One), 1927–28
Most capped players:
Past – Kevin Ratcliffe, 58, Wales
Present – Neville Southall, 60, Wales
Other leading internationals:
England: Alan Ball, 39 (72); Ray Wilson, 33 (63); Brian Labone, 26; Gary Stevens, 26 (46)
Scotland: Graeme Sharp, 12
Northern Ireland: Billy Scott, 16 (25)
Republic of Ireland: Kevin Sheedy, 41 (42)

Mo Johnston

PEN-PIX

GARY ABLETT (defender): Signed from Liverpool for £750,000 in January 1992, the England Under-21 international has already collected the game's top domestic honours. He opened his Everton goal-scoring account against West Ham. Born Liverpool 19.11.65.

STUART BARLOW (forward): Youngster who has progressed through the Everton ranks, working his way into the side via the substitutes' bench towards the end of last season. Born Liverpool 16.7.68.

PETER BEAGRIE (midfielder): England B international who found his way to Goodison Park via Middlesbrough, Sheffield United and Stoke City, signing for Everton for £750,000 in November 1989. Has also won two England Under-21 caps. Born Middlesbrough 28.11.65.

THE F.A. PREMIER LEAGUE

PETER BEARDSLEY (forward): Discovered by Carlisle, but after finding his best form with Newcastle, he was bought by Liverpool for £1.9 million in 1987 and subsequently won 49 England caps. Signed for Everton in August 1991. Has also played for Vancouver Whitecaps (twice) and Manchester United. Born Newcastle 18.1.61.

TONY COTTEE (forward): Signed for £2 million in 1988 from West Ham, where he had been the club's top-scorer for the previous four seasons. Won eight Under-21 caps before being promoted and making seven full England appearances. Born West Ham 11.7.65.

JOHN EBBRELL (midfielder): A graduate of the FA School of Excellence at Lilleshall, he is heading for his fifth season as a member of the Everton first team yet has only just grown beyond the England Under-21 age range. He has played

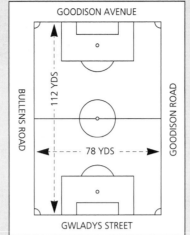

GOODISON AVENUE

112 YDS

BULLENS ROAD

GOODISON ROAD

78 YDS

GWLADYS STREET

Bootle New Strand Station
SOUTHPORT
RICE LANE
Bootle Oriel Rd Station
BALLIOL ROAD
STANLEY ROAD
QUEEN'S DRIVE
WALTON HALL AVE
Kirkdale Station
WALTON RD
COUNTY RD
EVERTON F.C.
Bank Hall Station
WALTON LANE
KIRKDALE RD
WALTON BRECK RD
TOWNSEND LANE
Sandhills Station

Ground capacity: 38,578
Number of seats: 35,235
Ground capacity (10 years ago): 53,091
Record attendance: 78,299 v Liverpool, Division One, 18 Sept, 1948

Directions to ground

By car: **From north**, exit M6 at Junction 28, then follow signs for Liverpool on A58 then A580 and forward into Walton Hall Avenue. **From east and south**, use M6 then M62 until end of motorway, then turn right (A5058) into Queen's Drive; in three-and-three-quarter miles turn left into Walton Hall Avenue. **From west**, use Mersey Tunnel until Liverpool city centre then follow signs Preston (A580) into Walton Hall Avenue.
By train: Lime Street, Liverpool Central and Kirkdale stations
By bus: From city bus station, Nos 1, 2, 19, 20, 21, F1, F2

for England B. Born Bromborough 1.10.69.

ALAN HARPER (defender): Can move to midfield; he is in his second spell with Everton whom he originally joined, from Liverpool, in 1983. He then made a round trip back to Goodison Park via Sheffield Wednesday and Manchester City, rejoining Everton for £300,000 in the summer of 1992. Born Liverpool 1.11.60.

ANDY HINCHCLIFFE (defender): Was nurtured by Manchester City and can also play in midfield. He joined Everton for a valuation of £1.2 million in the summer of 1990 in an exchange deal. Has won England Youth and Under-21 honours. Born Manchester 5.2.69.

BARRY HORNE (midfielder): Welsh international, signed from Southampton in July 1992. Started with Rhyl after obtaining a chemistry

Peter Beardsley

degree from Liverpool University. Has also played for Wrexham and Portsmouth. Born St Asaph 18.5.62.

MATTHEW JACKSON (defender): A Luton schoolboy who made such an impression for his home team in the early part of last season that Everton paid £760,000 for him in October 1991. Standing 6ft he is tall for a full-back. While at Luton he spent time on loan at Preston. Born Leeds 19.10.71.

IAIN JENKINS (defender): Everton trainee who had made only one appearance until last season and then made three (two from the substitutes' bench) in the closing weeks. Born Prescot 24.11.72.

MO JOHNSTON (forward): Free-scoring Scottish international who joined Everton from Glasgow Rangers for £1.5 million in November 1991. Has also played for Rangers' rivals Celtic, but began his career with Partick Thistle. Played in an FA Cup final with Watford and spent time with Nantes in France. Born Glasgow 30.4.63.

MARTIN KEOWN (defender): A key member of the England European Championship side, Keown joined Everton from Aston Villa in June 1989 for £750,000 and has burst on to the international scene only this year. Started career with Arsenal and had two spells on loan to Brighton. Born Oxford 24.7.66.

PAT NEVIN (forward): Art-loving winger who spent time last season on loan with Tranmere Rovers, he is a Scotland international who joined Everton for nearly £1 million from Chelsea in July 1988. Started career at Clyde. Born Glasgow 6.9.63.

GERRY PEYTON (goalkeeper): Signed in June, 1991 as cover for Southall, he has found openings few and far between and went on loan to Norwich towards the end of last season. Well-travelled, he has full Republic of Ireland caps and joined Everton from Bournemouth, having previously been with Burnley and Fulham. Born Birmingham 20.5.56.

NEVILLE SOUTHALL (goalkeeper): Plucked from non-League football with Winsford United by Bury, he signed for Everton in 1981 and had a spell on loan at Port Vale, before establishing himself with the Goodison club and at international level with Wales, for whom he has played 60 times. Born Llandudno 16.9.58.

DAVID UNSWORTH (defender): Trainee who made a spectacular debut against Tottenham last season, coming from the substitutes' bench to score in the 3–3 draw. He then earned a starting place for the last game of the season against Chelsea. Born Preston 16.10.73.

MARK WARD (midfielder): Served an apprenticeship with Everton before being released and going to non-League Northwich Victoria, where he was spotted and signed by Oldham in 1983. Moved to West Ham and then Manchester City before completing the circle in August 1991 when he returned to Goodison for £1 million. Born Prescot 10.10.62.

ROBERT WARZYCHA (forward): Established Polish international who joined Everton in the spring of 1991 and scored on his debut, against Leeds United in the Zenith Data Systems Cup northern final, and then again in the final against Crystal Palace at Wembley. Cost £500,000 from Gornik Zabrze. Born Poland 20.8.63.

DAVE WATSON (defender): The former England international moved to Goodison Park from Norwich for nearly £1 million in 1986. He started his career with Liverpool, although he did not make a first-team appearance while at Anfield. He won 12 England caps. Born Liverpool 20.11.61.

EVERTON: 10–YEAR RECORD

	Div	P	W	D	L	F	A	Pts	Pos	FA Cup	Lge Cup
1982–83	1	42	18	10	14	66	48	64	7	QF	3
1983–84	1	42	16	14	12	44	42	62	7	W	F
1984–85	1	42	28	6	8	88	43	90	1	F	4
1985–86	1	42	26	8	8	87	41	86	2	F	4
1986–87	1	42	26	8	8	76	31	86	1	5	QF
1987–88	1	40	19	13	8	53	27	70	4	5	SF
1988–89	1	38	14	12	12	50	45	54	8	F	4
1989–90	1	38	17	8	13	57	46	59	6	5	4
1990–91	1	38	13	12	13	50	46	51	9	QF	3
1991–92	1	42	13	14	15	52	51	53	12	4	4

Leading League scorers in last 10 seasons | *League hat-tricks*

	Leading League scorers	League hat-tricks
1982–83	Sharp 15	—
1983–84	Heath 12	Heath (1)
1984–85	Sharp 21	—
1985–86	Lineker 30	Lineker (3)
1986–87	Steven 14	Clarke (1)
1987–88	Sharp 13	Sharp (1 x 4)
1988–89	Cottee 13	Cottee (1)
1989–90	Cottee 13	—
1990-91	Cottee 10	—
1991-92	Beardsley 15	Beardsley (1), Cottee (1)

Ipswich Town

(The Blues)

Founded 1878

Portman Road,
Ipswich IP1 2DA

Telephone numbers
Ground: 0473 219211
Soccerline: 0839 664488
Ticket details: 0473 219211
Club shop: 0473 219211
Supporters' club: 0473 219211
Club fax: 0473 226835

*I*pswich Town, founded in 1878 but an amateur organisation until two years before their election, in 1938, to the Football League, will always be synonymous with two men who later managed England – Alf Ramsey (1955–63), who took them from Division Three (South) to the First Division title; and Bobby Robson (1969–82), whose team won the FA Cup, the UEFA Cup, and confirmed their top-grade credentials in the late 1970s and early 1980s. In 1954 the long-serving Scott Duncan (1937–55) led them into Division Two, where they survived only one season, but Ramsey's side clinched the Third Division (South) title on goal average in his second term (1957) and in 1961 they were Second Division Champions. A year later Ipswich astonished the football world by topping the First Division.

Ramsey's departure coincided with a slide to 17th, and under his initial successor, Jackie Milburn, Ipswich crashed to relegation in 1964, conceding 121 goals, which included traumatic setbacks at Fulham (1–10) and Stoke City (1–9), six-goal defeats at Arsenal, Bolton and Liverpool, and a 2–7 fall at home to Manchester United. Bill McGarry led them to another Division Two title in 1968, followed, after a modest start under Bobby Robson, by a run during which they finished lower than sixth only once in ten years. Ironically, that was in 1978 when they compensated (and made club history) with an FA Cup triumph over Arsenal at Wembley.

Runners-up in 1981 (when they won the UEFA Cup and reached the FA Cup semi-final) and 1982, they suffered a decline following Robson's departure, sliding in successive seasons until suffering relegation in 1986, and although they reached the 1987 play-offs they failed to gain promotion. However, John Lyall's arrival in 1990, while not immediately successful, led to the long-awaited upturn as Ipswich claimed their third Second Division title – and a place in the Premier League – in 1992. The other milestones in the season were completing 2,000 League matches and topping 3,000 goals!

THE MANAGER

John Lyall

Date of birth: 24 Feb, 1940
Birthplace: Ilford
Date of appointment: May 1990
Previous club: West Ham United

Managerial honours:
West Ham United: Division Two Champions 1981; FA Cup winners 1975, 1980; League Cup finalists 1981
Ipswich Town: Division Two Champions 1992

Barclays League Division 2 Champions 1991–92
Back row (left to right): Craig Forrest, Gavin Johnson, Steve Whitton, Eddie Youds, Neil Thompson, Phil Whelan, Romeo Zondervan, Steve Palmer, Frank Yallop, Glenn Pennyfather, John Wark, David Gregory. Front row (left to right): Mick Stockwell, Paul Goddard, Chris Kiwomya, David Linighan, Jason Dozzell, Simon Milton (and mascot, Sam Bullard)

RECORDS

Biggest wins:
League: 7–0 v Portsmouth, Division Two, Nov 1964; v Southampton, Division One, Feb 1974; v WBA, Division One, Nov 1976
FA Cup: 7–0 v Street, 1st round, March 1938 (Note: Ipswich once beat Cromer 11–0 in a qualifying round game in Oct 1936.)
Record defeat: 1–10 v Fulham, Division One, Dec 1963
Most appearances: Mick Mills, 740, League and Cup, 1966–83
Most goals (aggregate): Ray Crawford, 227, League and Cup, 1958–69
Most goals in a season: Ted Phillips, 46, League and Cup, 1956–57
Most capped player: Allan Hunter, 47 (53), Northern Ireland
Other leading internationals:
England: Terry Butcher, 45 (77); Mick Mills, 42; Paul Mariner, 33 (35)
Scotland: John Wark, 26 (29)
Wales: Mick Hill, 2
Northern Ireland: Bryan Hamilton, 21 (50)
Republic of Ireland: Kevin O'Callaghan, 17 (20)

THE F.A. PREMIER LEAGUE

Ground capacity: 23,000
Number of seats: 23,000
Ground capacity (10 years ago): 32,500
Record attendance: 38,010 v Leeds United, FA Cup, 6th round, 8 March, 1975

Directions to ground

By car: From junction at A12/A45 take A1214 signposted to Ipswich, go over two sets of traffic lights and at next set of traffic lights turn right into West End Road. Ground is on left approximately one-and-a-half miles.

By train: 5-minutes walk from station into Princes Street, across bridge and Portman Road is on the left.

By bus: Nos 12, 13, 15 (Ipswich Buses). Nos 90, 91, 92, 93, 94, 95, 96, 97 and 98 (Eastern Counties). All stop in Princes Street, 1-minute walk from the main stand in Portman Road.

Jason Dozzell

PEN-PIX

JASON DOZZELL (midfielder): Joined the club from school and at 16 was the youngest scorer in the First Division when making his debut against Coventry in 1984. Can play in attack or defence and has been capped at Under-21 level for England. Born Ipswich 9.12.67.

CRAIG FORREST (goalkeeper): Canadian international and former ice hockey player who joined the club in 1985–86 but had to wait for his League debut until a loan spell at Colchester in 1988. Stands at 6ft 4in. Was ever-present in the side during last season's Championship-winning campaign. Born Vancouver 20.9.67.

PAUL GODDARD (forward): Joined on a free transfer from Millwall in January 1991 when Ipswich became his sixth club after time at QPR, West Ham, Newcastle and Derby. Has one full England cap having played against Iceland in 1982. Born Harlington 12.10.59.

DAVID GREGORY (midfielder): A former YTS trainee. Yet to establish himself in first team, starting only one match last season, against Bristol Rovers in the Zenith Data Systems Cup. Born Sudbury 23.1.70.

LEE HONEYWOOD (defender): Son of Brian Honeywood, the former Ipswich and Colchester player, he has suffered with injuries over the last three seasons. A highly rated full-back who can double up in midfield, he has won England Youth honours. Born Chelmsford 3.8.71.

GAVIN JOHNSON (defender): Established himself last season, scoring six goals. He made his debut against Barnsley in February 1989 after joining the club straight from school. Born Ipswich 10.10.70.

CHRIS KIWOMYA (forward): Yorkshire player with explosive pace who was the club's top goalscorer in the 1990–91 season with 12 and in 1991–92 with 19. Has formed impressive partnerships with Dozzell and Goddard. A product of the club's youth policy, Kiwomya suffered a four-match break last term with injury. Born Huddersfield 2.12.69.

DAVID LINIGHAN (defender): Club captain and a former player of the year, whose brother Andy is on the books at Arsenal. David played for Hartlepool for five seasons, going on to Derby and then Shrewsbury before becoming, at the time, Ipswich's record signing at £300,000 in June 1988. Born Hartlepool 9.1.65.

DAVID LOWE (forward): Joined from Wigan for £100,000 in June 1987; he has been capped at England Youth and Under-21 level and was top goal-scorer in his first season at Portman Road. After suffering from injury, he found opportunities were limited last season. Born Liverpool 30.8.65.

SIMON MILTON (midfielder): Signed from non-League Bury Town, he spent time on loan at Exeter and Torquay before becoming a key member of the side. He made a delayed start to the 1991–92 campaign, not appearing until October. Born London 23.8.63.

STEVE PALMER (midfielder): Spotted while playing for Cambridge University against Ipswich, he has an honours degree in electrical information engineering and has played first-class cricket. Made his Ipswich debut in 1989–90 and was a vital member of last season's squad. Born Brighton 31.3.68.

GLENN PENNYFATHER (midfielder): Signed from Crystal Palace for £80,000 in October 1989, he has struggled against illness and injury and made only a few appearances last season. Started his career with Southend. Born Billericay 11.2.63.

MICK STOCKWELL (midfielder): Was a schoolboy with Leyton Orient but served out his apprenticeship at Portman Road. He has proved himself a versatile member of the squad, successful in attack and defence. Scored two goals last season and missed only one game. Born Chelmsford 14.2.65.

NEIL THOMPSON (defender): Started as an apprentice with Nottingham Forest but was released and joined Hull City, moving on to Scarborough and then Portman Road for £100,000 in the summer of 1989. The club's free-kick expert, he scored four goals last season. Born Beverley 2.10.63.

JOHN WARK (midfielder): A Scotland international and member of the Ipswich side which won the FA Cup and UEFA Cup in the late 1970s and early 1980s, he is in his third spell at the club after appearing for both Liverpool and Middlesbrough. He

started as an apprentice at Portman Road. Born Glasgow 4.8.57.

PHIL WHELAN (defender): Having scored on his League debut against Southend and again in his next match against Wolves, he established himself towards the end of the season playing eight consecutive games. He is studying accountancy at Norwich University and has played for England Schools at Under-18 level. Born Stockport 7.8.72.

STEVE WHITTON (forward): A much-travelled goalscorer who started out at Coventry and went to West Ham, Birmingham City and Sheffield Wednesday before becoming John Lyall's first signing in January 1991. Scored on his debut against WBA. Born East Ham 4.12.60.

GERAINT WILLIAMS (midfielder): Signed for a club record £650,000

from Derby County in July. Spent seven full seasons at Derby since signing from first club Bristol Rovers for £40,000 in March 1985. Capped 11 times by Wales. Born Treorchy 5.1.62.

FRANK YALLOP (defender): The club's other Canadian international, who was brought up in Vancouver. He joined Ipswich as a youth player and has made over 250 appearances in the No 2 shirt. Born Watford 4.4.64.

EDDIE YOUDS (defender): Signed from Everton for £250,000 but injured knee ligaments after 57 minutes of his debut against Derby in November 1991 and was out for the rest of the season. An Everton trainee, he had spells on loan at Cardiff and Wrexham before moving to Portman Road. Born Liverpool 3.5.70.

IPSWICH TOWN: 10-YEAR RECORD

	Div	P	W	D	L	F	A	Pts	Pos	FA Cup	Lge Cup
1982–83	1	42	15	13	14	64	50	58	9	5	2
1983–84	1	42	15	8	19	55	57	53	12	4	4
1984–85	1	42	13	11	18	46	57	50	17	QF	SF
1985–86	1	42	11	8	23	32	55	41	20 (R)	4	QF
1986–87	2	42	17	13	12	59	43	64	5	3	3
1987–88	2	44	19	9	16	61	52	66	8	3	4
1988–89	2	46	22	7	17	71	61	73	8	3	4
1989–90	2	46	19	12	15	67	66	69	9	4	2
1990–91	2	46	13	18	15	60	68	57	14	3	3
1991–92	2	46	24	12	10	70	50	84	1 (P)	5	2

Leading League scorers in last 10 seasons

1982–83	Wark 20
1983–84	Gates 13
1984–85	Gates 13
1935–86	Wilson 7
1986–87	Wilson 20
1987–88	Lowe 17
1988–89	Wark 13
1989–90	Lowe 13
1990–91	Kiwomya 10
1991–92	Kiwomya 16

League hat-tricks

Wark (1 x 4)

—

Wilson (1)

—

Deehan (1), Gleghorn (1), Wilson (2)

Atkinson (1)

Milton (1)

—

—

—

Leeds United
(United)

Founded 1919

Elland Road,
Leeds LS11 0ES

Telephone numbers
Ground: 0532 716037
Clubcall: 0898 121180
Ticket details: 0898 121680
Club shop: 0532 706844
Club fax: 0532 706560

Leeds United, formed in late 1919 after Leeds City (1904) were disbanded by the FA, completed 65 seasons in the Football League in 1992 by winning their third Championship, their first Division One title since 1974 confirming the remarkable extent of their renaissance under Howard Wilkinson.

When, in October 1988, Wilkinson became their eighth manager since Don Revie, Leeds were in their seventh season in Division Two – a far cry from the Revie glory years which, at the peak between 1968 and 1974, saw them win both the Championship and the Fairs Cup twice and lift the FA Cup and League Cup. Moreover, in Revie's 13 years, they were First Division runners-up five times, and beaten finalists in the FA Cup (three times), the Fairs Cup, and the European Cup Winners' Cup. In 1970 they were runners-up in both League and Cup, and in 1972 missed the double by losing their final League game.

Leeds spent 13 of 19 pre-war seasons in Division One, but passed nine of their first ten post-war years in Division Two. After falling again in 1960, following a four-year revival, they almost dropped into Division Three in Revie's first full season, 1961–62. However, following their return to the top in 1964, they promptly confirmed their determination to become a major force, and, though they endured so many near misses, not capturing their first top trophy until the League Cup win of 1968, their first Championship triumph in 1969 marked the beginning of a memorable phase.

After Revie went, they gradually lost their way, and an 18-year run in Division One ended in 1982. Though they reached the promotion play-offs and the FA Cup semi-final in 1987, their fortunes did not revive until Wilkinson's arrival. He swept away the last remnants of the Revie era, leading the side to their third Division Two title in 1990; and, after finishing fourth in 1991, brought the Championship to Elland Road a year later.

RECORDS

Biggest wins:
League: 8–0 v Leicester City, Division One, April 1934
FA Cup: 8–1 v Crystal Palace, 3rd round, Jan 1930
European Cup: 10–0 (aggregate 16–0) v Lyn Oslo, 1st round, 1st leg, Sept 1969
Record defeats: 1–8 v Stoke City, Division One, Aug 1934; 0–7 v Arsenal, League Cup, 2nd round, 2nd leg, Sept 1979; 0–7 v West Ham, League Cup, 4th round, Nov 1966
Most appearances: Jack Charlton, 771, League and Cup, 1953–73

Most goals (aggregate): Peter Lorimer, 239, League and Cup, 1965–79 and 1983–86
Most goals in a season: John Charles, 43 (42 League), 1953–54
Most capped players:
Past – Billy Bremner, 54, Scotland
Present – Gary Speed, 14, Wales; Gary McAllister, 15 (18), Scotland
Other leading internationals:
England: Jack Charlton, 35; Norman Hunter, 28; Trevor Cherry, 27
Scotland: Joe Jordan, 27 (52)
Wales: Brian Flynn, 32 (66); Gary Sprake, 32 (37)
Northern Ireland: Wilbur Cush, 15 (26
Republic of Ireland: Johnny Giles, 32 (60)

THE MANAGER

Howard Wilkinson

Date of birth: 13 Nov, 1943
Birthplace: Sheffield
Date of appointment: Oct 1988
Previous clubs: Boston United, Notts County, Sheffield Wednesday

Managerial honours:
Notts County: Promotion to Division One 1981
Sheffield Wednesday: Division Two runners-up 1984
Leeds United: Football League Champions 1992; Division Two Champions 1990

PEN-PIX

DAVID BATTY (midfielder): England international and Leeds trainee who broke into the first team in 1987 and has held a regular spot ever since. Born Leeds 2.12.68.

ERIC CANTONA (forward): Signed by Leeds in February 1992 after a trial with Sheffield Wednesday fell through. A first-choice striker for France. Born Auxerre, France, 24.5.66.

LEE CHAPMAN (forward): Top-scorer last season with 20 goals in his second consecutive campaign in goal-getting form. Transferred from Nottingham Forest in 1990 for £450,000. Previously with Stoke, Arsenal, Sunderland, Sheffield Wednesday and Niort, of France. Born Lincoln 5.12.59.

MERVYN DAY (goalkeeper): Having played more than 250 matches for Leeds, he is now understudy to Lukic, but did not play for the first team last season. Is also a coach at the club. Born Chelmsford 26.6.55.

David Batty (left) and Gary McAllister

THE F.A. PREMIER LEAGUE

TONY DORIGO (defender): Left-back in England's European Championship squad. Started his League career at Aston Villa, before moving to Chelsea in 1987. Joined Leeds at the start of last season for £1.3 million. Born Melbourne, Australia, 31.12.65.

CHRIS FAIRCLOUGH (defender): Central defender signed from Tottenham in 1989 for £500,000, he has formed a solid partnership with Chris Whyte. Started at Nottingham Forest where he won England Under-21 honours. Born Nottingham 12.4.64.

PETER HADDOCK (defender): A key member of the 1990 Second Division Championship team, he missed the whole of last season through injury. A versatile player, he cost £45,000 from Newcastle in 1986. Born Newcastle 9.12.61.

STEVE HODGE (midfielder): Won over 20 caps for England in the late 1980s. Cost Leeds £900,000 in a transfer from Nottingham Forest (with whom he had two spells) in the summer of 1991. Has also played for Aston Villa and Tottenham. Born Nottingham 25.10.62.

JOHN LUKIC (goalkeeper): Ever-present last season while winning his second Championship medal. The first was with Arsenal, from whom he became Leeds' first £1 million signing, in 1990, for his second spell with the club. Born Chesterfield 11.12.60.

GARY McALLISTER (midfielder): A £1 million signing from Leicester City in 1990 and ever-present in the Championship-winning side. A regular for the Scottish national team. Began his career at Motherwell in 1981. Born Motherwell 25.12.64.

JON NEWSOME (defender): Started as a trainee at Sheffield Wednesday. Joined Leeds along with David Wetherall in a £275,000 transfer at the start of last season and broke into the team in the Championship run-in. Born Sheffield 6.9.70.

SCOTT SELLARS (midfielder): Former England Under-21 international who spent four seasons at Elland Road before joining Blackburn for £25,000 in August 1986. Rejoined Leeds in July 1992. Born Sheffield 27.11.65.

CARL SHUTT (forward): Used mainly as a substitute last season, but has made over 50 League appearances since signing from Bristol City in 1989. Started with Sheffield Wednesday and was loaned out to Swedish side Malmo two years ago. Born Sheffield 10.10.61.

GARY SPEED (midfielder): Welsh international who progressed from the Elland Road youth set-up, and has missed only one League game in the last two seasons, scoring 11 goals in 1991–92. Can play in many positions, but usually left midfield. Born Hawarden 8.9.69.

MEL STERLAND (defender): Right-back capped once by England in 1987. Scored vital goals last season, but was injured for the last two months. Made over 250 appearances for Sheffield Wednesday and had a short stay at Glasgow Rangers in 1989 before returning to Yorkshire. Born Sheffield 1.10.61.

GORDON STRACHAN (midfielder): Would have captained Scotland in the 1992 European Championship but for a back injury. Won Scottish Championship, Scottish Cup and European Cup Winners' Cup medals with Aberdeen after leaving Dundee, then spent five years at Manchester United. A £330,000 move to Leeds in 1989 rejuvenated his career. Born Edinburgh 9.2.57.

RAY WALLACE (defender): Transferred from Southampton as part of the deal involving his twin brother, Rod. Valued at £100,000, he has yet to play for the first team, but had

LEEDS UNITED: 10–YEAR RECORD

	Div	P	W	D	L	F	A	Pts	Pos	FA Cup	Lge Cup
1982–83	2	42	13	21	8	51	46	60	8	4	3
1983–84	2	42	16	12	14	55	56	60	10	3	3
1984–85	2	42	19	12	11	66	42	69	7	3	3
1985–86	2	42	15	8	19	56	72	53	14	3	3
1986–87	2	42	19	11	12	58	44	68	4	SF	2
1987–88	2	44	19	12	13	61	51	69	7	3	3
1988–89	2	46	17	16	13	59	50	67	10	4	3
1989–90	2	46	24	13	9	79	52	85	1 (P)	3	2
1990–91	1	38	19	7	12	65	47	64	4	4	SF
1991–92	1	42	22	16	4	74	37	82	1	3	QF

Leading League scorers in last 10 seasons

		League hat-tricks
1982–83	Butterworth 11	—
1983–84	McCluskey 8, Wright 8	—
1984–85	Wright 14	Ritchie (2), Wright (1)
1985–86	Baird 12	—
1986–87	Baird 15, Sheridan 15	Baird (1)
1987–88	Sheridan 12	Pearson (1)
1988–89	Davison 14	Shutt (1)
1989–90	Strachan 16	Strachan (1)
1990–91	Chapman 21	Chapman (1)
1991–92	Chapman 16	Chapman (2)

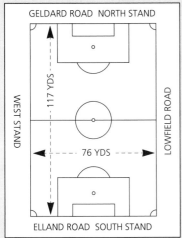

GELDARD ROAD NORTH STAND

117 YDS

76 YDS

WEST STAND

LOWFIELD ROAD

ELLAND ROAD SOUTH STAND

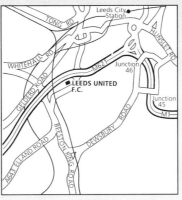

Ground capacity: 30,744
Number of seats: 20,400
Ground capacity (10 years ago): 40,000
Record attendance: 57,892 v Sunderland, FA Cup, 5th round replay, 15 March, 1967

Directions to ground
By car: **From north**, A58 or A61 to city centre; join M621 and take A643 from roundabout into Elland Road.
From south, M1, M621 to A643 into Elland Road.
From east, A62 or A64 into city centre then as from north.
From west, M62, M621 to A643 into Elland Road.
By train: Leeds City
By bus: From Vicar Lane Nos 49, 51, 51A, 52, 52A, 53, 53A, 54. From City Square No 96

Lee Chapman

a loan spell at Swansea. Born Lewisham 2.10.69.

ROD WALLACE (forward): Became Leeds United's most expensive player when signed for £1.6 million from Southampton at the start of last season. Scored 14 goals in all competitions. Has played for England at Under-21 and B level. Born Lewisham 2.10.69.

DAVID WETHERALL (defender): A member of the Great Britain team which won bronze at the 1991 World Student games. Signed from Sheffield Wednesday in a combined deal with Jon Newsome, but has yet to establish a first-team place. Born Sheffield 14.3.71.

CHRIS WHYTE (defender): Missed only one match in central defence last season. Cost £500,000 from WBA in 1990. Won Under-21 caps at Arsenal in the early 1980s and has also played for Los Angeles Raiders. Born Islington 2.9.61.

Liverpool

(The Reds)

Founded 1892

Anfield Road,
Anfield, Liverpool L4 0TH

Telephone numbers
Ground: 051-263 2361/2
Clubcall: 0898 121184
Ticket details: 051-260 9999
Club shop: 051-263 1760
Supporters' club: 051-263 6386
Club fax: 051-260 8813

Liverpool's achievements since 1963 are truly remarkable: 13 times League Champions, five FA Cup triumphs in eight finals, four League Cup wins (in successive years) in six finals, four European Cup successes in five finals, and two UEFA Cup victories - with a hat-trick of titles (1982, 1983, 1984), three major trophies in one year (1984) and a League and Cup double in another (1986).

Formed in March 1892 after Everton quit Anfield and the landlord chose to launch a new club, Liverpool FC. Won the Second Division three times and the First Division twice in their first 14 years; but then, though reaching their first FA Cup final in 1914 and being Champions in 1922 and 1923, they found the prizes largely elusive for the next 40 years. Indeed, though they were Champions again at last in 1947, their run of 38 consecutive seasons in Division One ended in 1954, and it was not until Bill Shankly's arrival in 1959 that the tide began to turn. They won the Second Division title in 1962, and by 1966 had claimed two Championships, won the FA Cup for the first time, and reached the European Cup Winners' Cup final. By the time Shankly retired in 1974, Liverpool had again won the League title and lifted the UEFA Cup. Under Bob Paisley, they were six times English Champions and three times European champions, with Joe Fagan's 1984 side completing that title hat-trick, as well as adding the European Cup and the fourth League Cup success.

Kenny Dalglish saw the double achieved in 1986, and almost repeated it in 1988 and 1989 (the year they were pipped to the title by Arsenal on goal difference), and his era brought Liverpool three Championships (making a record 18 in all) and two FA Cup wins. Last season, under Graeme Souness, Liverpool finished in their lowest position (sixth) since 1981, but, true to a tradition which has seen them fail to lift a trophy in only three seasons since 1975, they ended their programme with a fifth FA Cup triumph – to launch their Premier League era with their 23rd excursion into Europe.

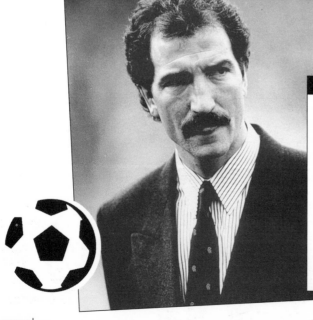

THE MANAGER

Graeme Souness

Date of birth: 6 May, 1953
Birthplace: Edinburgh
Date of appointment: April 1991
Previous club: Glasgow Rangers

Managerial honours:
Glasgow Rangers: Scottish League Champions 1987, 1989, 1990; Skol Cup winners 1987, 1988, 1989, 1991; Scottish Cup runners-up 1989
Liverpool: FA Cup winners 1992

Liverpool

Liverpool

RECORDS

Biggest wins:
League: 10–1 v Rotherham Town, Division Two, Feb 1896; 9–0 v Crystal Palace, Division One, Sept 1989
FA Cup: 8–0 v Swansea, 2nd round replay, Jan 1990
League Cup: 10–0 v Fulham, 3rd round, Sept 1986
European Cup Winners' Cup: 11–0 v Stromsgodset, 1st round, 1st leg, Sept 1974
Record defeat: 1–9 v Birmingham City, Division One, Dec 1954
Most appearances: Ian Callaghan, 848, League and Cup, 1959–78

Most goals (aggregate): Roger Hunt, 285, League and Cup, 1959–69
Most goals in a season: Ian Rush, 47, League and Cup, 1983–84
Most capped players:
Past – Emlyn Hughes, 59 (62), England
Present – Ian Rush, 49 (54), Wales
Other leading internationals:
England: Ray Clemence, 56 (61); Phil Neal, 50; Phil Thompson, 42; John Barnes, 36 (67)
Scotland: Kenny Dalglish, 55 (102)
Wales: John Toshack, 26
Northern Ireland: Elisha Scott, 27 (31)
Republic of Ireland: Ronnie Whelan, 42

PEN-PIX

JOHN BARNES (forward): Cost £900,000 from Watford in July 1987. He damaged an ankle while winning his 67th England cap, in Finland in June, after missing most of last season through injury. Born Jamaica 7.11.63.

DAVID BURROWS (defender): Left-back or midfielder, he signed from WBA for £500,000 in October 1988. Has been capped by England at B and Under-21 level. Born Dudley 25.10.68.

BRUCE GROBBELAAR (goalkeeper): Zimbabwean international, signed from Vancouver Whitecaps for £250,000 in March 1981. Originally played for Crewe before moving to Canada. Born Durban, South Africa, 6.10.57.

STEVE HARKNESS (midfielder): England Youth international midfielder. Spent one season with first club Carlisle before Liverpool signed him for £75,000 in July 1989. Born Carlisle 27.8.71.

Ray Houghton (left) and Mark Walters

THE F.A. PREMIER LEAGUE

Liverpool **51**

MIKE HOOPER (goalkeeper): Formerly with Bristol City and Wrexham, he signed for £40,000 in October 1985 and is a regular deputy for Grobbelaar. Born Bristol 10.2.64.

RAY HOUGHTON (midfielder): A Republic of Ireland international who started at West Ham before joining Fulham and then Oxford United. Signed for Liverpool for £800,000 in October 1987. Born Glasgow 9.1.62.

DAVID JAMES (goalkeeper): England Youth and Under-21 international who signed for Watford as a trainee. Pursued by several Premier League

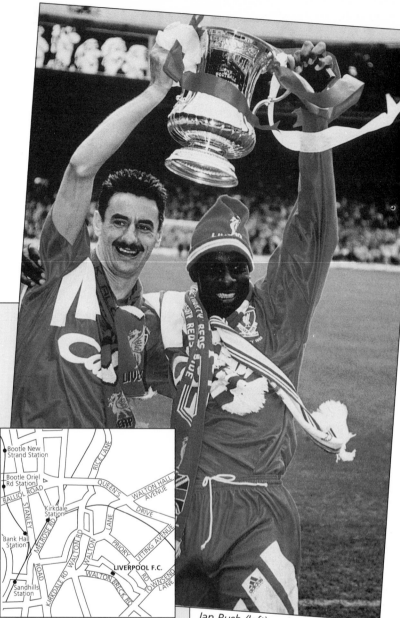

Ian Rush (left) and Michael Thomas with the FA Cup

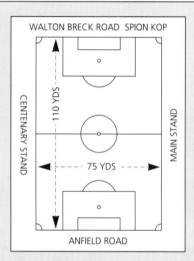

Ground capacity: 44,631
Number of seats: 28,451
Ground capacity (10 years ago): 50,133
Record attendance: 61,905 v Wolverhampton Wanderers, FA Cup, 4th round, 2 Feb, 1952

Directions to ground

By car: **From north**, exit M6 Junction 23 and follow Liverpool (A580) signs into Walton Hall Avenue; pass Stanley Park and turn left into Anfield Road.
From south and east, take M62 to end of motorway, turn right under flyover into Queen's Drive (A5058), turn left (3 miles) into Utting Avenue; continue into Arkles Lane; turn right into Anfield Road.
From North Wales, take Mersey tunnel into city centre and follow signs to Preston into Walton Hall Avenue; turn right into Anfield Road before Stanley Park.
By train: Merseyrail City centre to Kirkdale Station
By bus: Nos 17 and 26 from city centre

clubs before agreeing to sign for Liverpool in June 1992. Born Welwyn 1.8.70.

ROB JONES (defender): Signed from Crewe for £300,000 (a further £300,000 will be paid if he plays a specified number of games) in September 1991. An England international like his grandfather, who also played for Liverpool. Born Wrexham 5.11.71.

ISTVAN KOZMA (midfielder): Cost £300,000 from Dunfermline last season. A Hungarian international midfielder, he started with Ujpest Dozsa and moved to Scotland from Bordeaux, of France, in 1989. Born Paszto, Hungary, 3.12.64.

MIKE MARSH (midfielder): Has played at full-back, midfield and in attack. Joined from non-League Kirkby Town in March 1988. Born Liverpool 21.7.69.

STEVE McMANAMAN (forward): A former YTS trainee and Everton supporter, he is an England Under-21 international, who made his debut in December 1990. Born Liverpool 11.2.72.

JAN MOLBY (midfielder): Danish international, but not selected for the European Championship squad. He cost £225,000 from Ajax Amsterdam in August 1984. Born Kolding, Denmark, 4.7.63.

STEVE NICOL (defender): Scotland international utility player, signed from Ayr United in October 1981 for £300,000. Had a shoulder operation in summer 1992. Born Irvine 11.12.61.

JAMIE REDKNAPP (midfielder): Son of former Bournemouth manager Harry Redknapp, he cost £350,000 from Bournemouth in January 1991 – the biggest ever transfer fee in British football for a 17-year-old. Born Barton-on-Sea 25.6.73.

RONNY ROSENTHAL (forward): Israeli international striker, who signed for Liverpool for £650,000 from Belgium club Standard Liege in June 1990, following a two-month loan period. Born Haifa 11.10.63.

IAN RUSH (forward): A Welsh international striker who was originally with Chester, he rejoined Liverpool from Juventus for £2.8 million in August 1988, having been sold to them in June 1986 for a club record £3.2 million. Born St Asaph 20.10.61.

DEAN SAUNDERS (forward): Formerly with Swansea City, Brighton, Oxford United and Derby before signing for Liverpool in July 1991 for £2.9 million – a record fee between

British clubs. A Welsh international. Born Swansea 21.6.64.

NICK TANNER (defender): Began last season as a reserve but has become a first-team regular during Liverpool's injury crisis. Signed from Bristol Rovers for £20,000 in June 1988. Born Bristol 24.5.65.

MICHAEL THOMAS (midfielder): He signed from Arsenal in a £1.5 million transfer in December 1991, after being unable to command a regular place at Highbury. An England international. Born Lambeth 24.8.67.

MARK WALTERS (forward): Signed from Glasgow Rangers for £1.25 million in August 1991. Won three Premier League titles and three Skol Cup finals with Rangers. Previously with Aston Villa, he is an England international. Born Birmingham 2.6.64.

RONNIE WHELAN (midfielder): Signed by Bob Paisley in 1981, from Irish team Home Farm. A Republic of Ireland international, he has made more than 300 appearances for the club. Born Dublin 25.9.61.

MARK WRIGHT (defender): England international, who cost £2.2 million from Derby County last summer. Club captain who led Liverpool to their FA Cup final triumph in May. Previously with Oxford and Southampton. Born Dorchester 1.8.63.

LIVERPOOL: 10–YEAR RECORD

	Div	P	W	D	L	F	A	Pts	Pos	FA Cup	Lge Cup
1982–83	1	42	24	10	8	87	37	82	1	5	W
1983–84	1	42	22	14	6	73	32	80	1	4	W
1984–85	1	42	22	11	9	68	35	77	2	SF	3
1985–86	1	42	26	10	6	89	37	88	1	W	SF
1986–87	1	42	23	8	11	72	42	77	2	3	F
1987–88	1	40	26	12	2	87	24	90	1	F	3
1988–89	1	38	22	10	6	65	28	76	2	W	4
1989–90	1	38	23	10	5	78	37	79	1	SF	3
1990–91	1	38	23	7	8	77	40	76	2	5	3
1991–92	1	42	16	16	10	47	40	64	6	W	4

Leading League scorers in last 10 seasons		League hat-tricks
1982–83	Rush 24	Dalglish (1), Rush (1 x 4, 2 x 3)
1983–84	Rush 32	Robinson (1), Rush (1 x 5, 1 x 4, 1 x 3)
1984–85	Wark 18	Wark (1)
1985–86	Rush 23	Gillespie (1), Rush (1), Whelan (1)
1986–87	Rush 30	Rush (1), Walsh (1)
1987–88	Aldridge 26	Aldridge (1), Nicol (1)
1988–89	Aldridge 21	Aldridge (2)
1989–90	Barnes 22	Barnes (1), Rosenthal (1)
1990–91	Barnes 16, Rush 16	Beardsley (1)
1991–92	Saunders 10	—

Manchester City
(The Blues)
Founded 1887

Maine Road, Moss Side,
Manchester M14 7WN

Telephone numbers
Ground: 061-226 1191/2
Clubcall: 0898 121191
Ticket details: 061-226 2224
Ticketcall: 0898 121591
Club shop: 061-226 4824
Supporters' club: 061-226 5047
Club fax: 061-227 9418

anchester City, fifth in Division One (their highest place since 1978) in each of the last two years, were champions only twice, despite spending 68 of their 89 seasons in the Football League in the top grade. Yet they boast an eventful and sometimes frustrating history. Originating from two Gorton clubs of the early 1880s, as Ardwick FC (formed 1887) they were founder members of Division Two in 1892, and were re-formed as Manchester City in 1894 when Ardwick went bankrupt.

Although pipped to promotion in the 1896 Test matches, they were Division Two Champions in 1899, and having been relegated three years later, they promptly topped the lower grade again in 1903. In 1904 City finished Division One runners-up and FA Cup winners for the first time, which was to be their last major honour for 30 years.

By the time they next won the FA Cup in 1934 they had been Division One runners-up (1921), twice been relegated (once, in 1926, after reaching the FA Cup final), twice Division Two Champions (1910 and 1928), been pipped for promotion on goal average (1927), and lost a third FA Cup final (1933). They followed their 1934 Wembley defeat of Portsmouth with their first Division One title in 1937 . . . and then suffered relegation in 1938! Back in Division One in 1947, between 1950 and 1963 they were relegated twice and won the FA Cup once (1956) in successive finals; but their most famous peak came with the Mercer-Allison era, during which they won the Second Division (1966), the First Division (1968), the FA Cup (1969) and both the European Cup Winners' Cup and League Cup (1970).

The next 11 years brought three Wembley finals (of which they won one – the League Cup in 1976) and a Division One runners-up place (1977), but 17 years in the top flight ended in 1983, when Luton escaped by beating City in the final game at Maine Road.

Although they returned after promotion on goal difference in 1985, they fell again in 1987, only to climb back in 1989. Mel Machin left shortly after taking them up and, after Howard Kendall's brief stay, Peter Reid became City's 12th manager since Mercer and saw them finish in their best position since the days of Tony Book.

THE MANAGER

Peter Reid

Date of birth: 20 June, 1956
Birthplace: Liverpool
Date of appointment: Nov 1990

RECORDS

Biggest wins:
League: 10–1 v Huddersfield Town, Division Two, Nov 1987
FA Cup: 10–1 v Swindon Town, 4th round, Jan 1930 (Note: In 1890 Manchester City beat Liverpool Stanley 12–0 in the qualifying round.)
Record defeat: 1–9 v Everton, Division One, Sept 1906
Most appearances: Alan Oakes, 669, League and Cup, 1958–76
Most goals (aggregate): Eric Brook, 178, League and Cup, 1928–39
Most goals in a season: Tommy Johnson, 38, Division One, 1928–29

Most capped players:
Past – Colin Bell, 48, England
Present – Niall Quinn, 19 (31), Republic of Ireland
Other leading internationals:
England: Dave Watson, 30 (65); Francis Lee, 27; Frank Swift, 19
Scotland: Asa Hartford, 36 (50); Willie Donachie, 35
Wales: Roy Paul, 24 (33)
Northern Ireland: Johnny Crossan, 10 (24); Sammy McIlroy, 9 (88)
Republic of Ireland: Mick McCarthy, 20 (57)

David White

THE F.A. PREMIER LEAGUE

MARK BRENNAN (midfielder): Former England Under-21 player, who started at Ipswich and played for Middlesbrough before a £400,000 move to City in July 1990. Born Rossendale 4.10.65.

DAVID BRIGHTWELL (defender): Younger brother of team-mate Ian and son of former Olympic athletes Robbie Brightwell and Ann Packer. Former City trainee who made his League debut while on loan at Chester in 1990–91. Born Lutterworth 7.1.71.

IAN BRIGHTWELL (midfielder): A product of City's youth policy, like his brother David. Helped City win the

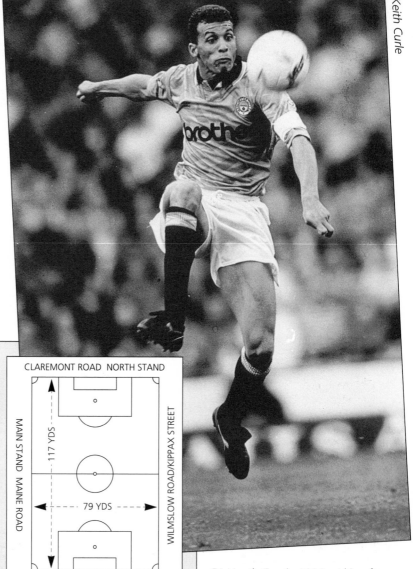

Keith Curle

Ground capacity: 34,300
Number of seats: 16,000
Ground capacity (10 years ago): 52,000
Record attendance: 84,569 v Stoke City, FA Cup, 6th round, 3 March, 1934

Directions to ground

By car: **From north and west**, take M61 and M63, exit Junction 9 following signs to Manchester (A5103); turn right at crossroads (two-and-three-quarter miles) into Claremont Road, after a third of a mile turn right into Maine Road. **From south,** exit M6 Junction 19 to A556 and M56 Junction 3, following signs to Manchester (A5103), then as above. **From east,** exit M62 Junction 17 and take A56 to A57 (Manchester Airport signs), follow Birmingham signs to A5103 and turn left into Claremont Road (one-and-a-quarter miles), then as above. *By train:* Manchester Piccadilly or Victoria station and then regular bus service to ground. *By bus:* No 111 from Piccadilly Square.

CLAREMONT ROAD NORTH STAND

MAIN STAND MAINE ROAD

WILMSLOW ROAD/KIPPAX STREET

117 YDS

79 YDS

PLATT LANE STAND

FA Youth Cup in 1986 and is a former England Under-21 international. Born Lutterworth 9.4.68.

TONY COTON (goalkeeper): A 6ft 2in goalkeeper signed from Watford for £1 million in July 1990, having started at Birmingham. A regular member of the England squad but yet to win his first cap. Born Tamworth 19.5.61.

KEITH CURLE (defender): City captain and England international. Became the most expensive defender in British football when he joined from Wimbledon for £2.5 million in August 1991. Has also played for both Bristol clubs, Torquay and Reading. Born Bristol 14.11.63.

ANDY DIBBLE (goalkeeper): Welsh international who began at Cardiff and then had four years at Luton, with whom he won a Littlewoods Cup winners' medal in 1988. Signed for City for £240,000 in July 1988. Born Cwmbran 8.5.65.

ANDY HILL (defender): Became Peter Reid's first signing in March 1991, when he joined from Bury for £200,000 after loan spell from December 1990. A full-back, he was released without making an appearance for his first club Manchester United. Born Maltby 20.1.65.

MICHAEL HUGHES (forward): Began at City as a trainee and made his club debut against Plymouth Argyle in October 1988, aged 17. Has also been used on left wing and is a Northern Ireland international. Born Larne 2.8.71.

STEVE McMAHON (midfielder): England international who cost £900,000 from Liverpool in December 1991. Won League and FA Cup honours with Liverpool and previously played with Everton and Aston Villa. Born Liverpool 20.8.61.

ADRIAN MIKE (midfielder): City youth product who made his debut against Notts County in the penultimate match of last season and scored in the next match against Oldham. Born Manchester 16.11.73.

NEIL POINTON (defender): Began his professional career at Scunthorpe and then played for Everton, with whom he won a League Championship medal in 1987. Left Everton for Manchester City in a £600,000 transfer in July 1990. Born Warsop Vale 28.11.64.

NIALL QUINN (forward): Republic of Ireland international who scored 14 goals for City last season. Joined the club from Arsenal in £800,000 transfer in March 1989. Born Dublin 6.10.66.

STEVE REDMOND (defender): Former England Under-21 international and another City youth product. Made his debut as an 18-year-old in February 1986 and

captained the club to victory in the FA Youth Cup final in the same season. Born Liverpool 2.11.67.

PETER REID (midfielder): Former England international who succeeded Howard Kendall as City manager in November 1990. Won League and Cup honours with Everton and signed for City on a free transfer from QPR in December 1989. Born Liverpool 20.6.56.

MIKE SHERON (forward): Former City trainee who made his senior debut while on loan at Bury in 1990–91. Scored on his first full appearance for the club against Notts County last season. Born Liverpool 11.1.72.

FITZROY SIMPSON (midfielder): Signed for City from Swindon in March 1992 in a deal worth

£500,000. Started at Swindon and made more than 100 League appearances for the Wiltshire club before his transfer. Born Bradford-on-Avon 26.2.70.

DAVID WHITE (forward): City's top scorer with a total of 21 goals in all competitions last season. An England B international and another member of City's 1986 FA Youth Cup-winning side. Born Manchester 30.10.67.

MANCHESTER CITY: 10–YEAR RECORD

	Div	P	W	D	L	F	A	Pts	Pos	FA Cup	Lge Cup
1982–83	1	42	13	8	21	47	70	47	20 (R)	4	3
1983–84	2	42	20	10	12	66	48	70	4	3	3
1984–85	2	42	21	11	10	66	40	74	3 (P)	3	4
1985–86	1	42	11	12	19	43	57	45	15	4	3
1986–87	1	42	8	15	19	36	57	39	21 (R)	3	3
1987–88	2	44	19	8	17	80	60	65	9	QF	QF
1988–89	2	46	23	13	10	77	53	82	2 (P)	4	4
1989–90	1	38	12	12	14	43	52	48	14	3	4
1990–91	1	38	17	11	10	64	53	62	5	5	3
1991–92	1	42	20	10	12	61	48	70	5	3	4

Leading League scorers in last 10 seasons		League hat-tricks
1982–83	Cross 12	—
1983–84	Parlane 16	Parlane (1)
1984–85	Phillips 12, Smith 12	—
1985–86	Lillis 11	—
1986–87	Varadi 9	—
1987–88	Stewart 24	Adcock (1), Stewart (1), Varadi (1), White (1)
1988–89	Moulden 13	Morley (1)
1989–90	Allen 10	—
1990–91	Quinn 20	Quinn (1), White (1 x 4)
1991–92	White 18	White (1)

Manchester United

(The Red Devils)

Founded 1878

Old Trafford,
Manchester M16 0RA

Telephone numbers
Ground: 061-872 1661
Clubcall: 0898 121161
Ticket details: 061-872 0199
Club shop: 061-872 3398
Supporters' club: 061-872 5208
Museum and tours: 061-877 4002
Club fax: 061-876 5502

Manchester United, formed in 1878 and known as Newton Heath until 1902, spent exactly half of their first 42 seasons in the Football League in Division Two; but since 1938 they have passed only one year outside the top grade – that being in 1974–75, the lowest point in the post-Busby era. Matt Busby, later knighted, was the architect of United's rise to a unique status within the game. Before his arrival in 1945, they had won the Championship twice and the FA Cup once, all between 1908 and 1911; but from 1948 to 1968 they lifted the Championship five times, were runners-up six times, won the FA Cup twice in four finals, and captured the European Cup to climax a glittering phase.

Busby's success stemmed from the building of a succession of outstanding teams: the first, led by skipper Johnny Carey, was followed by the legendary Busby Babes, and those sides which came after the horror of the 1958 Munich air disaster, in which eight of the squad were killed.

The 1948 FA Cup win, when United hit back to beat Blackpool, was their first major triumph for 37 years, and four years later they claimed the League title. Busby then broke up the old team and nurtured a new United side which, after winning the Championship in 1956, repeated the feat in 1957 and were denied a treble success with defeats in the FA Cup final and the European Cup semi-final. In the post-Munich period, United's first triumph was the 1963 FA Cup win, and they were Champions in 1965 and 1967, but the 1968 defeat of Benfica at Wembley which made them European Champions was the famous final peak in a golden era.

United had to wait until 1977 for their next major prize, the FA Cup, a success repeated in 1983, 1985 and 1990, leading to the European Cup Winners' Cup in 1991. They finally won the League Cup in 1992 after defeats in the finals of 1983 and 1991, but that most coveted of prizes, the League crown, eluded them at the last gasp in 1992 when they were First Division runners-up for the tenth time in their final season prior to the launch of the Premier League.

THE MANAGER

Alex Ferguson

Date of birth: 31 Dec, 1941
Birthplace: Govan, Glasgow
Date of appointment: Nov 1986
Previous clubs: East Stirling, St Mirren, Aberdeen

Managerial honours:
Aberdeen: Scottish League Champions 1980, 1984, 1985; Scottish Cup winners 1982, 1983, 1984, 1986; Scottish League Cup winners 1986, finalists 1980; European Cup Winners' Cup winners 1983, European Super Cup winners 1983
Manchester United: FA Cup winners 1990; Rumbelows Cup winners 1992, finalists 1991; European Cup Winners' Cup winners 1991; European Super Cup winners 1991

RECORDS

Biggest wins:
League: 10–1 v Wolverhampton Wanderers, Division Two, Oct 1892
FA Cup: 8–0 v Yeovil, 5th round, 1949
European Cup: 10–0 v Anderlecht, preliminary round, 2nd leg, Sept 1956
Record defeats: 0–7 v Blackburn Rovers, Division One, April 1926; v Aston Villa, Division One, Dec 1930; v Wolverhampton Wanderers, Division Two, Dec 1931
Most appearances: Bobby Charlton, 756, League and Cup, 1956–73
Most goals (aggregate): Bobby Charlton, 248, League and Cup, 1956–73 (+ a record 49 for England)

Most goals in a season: Denis Law, 46, League and Cup, 1963–64; Dennis Viollet, 32, Division One, 1959–60
Most capped players:
Past – Bobby Charlton, 106, England
Present – Bryan Robson, 77 (90), England
Other leading internationals:
England: Steve Coppell, 42; Ray Wilkins, 38 (84); Roger Byrne, 33
Scotland: Denis Law, 35 (55)
Wales: Mark Hughes, 35 (43); Clayton Blackmore, 33
Northern Ireland: Sammy McIlroy, 52 (88)
Republic of Ireland: Kevin Moran, 38 (62)

PEN-PIX

RUSSELL BEARDSMORE (midfielder): Started at Old Trafford as an apprentice in 1985 and signed professional forms in September 1986. An England Under-21 international, he had a spell on loan at Blackburn last season. Born Wigan 28.9.68.

CLAYTON BLACKMORE (midfielder): Welsh international who can also play in defence. Has risen through the ranks at United and has since won European Cup Winners' Cup and FA Cup-winners' medals. Born Neath 23.9.64.

STEVE BRUCE (defender): Former Norwich defender who cost United £800,000 in December 1987. Captain in Bryan Robson's absence. England B international who has won European Cup Winners' Cup, League Cup and FA Cup-winners' medals with United. Born Newcastle-upon-Tyne 31.12.60.

Ryan Giggs

THE F.A. PREMIER LEAGUE

MANCHESTER UNITED: 10–YEAR RECORD

	Div	P	W	D	L	F	A	Pts	Pos	FA Cup	Lge Cup
1982–83	1	42	19	13	10	56	38	70	3	W	F
1983–84	1	42	20	14	8	71	41	74	4	3	4
1984–85	1	42	22	10	10	77	47	76	4	W	3
1985–86	1	42	22	10	10	70	36	76	4	5	4
1986–87	1	42	14	14	14	52	45	56	11	4	3
1987–88	1	40	23	12	5	71	38	81	2	5	QF
1988–89	1	38	13	12	13	45	35	51	11	QF	3
1989–90	1	38	13	9	16	46	47	48	13	W	3
1990–91	1	38	16	12	10	58	45	59*	6	5	F
1991–92	1	42	21	15	6	63	33	78	2	4	W

1 pt deducted for disciplinary reasons

Leading League scorers in last 10 seasons   *League hat-tricks*

1982–83	Stapleton 14	—
1983–84	Stapleton 13	Stapleton (1)
1984–85	Hughes 16	Hughes (1)
1985–86	Hughes 17	Olsen (1)
1986–87	Davenport 14	—
1987–88	McClair 24	McClair (1)
1988–89	Hughes 14	—
1989–90	Hughes 13	Hughes (1)
1990–91	Bruce 13, McClair 13	—
1991–92	McClair 18	—

MAL DONAGHY (defender): Northern Ireland international signed from Luton in October 1988 for £650,000. Won League Cup (1988) with Luton and European Cup Winners' Cup (1991) medals with United. Started with Northern Irish club Larne. Born Belfast 13.9.57.

DARREN FERGUSON (midfielder): Son of United's manager Alex, he signed professional forms in July 1990, two years after joining as an apprentice. Scottish Under-21 international who made his first-team debut in February 1991. Born Glasgow 9.2.72.

RYAN GIGGS (forward): Youngest-ever Welsh international, at 17 years 321 days when he appeared as substitute against Germany in October 1991. Former *England* schoolboy, he signed as a trainee in July 1990, turning professional five months later. A League Cup winner last season. PFA Young Player of the Year 1991-92. Born Cardiff 29.11.73.

MARK HUGHES (forward): In second spell at United, his first club, following £1.5 million transfer in July 1988 from Barcelona to whom he had been sold for a club record £1.8 million in August 1986. Welsh international who has won FA Cup (1985, 1990), European Cup Winners' Cup (1991) and League Cup (1992) winners' medals. Born Wrexham 1.11.63.

PAUL INCE (midfielder): Cost United £800,000 (plus £5,000 for each game over 20 in each of first five seasons) from West Ham in September 1989. England B international who played in 1990 FA Cup, 1991 European Cup Winners' Cup and 1992 League Cup triumphs. Born Ilford 21.10.67.

DENIS IRWIN (defender): Republic of Ireland international signed from Oldham in June 1990 for £625,000. The former Leeds player was a member of the United side that won the European Cup Winners' Cup and League Cup. Born Cork 31.10.65.

ANDREI KANCHELSKIS (midfielder): Member of the CIS 1992 European Championship squad in Sweden. Signed for United in May 1991 for £650,000 and played in League Cup final win last season. Other clubs: Dynamo Kiev, Shakhytor Donetsk. Born Kirovograd 23.1.69.

LEE MARTIN (defender): Joined United in May 1986, when 18. Made his first-team debut in May 1988 and scored United's winner in 1990 FA Cup final against Crystal Palace. Injury has limited the England Under-21 player's appearances since. Born Hyde 5.2.68.

BRIAN McCLAIR (forward): Scottish international who joined United in July 1987 in £850,000 transfer from Celtic. Started at Motherwell and has played in all United's Cup triumphs since his move to Old Trafford. Top-scorer last season with 25 goals. Born Airdrie 8.12.63.

GARY PALLISTER (defender): PFA Player of the Year 1991–92. England international who started at Middlesbrough and moved to Old Trafford in club record £2.3 million transfer in August 1989. Has also played in all United's recent Cup triumphs. Born Ramsgate 30.6.65.

PAUL PARKER (defender): England international who was out injured for much of his first season at Old Trafford. Cost £2 million from QPR at the start of 1991–92 season. 1992 League Cup winner who started with Fulham. Born Essex 4.4.64.

MIKE PHELAN (midfielder): Signed for £750,000 from Norwich in July 1989. His only other club was Burnley. An England international who can also play in defence. Has won FA Cup, European Cup Winners' Cup and League Cup medals with United. Born Nelson 24.9.62.

Ground capacity: 33,981
Number of seats: 30,425
Ground capacity (10 years ago):
55,700
Record attendance: 82,950 v
Arsenal, FA Cup, 1st round, 1 Jan,
1949

Directions to ground
By car: **From M6/M56 (south),** M6
(Junction 19 Knutsford) on A556 to
M56, turn off on M63; continue to
intersection 7, leave motorway and
follow A56 to central Manchester,
turn into Warwick Road North.
**From M6/M61 (north), M62
east/west,** take M62 turn-off on
M602; follow Salford Quays signs,
over swing bridge and straight
along Trafford Park Road to traffic
lights, turn left into Warwick Road
North. From Manchester City
Centre, A56 Chester Road to
Stretford (Warwick Road North).
By train: From Manchester Oxford
Road Station direct to Football
Ground Station. Also service from
Oxford Road and Knott Hill,
Manchester, or from Altrincham,
Timperley and intermediate stations
running to Warwick Road Station
(2 minutes walk to ground).
By bus: From Victoria Railway
Station No 264. From Piccadilly Nos
84, 114, 115, 252, 253, 256, 257,
263.

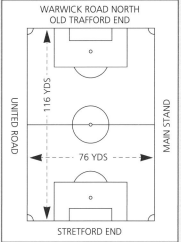

WARWICK ROAD NORTH
OLD TRAFFORD END

UNITED ROAD

MAIN STAND

116 YDS

76 YDS

STRETFORD END

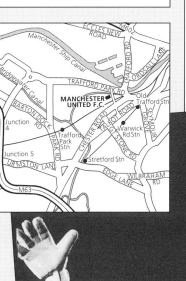

MARK ROBINS (forward): England Under-
21 striker who missed much of last season
through injury. Came to prominence with
his goals in United's 1990 FA Cup run. Risen
through the ranks at Old Trafford. Born
Ashton-under-Lyne 22.12.69.
BRYAN ROBSON (midfielder): Captain at
Old Trafford and the only player to win the
FA Cup three times with the same club.
Capped 90 times during England career.
Missed League Cup win last season but
lifted European Cup Winners' Cup in 1991.
Cost £1.5 million from WBA in October
1981. Born Chester-le-Street 11.1.57.
PETER SCHMEICHEL (goalkeeper):
£650,000 signing from Danish club Brøndby
in summer of 1991. A Danish international

who kept 26 clean sheets in 53
games last season, including the
Rumbelows Cup final. Born Denmark
18.11.63.
LEE SHARPE (forward): Former
Torquay winger signed by United for
£185,000 in June 1988. A hernia
injury kept the England international
out for much of last season. Born
Halesowen 27.5.71.
GARY WALSH (goalkeeper): Signed
professional forms with United and
made his League debut at Aston Villa
in December 1986. England Under-21
international who made four
appearances last season. Born Wigan
21.3.68.
NEIL WEBB (midfielder): England
international who was signed from
Nottingham Forest for £1.5 million in
July 1989. Started with Reading
before move to Portsmouth. An FA
Cup winner in 1990. Born Reading
30.7.63.

Peter Schmeichel

Middlesbrough

(The Boro)

Founded 1876

Ayresome Park, Middlesbrough,
Cleveland TS1 4PB

Telephone numbers
Ground: 0642 819659
Clubcall: 0898 121181
Ticket details: 0642 815996
Club shop: 0642 826664
Lottery department: 0642 850584
Club fax: 0642 820244

Although Middlesbrough spent 46 of their 82 seasons in the Football League in Division One, it is significant that since 1954 they have enjoyed only nine years in the top grade – eight of these between 1974 and 1982. Yet their last 10 years have certainly been eventful. Between 1982 and 1986 they fell from the First to the Third Division and almost folded. Then, after climbing two grades in successive seasons and reaching Division One in 1988 via the play-offs, they were relegated in 1989, escaped the drop to Division Three in 1990 by two points, and missed promotion in the 1991 play-offs.

Middlesbrough's promotion in 1992 was their sixth climb out of Division Two, of which they were Champions in 1927, 1929 and 1974. Those two titles in the late 1920s came in the middle of a run in which they spent 37 of 41 seasons in Division One, although in all that time they finished in the top four only twice, their best being third place in 1914.

Formed in 1876, Middlesbrough adopted professionalism for three years before reverting to amateur status in 1892 and winning the FA Amateur Cup in 1895 and 1898. They turned professional again in 1899 and joined the Football League, rising to Division One in 1902. The late 1920s and the 1930s were good years. More recently, following their brief fall into Division Three for the first time in 1966, the 1970s were perhaps the most eventful times. Under Jack Charlton Boro returned to Division One in 1974 after 20 years. It was in that decade, too, that they reached four of their eight FA Cup quarter-finals and a League Cup semi-final.

In 1992 Lennie Lawrence's side reached the last 16 in the FA Cup and made the League Cup semi-final. Fortunately this eventual double disappointment on the Wembley trail did not detract from their push for promotion.

RECORDS

Biggest wins
League: 9–0 v Brighton & Hove Albion, Division Two, Aug 1958
FA Cup: 9–3 v Goole Town, 1st round, Jan 1915
Record defeat: 0–9 v Blackburn Rovers, Division Two, Nov 1954
Most appearances: Tim Williamson, 600, League and Cup, 1902–23
Most goals (aggregate): George Camsell, 345, League and Cup, 1925–39 (+18 for England)
Most goals in a season: George Camsell, 64, League and Cup, 1926–27 (including 59 in Division Two)
Most capped players:
Past – Wilf Mannion, 26, England
Present – Bernie Slaven, 6, Republic of Ireland
Other leading internationals:
England: George Hardwick, 13; George Camsell, 9; Mick McNeil, 9
Scotland: John Marshall, 6 (7); Andy Wilson, 6 (12)
Wales: Bill Harris, 6
Northern Ireland: Jim Platt, 20 (23); Eric McMordie, 21
Republic of Ireland: Arthur Fitzsimons, 25 (26)

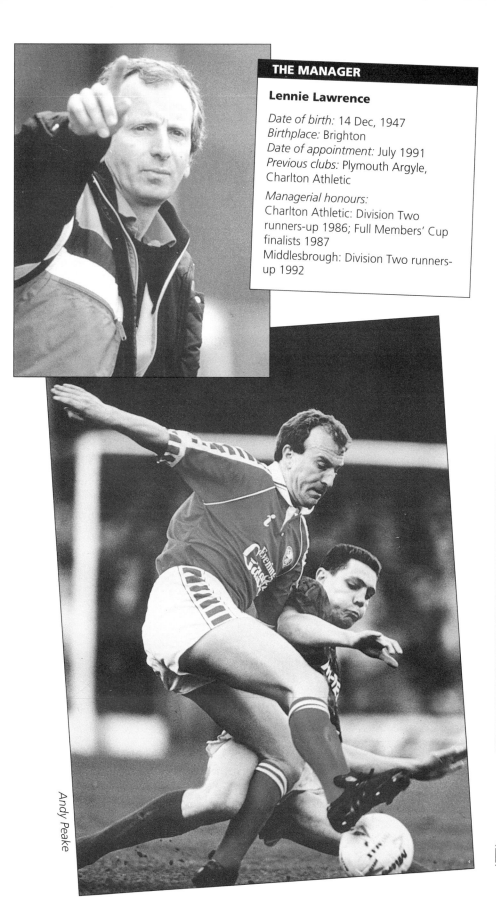

THE MANAGER

Lennie Lawrence

Date of birth: 14 Dec, 1947
Birthplace: Brighton
Date of appointment: July 1991
Previous clubs: Plymouth Argyle, Charlton Athletic

Managerial honours:
Charlton Athletic: Division Two runners-up 1986; Full Members' Cup finalists 1987
Middlesbrough: Division Two runners-up 1992

Andy Peake

THE F.A. PREMIER LEAGUE

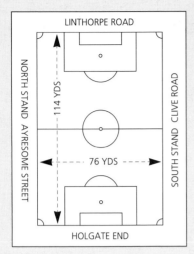

LINTHORPE ROAD

NORTH STAND AYRESOME STREET

114 YDS

76 YDS

SOUTH STAND CLIVE ROAD

HOLGATE END

Ground capacity: 26,550
Number of seats: 13,070
Ground capacity (10 years ago): 35,000
Record attendance: 53,596 v Newcastle United, Division One, 27 Dec, 1949

Directions to ground

By car: **From north,** A19 across Tees Bridge to A66, take third exit from roundabout into Heywood Street; left into Ayresome Street for Ayresome Park.
From south, A1/A19 to junction with A1130, then as for the north.
From west, take A66 then one-and-a-half miles after Teesside Park Racecourse, take 4th exit at roundabout into Ayresome Park.
By train: Middlesbrough (1 mile)
By bus: From town centre to Ayresome Street, Nos 5, 22, 27, 63, 236, 263, 267, 271, 272

PEN-PIX

WILLIE FALCONER (midfielder): Started at Aberdeen and played for Watford before a £300,000 transfer to Boro in July 1991. Has been capped by Scotland at Under-21 level. Born Aberdeen 5.4.66.
CURTIS FLEMING (defender): Full-back who signed for Boro in a £50,000 deal in August 1991 from Irish club St Patrick's, Dublin, where he spent four years. Born Manchester 8.10.68.
JON GITTENS (defender): Joined Boro for £250,000 from Southampton in July 1992 after a three month loan spell at the end of the previous season. Has also played for Swindon. Born 22.1.64.

John Hendrie

Left: Steve Hodge shows his joy at scoring the goal that gives Leeds United victory over Liverpool

Below: Thanks for the memories. Gary Lineker scores in Tottenham's 2–0 win over QPR in his final season in English football

Left: It's decision day in the First Division and Jon Newsome celebrates his second goal as Leeds beat Sheffield United 3–2 to lift the Championship

Left: Take your partners for the Premier League. Jamie Pollock scores and Stuart Ripley congratulates as Middlesbrough reach for the top

Below: Des Walker demonstrates that the use of arms and legs can help make you a target of the top Italian clubs in this duel with Leeds' Lee Chapman

Opposite above: An increasingly familiar sight in football as Manchester United's talented Ryan Giggs, the Young Player of the Year, wriggles past Luton Town's John Dreyer

Opposite below: Arsenal's Ian Wright slides in with Southampton's Glenn Cockerill on his way to becoming the top scorer in the First Division

This is the way to do it, lads. Sheffield Wednesday player-manager Trevor Francis shows his team the way with an 89th minute winner against Nottingham Forest

Niall Quinn's version of an Irish jig as he celebrates his part in Manchester City's shock 4–0 victory over Leeds that put a temporary brake on their title drive

Below: Reach out and touch. Dennis Wise runs to meet his admirers during Chelsea's game against Liverpool

Hands, knees and bumps ... Arsenal's Steve Bould and Leeds' Eric Cantona involved in a painful collision

Vinnie Jones and Graeme Le Saux have a ham-fisted celebration during Chelsea's game against Luton

Below: David Speedie celebrates the hat-trick for Blackburn Rovers that brought Kevin Keegan down to earth in his second game as New-castle manager

Chris Kiwomya gags Brighton's Gary Chivers as he and his Ipswich team-mates head for the new Premier League

Oldham's Mike Milligan and Forest's Nigel Clough indulge in arm wrestling as they fight for the right of possession

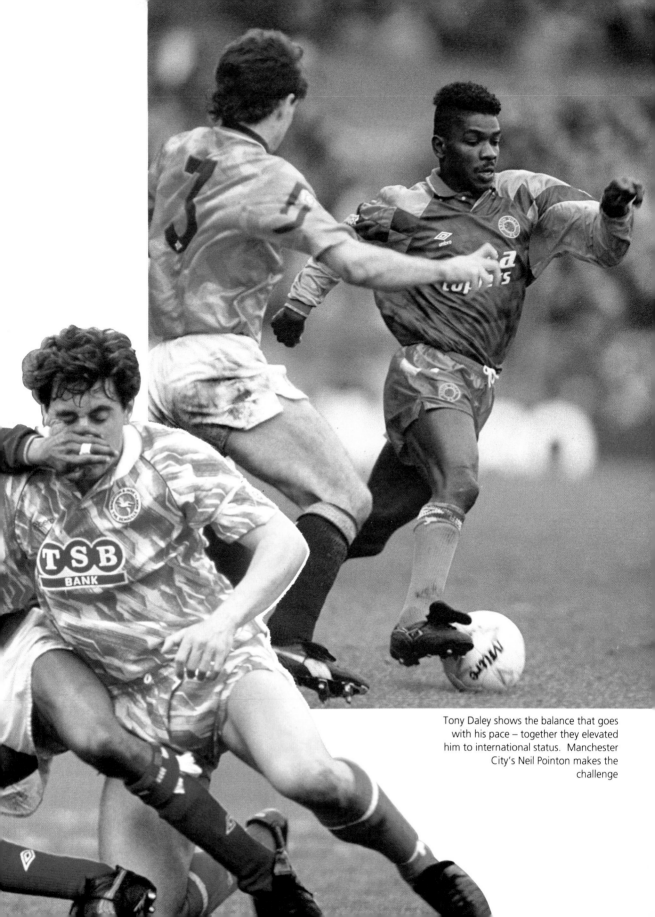

Tony Daley shows the balance that goes with his pace – together they elevated him to international status. Manchester City's Neil Pointon makes the challenge

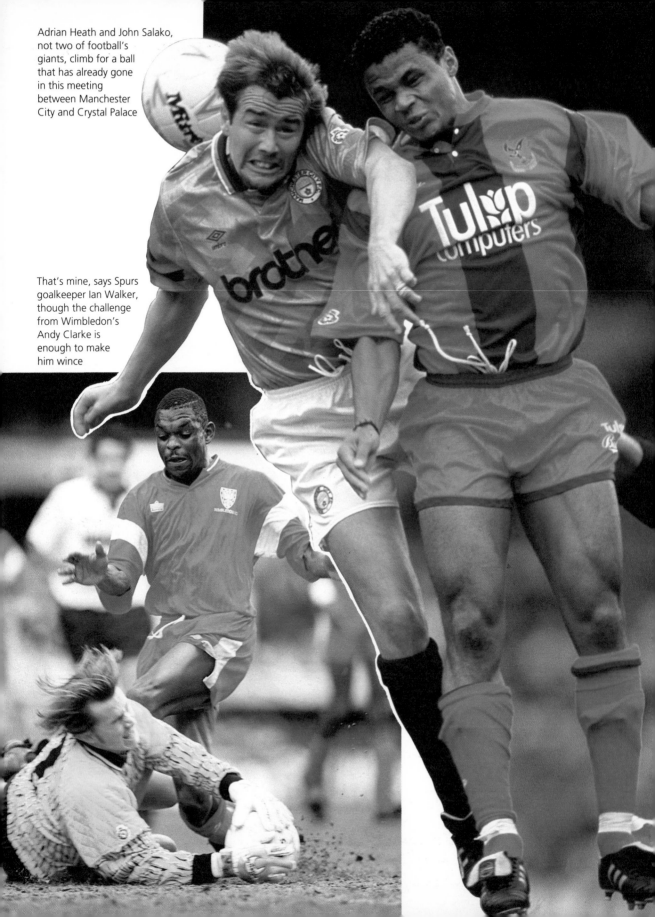

Adrian Heath and John Salako, not two of football's giants, climb for a ball that has already gone in this meeting between Manchester City and Crystal Palace

That's mine, says Spurs goalkeeper Ian Walker, though the challenge from Wimbledon's Andy Clarke is enough to make him wince

JOHN HENDRIE (forward): A Scottish winger who joined Boro for £500,000 in July 1990 after helping Leeds to promotion. Has also played for Coventry, Hereford (loan), Bradford and Newcastle. Born Lennoxtown 24.10.63.

IAN IRONSIDE (goalkeeper): A 6ft 2in understudy to Stephen Pears. Starting as an apprentice at Barnsley, he moved to Boro from Scarborough in an £80,000 deal in July 1991. Born Sheffield 8.3.64.

ALAN KERNAGHAN (defender): Centre-half who took over the club captaincy following Tony Mowbray's transfer to Celtic in November 1991. Former Boro apprentice, who began his career as a striker. Born Otley 25.4.67.

NICKY MOHAN (defender): A centre-half who established himself in the Boro side after Tony Mowbray's departure, having started there as a trainee. Born Middlesbrough 6.10.70.

ROBBIE MUSTOE (midfielder): Was a first-team regular for two seasons at home-town club Oxford before he signed for Boro for £375,000 in July 1990. Born Oxford 28.8.68.

GARY PARKINSON (defender): A right-back who started at Everton but did not make a first-team appearance for the Goodison Park club, moving to Boro in December 1985. Born Middlesbrough 10.1.68.

ANDY PAYTON (forward): Hull's top-scorer for the past two seasons before Boro signed him for a club record £750,000 in November 1991. Contributed three goals towards Boro's promotion challenge. Born Burnley 23.10.66.

ANDY PEAKE (midfielder): Was re-united with Lennie Lawrence when Boro paid Charlton £350,000 for him in November 1991. This former England Under-21 international started at Leicester and moved on to Grimsby. Born Market Harborough 1.11.61.

STEPHEN PEARS (goalkeeper): Was limited to four appearances in seven years at first club Manchester United and joined Boro for £80,000 in July 1985. Earned a call-up into the England squad last season. Born Brandon 22.1.62.

JIMMY PHILLIPS (defender): Started at Bolton and had spells with Glasgow Rangers and Oxford, moving to Boro in a £250,000 transfer in March 1990. Born Bolton 8.2.66.

JAMIE POLLOCK (midfielder): One of a number of talented young players on the Boro staff. Made his Boro debut against Wolves in April 1991. Born Stockton 16.2.74.

MARK PROCTOR (midfielder): Former England Under-21 player. Now in his second spell at Boro, he re-joined the club from Sheffield Wednesday for £300,000 in March 1988. Has also played for Nottingham Forest and Sunderland. Born Middlesbrough 30.1.61.

BERNIE SLAVEN (forward): Republic of Ireland international and Boro's top League scorer for the last six seasons. Formerly with Morton, Airdrie, Queen of the South and Albion Rovers, he moved to Boro for £250,000 in October 1985. Born Paisley 13.11.60.

PAUL WILKINSON (forward): Boro's leading scorer with 24 goals in *all* competitions last season. Cost £500,000 from Watford in August 1991, having previously played for Grimsby, Everton and Nottingham Forest. Born Louth 30.10.64.

TOMMY WRIGHT (forward): Former Scottish Under-21 winger signed from Leicester for £650,000 in July 1992. Began his career with Leeds before moving to Oldham in October 1986 and signed for Leicester for £300,000 in August 1989. Born Dunfermline 10.1.66.

MIDDLESBROUGH: 10-YEAR RECORD

	Div	P	W	D	L	F	A	Pts	Pos	FA Cup	Lge Cup
1982–83	2	42	11	15	16	46	67	48	16	5	2
1983–84	2	42	12	13	17	41	47	49	17	5	1
1984–85	2	42	10	10	22	41	57	40	19	3	1
1985–86	2	42	12	9	21	44	53	45	21(R)	3	1
1986–87	3	46	28	10	8	67	30	94	2(P)	3	2
1987–88	2	44	22	12	10	63	36	78	3(P)	4	2
1988–89	1	38	9	12	17	44	61	39	18(R)	3	2
1989–90	2	46	13	11	22	52	63	50	21	3	3
1990–91	2	46	20	9	17	66	47	69	7	4	4
1991–92	2	46	23	11	12	58	41	80	2(P)	5	SF

Leading League scorers in last 10 seasons		League hat-tricks
1982–83	Otto 9, Shearer 9	—
1983–84	Currie 15	—
1984–85	Mills 14	—
1985–86	Rowell 10	—
1986–87	Slaven 17	—
1987–88	Slaven 21	Ripley (1), Slaven (2)
1988–89	Slaven 15	Slaven (1)
1989–90	Slaven 21	Kernaghan (1)
1990–91	Slaven 16	Baird (1), Slaven (1)
1991–92	Slaven 17	Slaven (1)

NORWICH CITY FC

Norwich City

(The Canaries)
Founded 1902

Carrow Road, Norwich NR1 1JE

Telephone numbers
Ground: 0603 612131
Clubcall: 0898 121144
Ticket details: 0603 761661
Ticket information: 0898 121514
Club shop: 0603 761125
Supporters' club: 0603 612131
Marketing: 0603 761126
Club fax: 0603 665510

Norwich City, formed in 1902 and members of the Football League from 1920, reached Division One for the first time as recently as 1972. Since then they have spent only three seasons outside the top grade, clinching promotion immediately each time they have fallen back into Division Two. Yet before 1960 they had spent only five seasons ranked higher than Division Three. Tom Parker guided them into Division Two in 1934, but they went down again in 1939 – and it took a memorable run to the FA Cup semi-final in 1959 (two years after they had faced the threat of closure) to alert the football world that Norwich were set to rise again.

Archie Macaulay's side left Division Three behind in 1960 and then, with Ron Ashman at the helm, City won the League Cup in 1962. But it was when Ron Saunders led them to the Second Division title in 1972 that a new era began at Carrow Road. Norwich reached the final of the upgraded League Cup in 1973 and 1975, the latter milestone coinciding with promotion to atone for relegation in 1974. This time they survived in Division One for six years, following relegation in 1981 with promotion in 1982 only to fall again in 1985. That was the year when, distracted by a triumphant run in the League Cup in which they beat Sunderland in the final, they stumbled into a losing streak which sent them down with their Wembley opponents.

Since winning the Second Division title in 1986, Norwich have experienced mixed fortunes. While they finished fifth in 1987 and fourth in 1989, and reached the FA Cup semi-finals of 1989 and 1992, their slide to 15th and 18th in the last two seasons has emphasised how narrow is the gap between success and failure – a point which will not be lost on new City manager Mike Walker.

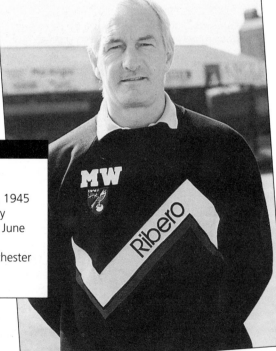

THE MANAGER

Mike Walker

Date of birth: 28 Nov, 1945
Birthplace: Colwyn Bay
Date of appointment: June 1992
Previous club: Colchester United

RECORDS

Biggest wins:
League: 10–2 v Coventry City, Division Three (S), March 1930
FA Cup: 8–0 v Sutton United, 4th round, Jan 1989
Record defeats: 2–10 v Swindon Town, Southern League, Sept 1908; 0–7 v Sheffield Wednesday, Division Two, Nov 1938; 0–7 v Walsall, Division Three (S), Sept 1930
Most appearances: Kevin Keelan, 673, League and Cup, 1963–80; Ron Ashman, 592, League, 1947–64
Most goals (aggregate): Johnny Gavin, 132, League and Cup, 1945–54 & 1955–58
Most goals in a season: Ralph Hunt, 31, Division Three (S), 1955–56
Most capped players:
Past – Martin O'Neill, 18 (64), Northern Ireland
Present – Mark Bowen, 17 (19), Wales; David Phillips, 17 (39), Wales
Other leading internationals:
England: Dave Watson, 6 (12); Chris Woods, 4 (31)
Scotland: Robert Fleck, 4
Wales: David Jones, 8
Republic of Ireland: Andy Townsend, 17 (31)

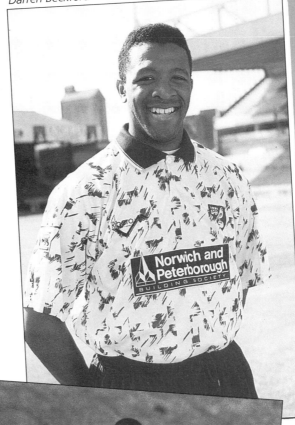

Darren Beckford

Robert Fleck

THE F.A. PREMIER LEAGUE

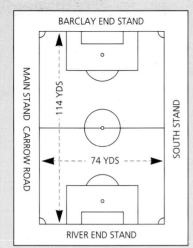

BARCLAY END STAND

MAIN STAND CARROW ROAD

114 YDS

74 YDS

SOUTH STAND

RIVER END STAND

Ground capacity (from January 1993): 20,559
Number of seats (from January 1993): 20,559 (Extensive work on River End Terrace and Barclay End Stand should be completed by Christmas 1992)
Ground capacity (10 years ago): 29,000
Record attendance: 43,984 v Leicester City, FA Cup, 6th round, 30 March, 1963

Directions to ground
By car: Situated on the ring road between the exits to Great Yarmouth and Lowestoft.
By train: Norwich Station, half-a-mile from ground.
By bus: Nearest stop, Norwich Bus Station, Surrey Street.

at Coventry before signing for Nottingham Forest. Signed for Norwich from Forest for £160,000 in November 1986. Born Nantwich 25.1.64.

IAN CROOK (midfielder): An England B international and versatile player. Signed from Tottenham for £90,000 in June 1986. Born Romford 18.1.63.

IAN CULVERHOUSE (defender): Versatile full-back who has played more League games for Norwich than any other current player. England Youth international who played two League games for Tottenham before a £50,000 transfer in October 1985. Born Bishop's Stortford 22.9.64.

ROBERT FLECK (forward): Scottish international who was top-scorer last season with 19 goals. Started his career at Partick Thistle before joining Glasgow Rangers, and signed for

PEN-PIX

DARREN BECKFORD (forward): Signed from Port Vale for a tribunal-set fee of £925,000 in June 1991. Was top-scorer at Vale in his last three seasons there. A former England Youth international who began his career at Manchester City. Born Manchester 12.5.67.

PAUL BLADES (defender): Signed for Norwich for £700,000 from Derby in July 1990. England Youth international who had eight seasons at Derby after starting as an apprentice. Born Peterborough 5.1.65.

MARK BOWEN (defender): A Welsh international and Norwich captain, he is an adaptable full-back. Signed for £90,000 in July 1987 from Tottenham, where he spent six seasons and earned Schools, Youth and Under-21 honours. Born Neath 7.12.63.

IAN BUTTERWORTH (defender): Former club captain. Central defender who won England Under-21 honours. Began his career

Bryan Gunn

Norwich for £580,000 in December 1987. Born Glasgow 11.8.65.

RUEL FOX (forward): Winger turned central striker who signed professional forms in 1985 and burst on the scene two seasons ago after a promising start in 1987–88. Now firmly established in the first team. Born Ipswich 14.1.68.

JEREMY GOSS (midfielder): Cypriot-born but capped by Wales. With ten seasons at Norwich behind him, he finally sealed a permanent place in the side early last season. Born Cyprus 11.5.65.

BRYAN GUNN (goalkeeper): Scottish international signed from Aberdeen for £100,000 in October 1986. A member of the Scottish 1990 World Cup squad, he was spotted by Aberdeen playing for Invergordon BC. Born Thurso 22.12.63.

GARY MEGSON (midfielder): Joined Norwich on a free transfer from Manchester City in July 1992. Much travelled midfielder formerly with Plymouth, Everton, Sheffield Wednesday (twice), Nottingham Forest and Newcastle. Born Manchester 2.5.59.

ROB NEWMAN (midfielder): Former Bristol City apprentice who went on to captain their side. Can play in defence, midfield or attack and cost Norwich £600,000 in July 1991. Born Bradford-on-Avon 13.12.63.

DAVID PHILLIPS (midfielder): Welsh international signed from Coventry for £550,000 in July 1989. Was a member of Coventry's 1987 FA Cup-winning team. Previously played for Plymouth and Manchester City. Born Wegberg, Germany, 29.7.63.

JOHN POLSTON (defender): Former England Youth international signed from Tottenham for £300,000 in July 1990. A former Tottenham apprentice who spent five seasons on their full-time playing staff. Born London 10.6.68.

LEE POWER (forward): A Republic of Ireland Youth and Under-21 international who played four matches last season, scoring once. A former Norwich trainee with a bright future. Born Lewisham 30.6.72.

NORWICH CITY: 10-YEAR RECORD

	Div	P	W	D	L	F	A	Pts	Pos	FA Cup	Lge Cup
1982–83	1	42	14	12	16	52	58	54	14	QF	4
1983–84	1	42	12	15	15	48	49	51	14	5	QF
1984–85	1	42	13	10	19	46	64	49	20(R)	4	W
1985–86	2	42	25	9	8	84	37	84	1(P)	3	4
1986–87	1	42	17	17	8	53	51	68	5	4	4
1987–88	1	40	12	9	19	40	52	45	14	3	3
1988–89	1	38	17	11	10	48	45	62	4	SF	3
1989–90	1	38	13	14	11	44	42	53	10	4	3
1990–91	1	38	13	6	19	41	64	45	15	QF	3
1991–92	1	42	11	12	19	47	63	45	18	SF	QF

Leading League scorers in last 10 seasons		League hat-tricks
1982–83	Deehan 20	—
1983–84	Deehan 15	Deehan (1 x 4)
1984–85	Deehan 13	Deehan (1)
1985–86	Drinkell 22	—
1986–87	Drinkell 16	—
1987–88	Drinkell 12	—
1988–89	Fleck 10	—
1989–90	Bowen 7, Fleck 7	—
1990–91	Gordon 7, Sherwood 7	—
1991–92	Fleck 11	Beckford (1)

DAVID SMITH (midfielder): Versatile player who has made five League appearances for the club, one of them last season. A former trainee at the club. Born Liverpool 26.12.70.

DARYL SUTCH (forward): A former trainee and England Youth international who can also play in midfield. Made ten appearances in 1991–92, his third full season at Carrow Road. Born Lowestoft 11.9.71.

CHRIS SUTTON (forward): Signed as a full-time professional in the summer of 1991 and quickly established himself in the side. The son of former Norwich player Mike Sutton, is equally effective in central defence. Born Nottingham 10.3.73.

ROBERT ULLATHORNE (defender): A tenacious Yorkshireman who began his Norwich career as a trainee. Won his chance in the first team last season and played 24 times. Born Wakefield 11.10.71.

MARK WALTON (goalkeeper): Took over in goal from Bryan Gunn for the second half of the season. Wales Under-21 international who started his career at Luton but moved to Colchester after failing to play a League match. Signed from Colchester for £75,000 in July 1989. Born Merthyr Tydfil 1.6.69.

COLIN WOODTHORPE (defender): A versatile player signed in summer 1991 from Chester City for £175,000. A former apprentice at Chester where he enjoyed four full seasons. Born Ellesmere Port 13.1.69.

Nottingham Forest

(The Reds)

Founded 1865

City Ground,
Nottingham NG2 5FJ

Telephone numbers
Ground: 0602 822202
Clubcall: 0898 121174
Ticket details: 0602 813801
Club shop: 0602 822664
Supporters' club: 0602 252436
Commercial office: 0602 820444
Lottery department: 0602 816458
Junior reds: 0602 455206
Club fax: 0602 455581

Nottingham Forest, formed in 1865 and elected to Division One in 1892, had won only two major honours (the FA Cup in 1898 and 1959) in 110 years before Brian Clough arrived as manager in January 1975. Ironically, the FA Cup is the only trophy to elude Forest under Clough who, since ending their fifth spell in Division Two in 1977, has led them to two European Cup triumphs (1979 and 1980), a League Championship (1978) and four League Cup wins in six finals between 1978 and 1992.

The years immediately following that 1977 promotion were probably the best, in that Forest won both the First Division title and the League Cup in 1978; achieved the European Cup and League Cup double in 1979, when they also finished Division One runners-up; and won the European Cup but lost in the League Cup final in 1980. Those were the days, too, when Forest had the first £1 million player, Trevor Francis. Since then they have finished third in Division One four times and won the League Cup twice (1989 and 1990), but though they have reached the semi-final twice and played the final in 1991, the coveted FA Cup has continued to elude Clough and Forest.

Their first FA Cup triumph in 1898 – beating Derby County at Crystal Palace – was Forest's only major success in their first 66 years in the Football League, although they were Second Division Champions in 1907 and 1922. However, before winning promotion again in 1957 (ending 32 years exile from Division One), they had spent two years in Division Three (South) between 1949 and 1951. That 1957 climb marked the beginning of a bright phase for Forest, with Billy Walker leading them to FA Cup success in 1959. Johnny Carey's side were Division One runners-up and FA Cup semi-finalists in 1967, and Forest, having made their European debut in 1961, were again in the Fairs Cup in 1967-68. Clough's appointment ultimately set higher and more consistent standards, but it is a source of dismay that their recent League form has not matched their Cup form. They have finished higher than eighth only twice in the last eight seasons.

RECORDS

Biggest wins:
League: 12–0 v Leicester Fosse, Division One, April 1909
FA Cup: 14–0 v Clapton, 1st round, Jan 1891
Record defeat: 1–9 v Blackburn Rovers, Division Two, April 1937
Most appearances: Bob McKinlay, 685, League and Cup, 1951–70
Most goals (aggregate): Grenville Morris, 217, League and Cup, 1898–1913
Most goals in season: Wally Ardron, 36, Division Three (S), 1950–51

Most capped players:
Past – Martin O'Neill, 36 (64), Northern Ireland
Present – Stuart Pearce, 47, England
Other leading internationals:
England: Des Walker, 41 (44); Peter Shilton, 19 (125); Neil Webb, 18 (24)
Scotland: John Robertson, 26 (28)
Wales: Ronnie Rees, 16 (39); Terry Hennessey, 15 (39)
Northern Ireland: Liam O'Kane, 20
Republic of Ireland: Miah Dennehy, 7 (11); Roy Keane, 5

THE MANAGER

Brian Clough

Date of birth: 21 March, 1935
Birthplace: Middlesbrough
Date of appointment: Jan 1975
Previous clubs: Hartlepool United, Derby County, Brighton & Hove Albion, Leeds United

Managerial honours:
Derby County: Division One Champions 1972; Division Two Champions 1969 Nottingham Forest: Division One Champions 1978; promotion to Division One 1977; FA Cup finalists 1991; League Cup winners 1978, 1979, 1989, 1990, finalists 1980; Simod Cup winners 1989; Zenith Data Systems Cup winners 1992; Anglo-Scottish Cup winners 1977; European Cup winners 1979, 1980

Roy Keane

THE F.A. PREMIER LEAGUE

KINGSLEY BLACK (forward): Northern Ireland international left-winger, he moved to Forest from Luton for £1.5 million in August 1991. Made more than 120 League appearances for Luton, whom he joined from school. Born Luton 22.6.68.

GARY CHARLES (defender): Right-back who won his first England cap on the tour of Australasia in summer 1991. Joined Forest from school, making his debut in November 1988. Born London 13.4.70.

STEVE CHETTLE (defender): An England Under-21 international, he started as an apprentice at Forest and made his debut for the club in September 1987. Has played more than 130 first-team games for Forest. Born Nottingham 27.9.68.

NIGEL CLOUGH (forward): Son of Forest manager, Brian, and an England international. Has been the club's top-scorer for five of the last seven seasons but usually plays behind the Forest strikers. Born Sunderland 19.3.66.

GARY CROSBY (forward): This right-winger cost a bargain £15,000 from non-League Grantham Town in December 1987. He had started his League career with Lincoln City but made just seven appearances before moving to Grantham. Born Sleaford 8.5.64.

MARK CROSSLEY (goal-keeper): A 6ft England Under-21 international goalkeeper who has progressed through Forest's junior ranks. Saved a penalty from Gary Lineker in 1991 FA Cup final defeat by Tottenham. Born Barnsley 16.6.69.

TOMMY GAYNOR (forward): Signed for Doncaster from Limerick before joining Forest for £25,000 in October 1987. Also spent a loan spell with Newcastle in 1990–91. Born Limerick 29.1.63.

SCOT GEMMILL (midfielder): A Scottish Under-21 international, he is the son of former Scottish star and now Forest coach, Archie Gemmill. A former Forest trainee, he scored twice in the club's Zenith Data Systems Cup final win over Southampton last season. Born Paisley 2.1.71.

LEE GLOVER (forward): Another Scottish Under-21 player who joined the club straight from school and has since had loan periods with Leicester, Barnsley and Luton. Born Kettering 24.4.70.

ROY KEANE (midfielder): One of the most exciting talents to emerge in recent seasons. A Republic of Ireland international, he cost £25,000 from Cobh Ramblers in May 1990, and scored 14 goals last season. Born Cork 10.8.71.

BRIAN LAWS (defender): A full-back who began as an apprentice with Burnley, moving to Huddersfield and then to Middlesbrough. Joined Forest for £120,000 in June 1988. Born Wallsend 14.10.61.

RAY McKINNON (midfielder): Scottish Under-21 international signed from Dundee United for £750,000 in June 1992. Was on schoolboy forms with Dundee United. Born Dundee 5.8.70.

ANDREW MARRIOTT (goalkeeper): A former trainee at Arsenal, he did not make a first-team appearance for the Gunners before moving to Forest. Made his League debut while on loan at WBA in the 1989–90 season and has also been on loan to Blackburn and Colchester. Born Sutton-in-Ashfield 11.10.70.

Ground capacity: 21,000 approx (from August 1992); 28,000 approx (from November 1992)
Number of seats: unknown, owing to ground development
Ground capacity (10 years ago): 35,000
Record attendance: 49,946 v Manchester United, Division One, 28 Oct, 1967

Directions to ground
By car: **From north**, exit M1 Junction 26, follow Nottingham signs (A610) then Melton Mowbray and Trent Bridge (A606) signs, cross river, left into Radcliffe Road, then left into Colwick Road.
From south, exit M1 Junction 24, follow signs Nottingham (South) to Trent Bridge, right into Radcliffe Road, then left into Colwick Road.
From east, use A52 to West Bridgford, turn right into Colwick Road.
From west, use A52 into Nottingham, follow signs to Melton Mowbray and Trent Bridge, cross river (then as north).
By train: Nottingham Midland (half-a-mile).
By bus: From Broadmarsh Nos 1, 2. From city centre Nos 10, 12, 85, 86.

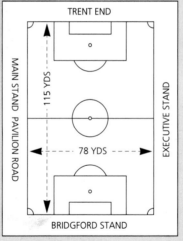

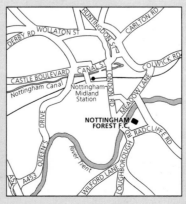

NOTTINGHAM FOREST: 10-YEAR RECORD

	Div	P	W	D	L	F	A	Pts	Pos	FA Cup	Lge Cup
1982–83	1	42	20	9	13	62	50	69	5	3	QF
1983–84	1	42	22	8	12	76	45	74	3	3	2
1984–85	1	42	19	7	16	56	48	64	9	4	3
1985–86	1	42	19	11	12	69	53	68	8	3	4
1986–87	1	42	18	11	13	64	51	65	8	3	QF
1987–88	1	40	20	13	7	67	39	73	3	SF	3
1988–89	1	38	17	13	8	64	43	64	3	SF	W
1989–90	1	38	15	9	14	55	47	54	9	3	W
1990–91	1	38	14	12	12	65	50	54	8	F	4
1991–92	1	42	16	11	15	60	58	59	8	QF	F

Leading League scorers in last 10 seasons		*League hat-tricks*
1982–83	Wallace 13	—
1983–84	Birtles 15, Davenport 15	Walsh (1)
1984–85	Davenport 16	Christie (1), Davenport (1)
1985–86	Clough 15	Davenport (1), Webb (1)
1986–87	Birtles 14, Clough 14, Webb 14	Birtles (1), Webb (1)
1987–88	Clough 19	Clough (1)
1988–89	Clough 14	—
1989–90	Hodge 10	—
1990–91	Clough 14	—
1991–92	Sheringham 13	—

loan spells at Stockport, Northampton and Hereford. Born Dudley 19.3.68.

TERRY WILSON (midfielder): Was limited to just one appearance last season – in Forest's final League game against West Ham – owing largely to injury. A Scottish Under-21 international, he started as an apprentice with Forest. Born Broxburn 8.2.69.

IAN WOAN (forward): Signed from GM Vauxhall Conference side Runcorn for £70,000 in March 1990, and spent last season vying with Kingsley Black for a place on the left wing. Born Wirral 14.12.67.

Stuart Pearce

THORVALDUR ORLYGSSON (midfielder): Danish-born Icelandic international. The consistency of Gemmill and Keane restricted him to just five appearances last season. Signed from KA Akureyri for £175,000 in December 1989. Born Odense, Denmark, 2.8.66.

STUART PEARCE (defender): England's left-back and the club captain. Began with non-League Wealdstone, moved to Coventry during the 1983–84 season and joined Forest in May 1985 in a joint £450,000 deal with Ian Butterworth (now Norwich). Born Shepherd's Bush 24.4.62.

TEDDY SHERINGHAM (forward): Forest's leading scorer last season with 22 goals. Joined Forest for a club record £2 million in July 1991 after he finished as the League's highest scorer with 33 goals for Millwall in 1990–91. Born Highams Park 2.4.66.

CARL TILER (defender): Centre-half who became Brian Clough's first million-pound plus buy for more than a decade when he signed for £1.4 million from Barnsley in May 1991. Capped at Under-21 level by England. Born Sheffield 11.2.70.

BRETT WILLIAMS (defender): As understudy to Stuart Pearce, he has had few chances to impress. Made his debut as a 17-year-old, having joined the club straight from school. Has had

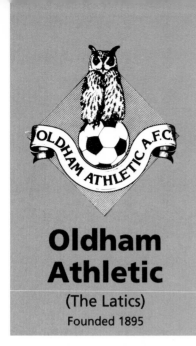

Oldham Athletic

(The Latics)
Founded 1895

Boundary Park,
Sheepfoot Lane,
Oldham OL1 2PA

Telephone numbers
Ground: 061-624 4972
Clubcall: 0898 121142
Ticket details: 0898 121582
Club shop: 061-652 0966
Commercial Department:
061-627 1802
Community programme:
061-678 8464

Oldham Athletic, who started out in 1895 as Pine Villa, have spent 85 years in the Football League, but it is fair to suggest that the last three seasons constitute the most colourful phase in their history. Perhaps it is fitting that Joe Royle should celebrate his tenth anniversary as manager by leading them into the Premier League era.

Elected to Division Two in 1907, Oldham just missed promotion in their first season, but in 1910 they pipped Hull and Derby into runners-up place on goal average. They reached the FA Cup semi-final in 1913, finished fourth in 1914, and in 1915 would have been First Division Champions had they not lost their final game against Liverpool.

Between the wars Oldham slipped down two grades, and though George Hardwick led them to the Third Division (North) title in 1953, they went straight back down, finishing the 1950s struggling at the foot of the new Fourth Division. They had a six-year spell in Division Three in the 1960s before their revival really began in the 1970s, when Jimmy Frizzell led them from the Fourth to the Second Division and, following Joe Royle's arrival in 1982, they gradually began to look likely contenders for a place in the top grade.

Two lean seasons followed their failure in the 1987 play-offs, but they gained respect and admiration in 1990 when they reached their first FA Cup semi-final since 1913 (they lost to Manchester United in a replay after a memorable 3–3 draw) and went all the way to Wembley in the League Cup before losing 1–0 to Nottingham Forest. A year later they were Second Division Champions, and in 1991–92, their first season in Division One since 1923, they produced the kind of drama and excitement which has become customary at Boundary Park. But Oldham consolidated and, had their away record not been poor, they would have finished much higher than 17th.

THE MANAGER

Joe Royle

Date of birth: 8 April, 1949
Birthplace: Liverpool
Date of appointment: July 1982

Managerial honours:
Oldham Athletic: Division Two Champions 1991; Littlewoods Cup finalists 1990

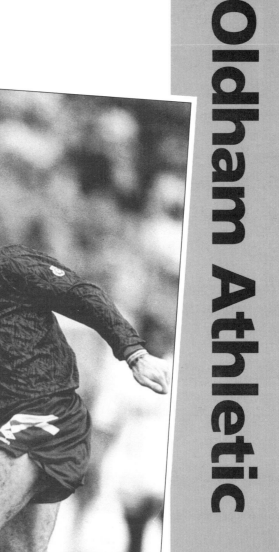

RECORDS

Biggest wins:
League: 11–0 v Southport, Division Four, Dec 1962
FA Cup: 10–1 v Lytham, 1st round, Nov 1925
Record defeat: 4–13 v Tranmere Rovers, Division Three (N), Dec 1935
Most appearances: Ian Wood, 564, League and Cup, 1966–80
Most goals (aggregate): Roger Palmer, 157, League and Cup, 1980–92
Most goals in a season: Tommy Davis, 35, League and Cup, 1936–37
Most capped player: Albert Gray, 9 (24), Wales
Other leading internationals:
England: John Hacking, 3
Scotland: Andy Goram, 4 (20)
Northern Ireland: Ron Blair, 5
Republic of Ireland: Tommy Davis, 2 (4)

ck Holden

THE F.A. PREMIER LEAGUE

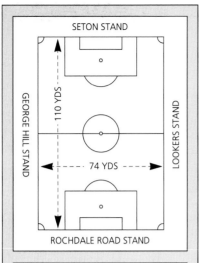

SETON STAND

GEORGE HILL STAND

110 YDS

74 YDS

LOOKERS STAND

ROCHDALE ROAD STAND

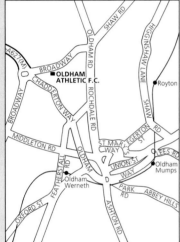

Ground capacity: 16,498
Number of seats: 11,498
Ground capacity (10 years ago):
26,000
Record attendance: 47,671 v
Sheffield Wednesday, FA Cup, 4th
round, 25 Jan 1930

Directions to ground
By car: Use M62, Junction 20, then
A627 to junction with A664; leave
motorway at roundabout and take
first exit into Broadway; turn right
at Hilbre Avenue for club car park.
By train: BR Mumps or BR
Werneth.
By bus: Nos 24, 181 or 182 from
Manchester Broadway.

PEN-PIX

NEIL ADAMS (forward): Versatile
player who started at Stoke before
moving to Everton. Signed for
Oldham in August 1989 for
£100,000 and is an England Under-
21 cap. Born Stoke 23.11.65.
ANDY BARLOW (defender): Home-
grown player who has gone on to
win England B honours. Born
Oldham 24.11.65.
PAUL BERNARD (midfielder): A
Scotland Youth and Under-21
international who joined Oldham as a
trainee. Born Edinburgh 30.12.72.
WILLIE DONACHIE (defender):
Evergreen former Manchester City,
Portland Timbers, Norwich and
Burnley left-back. A player-coach at

Neil McDonald

Boundary Park, he won 35 Scottish caps. Born Glasgow 5.10.51.

CRAIG FLEMING (defender): A midfielder for Halifax, who has moved back into defence since his arrival at Boundary Park for £80,000 in August 1991. Born Halifax 6.10.71.

GUNNAR HALLE (defender): Norwegian Youth, Under-21 and senior international, signed from Lillestroem for £280,000 in January 1991. Missed most of last season after breaking a leg against Torquay in the Rumbelows Cup in September. Born Oslo 11.8.65.

JON HALLWORTH (goalkeeper): Began his career at Ipswich and after loan spells at Swindon, Bristol Rovers and Fulham moved to Boundary Park for £125,000 in 1989. Born Stockport 26.10.65.

NICK HENRY (midfielder): A product of Oldham's youth section, who made his debut against Hull in September 1987. An England Under-21 international. Born Liverpool 21.2.69.

RICK HOLDEN (forward): Played for Burnley, Halifax and Watford before joining Oldham for £165,000 in August 1989. Born Skipton 9.9.64.

RICHARD JOBSON (defender): Central defender who began his career with Burton Albion before moving to Watford and Hull City. Joined Oldham for £460,000 in August 1990. Born Hull 9.5.63.

JOHN KEELEY (goalkeeper): Experienced former Southend United and Brighton goalkeeper who signed for Oldham from Brighton for £240,000 in August 1990. Made his first League appearance for the club in a 5–2 defeat by Manchester City on the final day of last season. Born Plaistow 27.7.61.

IAN MARSHALL (defender): Utility player who is often switched to attack. Signed from Everton for £100,000 in March 1988. Born Oxford 20.3.66.

NEIL McDONALD (midfielder): Former Newcastle and Everton player who moved to Oldham for £500,000 in September 1991. England Under-21 international. Born Wallsend 2.11.65.

OLDHAM ATHLETIC: 10–YEAR RECORD

	Div	P	W	D	L	F	A	Pts	Pos	FA Cup	Lge Cup
1982–83	2	42	14	19	9	64	47	61	7	3	2
1983–84	2	42	13	8	21	47	73	47	19	3	3
1984–85	2	42	15	8	19	49	67	53	14	4	1
1985–86	2	42	17	9	16	62	61	60	8	3	2
1986–87	2	42	22	9	11	65	44	75	3	3	3
1987–88	2	44	18	11	15	72	64	65	10	3	4
1988–89	2	46	11	21	14	75	72	54	16	3	3
1989–90	2	46	19	14	13	70	57	71	8	SF	F
1990–91	2	46	25	13	8	83	53	88	1 (P)	4	3
1991–92	1	42	14	9	19	63	67	51	17	3	4

Leading League scorers in last 10 seasons   *League hat-tricks*

1982–83	Wylde 19	Wylde (1)
1983–84	Palmer 13	—
1984–85	Quinn 18	Quinn (1)
1985–86	Futcher 17	—
1986–87	Palmer 16	Cecere (1)
1987–88	Ritchie 19	Palmer (2)
1988–89	Palmer 15	Palmer (1)
1989–90	Palmer 16	R. Holden (1)*
1990–91	Marshall 17	Marshall (1)
1991–92	Sharp 12	Sharp (1 x 4)

*Note: Bunn scored 6 v Scarborough in the League Cup, 25 Oct, 1989.

MIKE MILLIGAN (midfielder): Republic of Ireland international who captained Oldham in the 1990 Littlewoods Cup final against Nottingham Forest. Transferred to Everton for £850,000, but was unable to command a regular place and returned for £600,000. Born Manchester 20.2.67.

PAUL MOULDEN (forward): England Youth and Under-19 cap who started his career with Manchester City, then joined Bournemouth. He signed for Oldham for £225,000 in March 1990. Born Farnworth 6.9.67.

IAN OLNEY (forward): England Under-21 cap who signed for Oldham from Aston Villa for £700,000 in May. Born Luton 17.12.69.

ROGER PALMER (forward): Oldham's record scorer in all competitions, who began with Manchester City in 1977 and cost £70,000 in November 1980. Born Manchester 30.1.59.

ANDY RITCHIE (forward): Experienced striker who has previously played for Manchester United, Brighton and Leeds. Signed for Oldham in August 1987 from Leeds for £50,000. Born Manchester 28.11.60.

GRAEME SHARP (forward): Experienced Scottish international striker who signed from Everton for £500,000 in July 1991. Won FA Cup, League and European Cup Winners' Cup medals with Everton. Top scorer with 15 goals last season. Born Glasgow 16.10.60.

Queen's Park Rangers

(Rangers or Rs)

Founded 1885

Rangers Stadium,
South Africa Road,
Shepherd's Bush,
London W12 7PA

Telephone numbers
Ground: 081-743 0262
Clubcall: 0898 121162
Ticket details: 081-749 7798
Club shop: 081-749 6862
Supporters' club: 081-749 6771
Club fax: 081-749 0994
Marketing: 081-740 5737

Queen's Park Rangers, who kicked off in the mid-1880s as St Jude's Institute, won election to the Football League in 1920. Of their first 40 seasons, only four were spent outside the Third Division, and their emergence as a top club did not occur until the late 1960s – even then they faced a battle to prove their credentials.

A turning point in Rangers' history was the arrival of Alec Stock as manager in 1959. After three near misses, they romped to the Third Division title in 1967, the year they completed a memorable double by coming from behind to win the first League Cup final staged at Wembley, beating WBA 3–2. A year later they squeezed into Division One for the first time, pipping Blackpool to promotion on goal average. Then, with Stock gone, they went straight back down after winning only four games. They returned in 1973 but (despite having finished only one point behind League champions Liverpool in 1976) they were relegated again in 1979.

However, during their fourth and most recent spell in Division Two, QPR reached their first FA Cup final in 1982, losing 1–0 to Spurs after a 1–1 draw, and a year later they were Second Division Champions by ten clear points. After that they spent nine years in Division One, twice finishing in the top five yet generally looking a solid mid-table side capable of occasional extremes in fortune. In 1986 they reached the League Cup final again, only to lose to Oxford.

QPR reached their first FA Cup quarter-final as early as 1923, although they did not make the last eight again until 1948 – the year they were Division Three (South) Champions. On that occasion Dave Mangnall's side survived in Division Two through four disappointing seasons, but subsequently QPR had the indignity of finishing in the bottom four in Division Three (South) before things began to improve again. However, it is in the last 25 years that they have built a reputation for producing cultured performers and some famous stars. Gerry Francis returned to QPR in June 1991 to become their 15th manager since Alec Stock's departure in 1968.

RECORDS

Biggest wins:
League: 8–0 v Merthyr Tydfil, Division Three (S), March 1929; 9–2 v Tranmere Rovers, Division Three, Dec 1960
FA Cup: 8–1 v Bristol Rovers, 1st round, Nov 1937
UEFA Cup: 7–0 v Brann Bergen, 1st round, 1976–77
Record defeats: 1–8 v Manchester United, Division One, March 1969; 1–8 v Mansfield Town, Division Three, March 1965
Most appearances: Tony Ingham, 548, League and Cup, 1950–63

Most goals (aggregate): George Goddard, 186, League and Cup, 1926–34
Most goals in a season: George Goddard, 37, Division Three (S), 1929–30
Most capped player: Alan McDonald, 33, Northern Ireland
Other leading internationals:
England: Terry Fenwick, 19 (20); Paul Parker, 16 (17); Gerry Francis, 12
Scotland: Don Masson, 14 (17)
Wales: Ivor Powell, 4 (8)
Northern Ireland: Ian Stewart, 22 (31)
Republic of Ireland: Don Givens, 26 (56)

THE MANAGER

Gerry Francis

Date of birth: 6 Dec, 1951
Birthplace: Chiswick
Date of appointment: June 1991
Previous club: Bristol Rovers

Managerial honours:
Bristol Rovers: Division Three Champions
1990; Leyland Daf Cup finalists 1990

Bradley Allen

PEN-PIX

BRADLEY ALLEN (forward): England Under-21 international and one of the Allen football dynasty. Son of Les, brother of Clive and cousin of Martin and Paul, Bradley was a former trainee at Loftus Road. Born Harold Wood 13.9.71.

DENNIS BAILEY (forward): Signed from Birmingham City in summer 1991 for £175,000, he finished the season as the club's top scorer with 11 goals. Had started his League career at Crystal Palace, with two loan spells at Bristol Rovers. Born Lambeth 13.11.65.

DAVID BARDSLEY (defender): England Youth and B international who started at Blackpool and then joined Watford. Played for them at right-back in the 1984 FA Cup final defeat by Everton. Later played for Oxford and joined QPR in an exchange deal (for Mark Stein) in September 1989. Born Manchester 11.9.64.

SIMON BARKER (midfielder): England Under-21 international who was a high-goalscoring midfielder at his first club, Blackburn, before joining QPR for £400,000 in July 1988. Born Farnworth 4.11.64.

THE F.A. PREMIER LEAGUE

RUFUS BREVETT (defender): A YTS player at Doncaster who was signed by QPR in February 1991 for £250,000. A left-back, who began his career as a trainee with Derby. Born Derby 24.9.69.

JUSTIN CHANNING (defender): An England Youth international, who was an apprentice at Loftus Road. Turned professional in 1986. Has made 53 League appearances for QPR but last season made just one appearance, in the Zenith Data Systems Cup. Born Reading 19.11.68.

LES FERDINAND (forward): Having signed from non-League Hayes for £30,000 in 1989, he later had loan spells with Brentford and Turkish club Besiktas. Has now established himself in the QPR set-up. Born London 18.12.66.

IAN HOLLOWAY (midfielder): Gerry Francis signed him from Bristol Rovers, the manager's previous club, for £250,000 in August 1991. Began his career at Rovers in 1981 and was later with Wimbledon, Brentford and Torquay (loan) before returning to

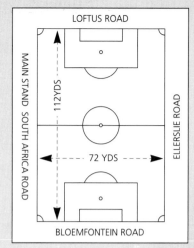

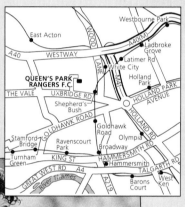

Ground capacity: 23,000
Number of seats: 14,546
Ground capacity (10 years ago): 30,000
Record attendance: 35,353 v Leeds Utd, Division One, 27 April, 1974

Directions to ground

By car: **From north**, M1 and A406 North Circular Road for Neasden, then A404 towards Hammersmith, right into White City Road, left into South Africa Road.

From east, join A40(M) and branch left to join M41, take third exit at roundabout A40, then join A4020 for Acton and turn right into Loftus Road.

From south, A3 follow signs for Hammersmith, then A219 to Shepherd's Bush, join A4020 towards Acton, turn right into Loftus Road.

From west, M4 to Chiswick, A315 and A402 to Shepherd's Bush and A4020 towards Acton, right into Loftus Road.

By train: Acton Central Station, then bus.

By bus: 283 to Bloemfontein Road; 72, 105, 220 to White City Station.

By tube: Shepherd's Bush (Hammersmith & City Line) or White City (Central Line)

Alan McDonald

Rovers in 1987. Born Kingswood 12.3.63.

ANDREW IMPEY (midfielder): Cost £35,000 from non-League Yeading in July 1990. Played his first game for the club in December 1991 and finished the season starting the last 11 matches. Born Hammersmith 30.9.71.

ALAN McCARTHY (defender): Signed from a trainee three seasons ago and has since made five League appearances for the club. Born London 11.1.72.

ALAN McDONALD (defender): Northern Ireland international who progressed through the ranks at Loftus Road but made his League debut while on loan at Charlton during season 1982–83. The longest-serving player on the staff. Born Belfast 12.10.63.

DANNY MADDIX (defender): Played just twice since December 1991 because of a knee ligament injury. Started his career at Tottenham but did not play a senior game for them and made his League debut on loan to Southend. Joined QPR on a free transfer in July 1987. Born Ashford, Kent, 11.10.67.

MICHAEL MEAKER (forward): A former trainee who has had three seasons at Loftus Road and made nine League appearances. Born Greenford 18.8.71.

DARREN PEACOCK (defender): Central defender who signed for QPR for £200,000 from Hereford in December 1990. Began his career with Newport County while they were still a Football League side. Born Bristol 3.2.68.

GARY PENRICE (forward): Played under Gerry Francis at his first club, Bristol Rovers, before moving to Watford in 1989. Signed for Aston Villa for £1 million in March 1991 before joining QPR for £625,000 in October 1991. Born Bristol 23.3.64.

TONY ROBERTS (goalkeeper): Understudy to Jan Stejskal, Roberts joined the club as a trainee and made his League debut in December 1987. Drifted back into reserve team football and made two appearances last season. Born Bangor 4.8.69.

ANDY SINTON (midfielder): A £2 million-rated England international winger who was signed from Brentford for £350,000 in March 1989. Started his career at Cambridge before moving to Brentford in 1985. Born Newcastle 19.3.66.

JAN STEJSKAL (goalkeeper): Czech goalkeeper who helped his country to the quarter-finals of the 1990 World Cup. His performances in Italy earned him a £625,000 move from Sparta Prague to QPR in July 1990. Born Brunn, Czechoslovakia, 15.1.62.

GARRY THOMPSON (forward): Signed from Crystal Palace for £100,000 in August 1991. He began his career at Coventry where Gerry Francis was player/coach and later

had spells at WBA, Sheffield Wednesday, Aston Villa and Watford before joining Palace. Born Birmingham 7.10.59.

ANDY TILLSON (defender): Brought into League football by Grimsby Town, who signed him from Kettering Town in July 1988. Signed for QPR from Grimsby for £400,000 in December 1990. Born Huntingdon 30.6.66.

GARY WADDOCK (midfielder): Republic of Ireland international who started his career at Loftus Road in 1979, and spent nine seasons there before joining Belgian club Charleroi and then Millwall. Signed from Millwall for £50,000 in December 1991 and finished the season on loan at Swindon. Born Kingsbury 17.3.62.

RAY WILKINS (midfielder): Club captain who won 84 England caps

between 1976 and 1987. His career began at Chelsea, where he was the youngest-ever captain. He later played for Manchester United, AC Milan, Paris St Germain and Glasgow Rangers, before signing on a free transfer in November 1989. Born Hillingdon 14.9.56.

CLIVE WILSON (defender): Started his career at Manchester City before joining Chelsea in March 1987, with a loan spell at Chester. Signed for QPR for £450,000 in July 1990. Born Manchester 13.11.61.

TONY WITTER (defender): Signed from Crystal Palace with Garry Thompson in August 1991. He cost £125,000 without playing a senior game for Palace, having joined them from non-League Grays. He made his debut last season while on loan at Plymouth. Born London 12.8.65.

QUEEN'S PARK RANGERS: 10-YEAR RECORD

	Div	P	W	D	L	F	A	Pts	Pos	FA Cup	Lge Cup
1982–83	2	42	26	7	9	77	36	85	1 (P)	3	2
1983–84	1	42	22	7	13	67	37	73	5	3	3
1984–85	1	42	13	11	18	53	72	50	19	3	QF
1985–86	1	42	15	7	20	53	64	52	13	3	F
1986–87	1	42	13	11	18	48	64	50	16	5	3
1987–88	1	40	19	10	11	48	38	67	5	5	3
1988–89	1	38	14	11	13	43	37	53	9	3	QF
1989–90	1	38	13	11	14	45	44	50	11	QF	3
1990–91	1	38	12	10	16	44	53	46	12	3	4
1991–92	1	42	12	18	12	48	47	54	11	3	3

Leading League scorers in last 10 seasons

1982–83	Sealy 16
1983–84	Allen 14
1984–85	Bannister 17
1985–86	Bannister 16
1986–87	Bannister 15
1987–88	Bannister 8
1988–89	Falco 12
1989–90	Clarke 6, Sutton 6, Wegerle 6
1989–91	Wegerle 18
1991–92	Ferdinand 10

League hat-tricks

Allen (1)
Allen (1)
—
Bannister (1)
Bannister (1)
Bannister (1)
—
Francis (1)
—
Bailey (1)

Sheffield United

(The Blades)

Founded 1889

Bramall Lane,
Sheffield S2 4SU

Telephone numbers
Ground: 0742 738955
Clubcall: 0898 888650
Ticket details: 0742 766771
Club shop: 0742 750596
Pools office: 0742 727901
Executive suite: 0742 755277
Community soccer: 0742 769314
Club fax: 0742 723030

Sheffield United, formed in 1889 by Yorkshire County Cricket Club, were elected to Division Two in 1892, promptly won promotion via the Test match system (equivalent to the modern play-offs), and spent the next 41 years in Division One. In six seasons between 1896 and 1902 they enjoyed a remarkable run in which they won their only League title (1898), twice finished runners-up (1897 and 1900), and won the FA Cup twice (1899 and 1902) in three finals in four years. Since then the Blades' only major honours have been FA Cup triumphs in 1915 and 1925, and they last reached the final in 1936.

It was in 1934 after the end of the Gillespie era that United's 37-season run at the top ended. They regained promotion in 1939, were relegated in 1949, won the Division Two championship in 1953 and then dropped down again in 1956 in what was a yo-yo decade for Sheffield football. John Harris, manager from 1959 until 1973 (apart from a one-year break) took them up in 1961, when they also reached the FA Cup semi-final, and led them to promotion again in 1971 after their unexpected fall of 1968; and though they finished sixth under Jimmy Sirrel in 1976, the years immediately after the end of the cricket era at Bramall Lane in 1973 were essentially a period of decline for Sheffield United.

Between 1976 and 1981 the club slid from the First to the Fourth Division and, though they were back in Division Two by 1984 under Ian Porterfield, they again fell into Division Three via the play-offs in 1988. Dave Bassett had arrived as manager by then, and he led them to successive promotions in 1989 and 1990. Indeed, in 1990 they were pipped to the Second Division title only on goal difference and reached their first FA Cup quarter-final since 1968.

The first years back in Division One since the mid-1970s were remarkable. In 1990–91 they finished 13th after failing to win in their first 16 games, while in 1991–92 they recovered to finish ninth, despite winning only one of their first 12 matches. In recognition of this feat, Bassett earned a special award from his fellow managers – plus a contract extended to 1996.

THE MANAGER

Dave Bassett

Date of birth: 4 Sept, 1944
Birthplace: Wembley
Date of appointment: Jan 1988
Previous clubs: Wimbledon, Watford

Managerial honours:
Wimbledon: Division Four Champions 1983; promotion to Division Three 1981; promotion to Division One 1986; promotion to Division Two 1984
Sheffield United: Promotion to Division One 1990; promotion to Division Two 1989

Simon Tracey

RECORDS

Biggest wins:
League: 10–1 v Burslem Port Vale, Division Two, Dec 1892; 11–2 v Cardiff City, Division One, Jan 1926
FA Cup: 5–0 v Newcastle United, 1st round, Jan 1914; 5–0 v Corinthians, 1st round, Jan 1925; 5–0 v Barrow, 3rd round, Jan 1956
Record defeats: 0–13 v Bolton Wanderers, FA Cup, 2nd round, Feb 1890; 3–10 v Middlesbrough, Division One, Nov 1933
Most appearances: Joe Shaw, 689, League and Cup, 1948–66
Most goals (aggregate): Harry Johnson, 225, League and Cup, 1919–30
Most goals in a season: Jimmy Dunne, 46, League and Cup, 1930–31
Most capped players:
Past – Billy Gillespie, 25, Northern Ireland
Present – Colin Hill, 6, Northern Ireland
Other leading internationals:
England: Ernest Needham, 16; George Green, 8; Fred Tunstall, 7; Tony Currie, 7 (17)
Scotland: Eddie Colquhoun, 9
Wales: Gil Reece, 16 (29)
Northern Ireland: Jimmy Dunne, 7 (+1 for Republic of Ireland)
Republic of Ireland: Alf Ringstead, 20 (Note: Bob Evans, who won four of his ten Welsh caps while with Sheffield United, also played four times for England.)

Sheffield United

THE F.A. PREMIER LEAGUE

DAVID BARNES (defender): Much-travelled full-back, who began his professional career at Coventry and then had spells at Ipswich, Wolves and Aldershot before moving to United for £50,000 in July 1989. Born London 16.11.61.

PAUL BEESLEY (defender): Joined United in £300,000 transfer from Leyton Orient in July 1990. Started his professional career at Wigan, for whom he made 185 appearances in all competitions in five years. Born Wigan 21.7.65.

CARL BRADSHAW (forward): Began at neighbouring Sheffield Wednesday and then played for Barnsley (loan) and Manchester City, moving to United in a £50,000 deal in October 1989. Born Sheffield 2.10.68.

IAN BRYSON (midfielder): Scottish winger signed from Kilmarnock for £40,000 in July 1988. Started with them and was their top scorer for two seasons (1985–86, 1986–87) before his transfer to United. Born Kilmarnock 26.11.62.

ALAN CORK (forward): Signed on a free transfer from Wimbledon in March 1992. Was a member of the Wimbledon side which rose from the Fourth Division to the First, and beat Liverpool 1–0 in the 1988 FA Cup final. Born Derby 4.3.59.

TOM COWAN (defender): Full-back who started his career at Clyde and cost £350,000 from Glasgow Rangers in the summer of 1991. Made 20 League appearances last season. Born Bellshill 28.8.69.

BRIAN DEANE (forward): Has been United's top-scorer for the last two seasons, scoring 17 League and Cup goals during the 1991–92 season. Cost £30,000 from Doncaster in July 1988 and won his two England caps on the 1991 summer tour to Australasia and Malaysia. Born Leeds 7.2.68.

KEVIN GAGE (defender): Joined from Aston Villa for £150,000 in January 1991 after an initial loan spell, having started his career at Wimbledon. A utility player, he was used mainly at right-back last season. Born Chiswick 21.4.64.

JOHN GANNON (midfielder): Was given his senior debut by manager Dave Bassett while at Wimbledon. Spent a period on loan at Crewe in 1986–87 and moved to United on a free transfer in February 1989. Born Wimbledon 18.12.66.

BRIAN GAYLE (defender): Reunited with Dave Bassett when he joined United in September 1991 for £700,000 from Ipswich. Began career at Wimbledon, moving to Manchester City in the summer of 1988 for £325,000. Born London 6.3.65.

CHARLIE HARTFIELD (forward): Joined the club on a free transfer from Arsenal in July 1991 and made his United debut a month later against Crystal Palace. Born Lambeth 4.9.71.

COLIN HILL (defender): Northern Ireland international who cost £85,000 from Colchester in October 1987. Started his career at Arsenal and has also played for Brighton (loan) and for Maritimo, Portugal. Born Hillingdon 12.11.63.

GLYN HODGES (midfielder): Welsh international who began as an apprentice with Wimbledon. Had spells with Newcastle, Watford and Crystal Palace before joining United in April 1991 for £410,000, following a loan period. Born Streatham 30.4.63.

JAMIE HOYLAND (midfielder): Signed for United, the team he supported as a boy, for £250,000 from Bury in June 1990. His father also played for the club in the 1950s. Born Sheffield 23.1.66.

PHIL KITE (goalkeeper): Began career as an apprentice with Bristol Rovers

SHOREHAM STREET SPION KOP

JOHN STREET

113YDS

75 YDS

NEW SOUTH STAND CHERRY STREET

BRAMALL LANE

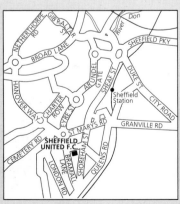

Ground capacity: 32,213
Number of seats: 22,862
Ground capacity (10 years ago): 49,000
Record attendance: 68,287 v Leeds United, FA Cup, 5th round, 15 Feb, 1936

Directions to ground

By car: **From north**, exit M1 Junction 34. Follow signs to Sheffield (A6109), turn left after three-and-a-half miles. Take 4th exit at roundabout into Sheaf Street, 5th exit at second roundabout into St Mary's Road (for Bakewell), turn left half-a-mile along Bramall Lane. **From south and east**, exit M1 Junction 31 or 33 and take A57 to roundabout, 3rd exit from Sheaf Street (then as above). **From west**, take A57 into Sheffield, 4th exit at roundabout into Upper Hanover Street; at second roundabout take 3rd exit into Bramall Lane.

By train: Sheffield Midland – within a mile from ground.

By bus: From main bus station, opposite BR, or city centre, Nos 20, 34, 38, 39, 42 and 259.

SHEFFIELD UNITED: 10–YEAR RECORD

	Div	P	W	D	L	F	A	Pts	Pos	FA Cup	Lge Cup
1982–83	3	46	19	7	20	62	64	64	11	3	3
1983–84	3	46	24	11	11	86	53	83	3 (P)	3	2
1984–85	2	42	10	14	18	54	66	44	18	3	2
1985–86	2	42	17	11	14	64	63	62	7	4	2
1986–87	2	42	15	13	14	50	49	58	9	4	3
1987–88	2	44	13	7	24	45	74	46	21 (R)	4	2
1988–89	3	46	25	9	12	93	54	84	2 (P)	5	3
1989–90	2	46	24	13	9	78	58	85	2 (P)	QF	1
1990–91	1	38	13	7	18	36	55	46	13	3	4
1991–92	1	42	16	9	17	65	63	57	9	5	3

Leading League scorers in last 10 seasons		*League hat-tricks*
1982–83	Morris 14	Morris (1)
1983–84	Edwards 33	Edwards (1 x 4, 2 x 3), Morris (1)
1984–85	Edwards 13	—
1985–86	Edwards 20	Edwards (1)
1986–87	Beagrie 9, Foley 9	—
1987–88	Philliskirk 9	—
1988–89	Agana 24	Agana (2), Deane (1)
1989–90	Deane 21	—
1990–91	Deane 13	—
1991–92	Deane 13	—

MITCH WARD (defender): Joined United as an apprentice and has now made ten League appearances for the club, scoring twice. Had a spell on loan at Crewe. Born Sheffield 18.6.71.

DANE WHITEHOUSE (midfielder): Normally a left-sided midfielder, he can also play in defence. Joined the club as an apprentice. Scored ten goals last season, including a goal in each Sheffield derby game. Born Sheffield 14.10.70.

CHRIS WILDER (defender): Began his career as an apprentice with Southampton, but moved to Sheffield United after failing to gain first-team recognition at The Dell. Has had loan spells at Walsall and Charlton. Born Wortley 2.9.67.

Brian Deane

before moving to Southampton in 1984. After short spells at Gillingham and Bournemouth was signed by United for £25,000 in August 1990. Has also had loan spells at Tottenham and Middlesbrough. Born Bristol 26.10.62.

MICHAEL LAKE (midfielder): Brother of Manchester City's Paul, he was signed from non-League Macclesfield in October 1989 for £40,000. Made 17 appearances last season – nine as a substitute. Born Manchester 16.11.66.

BRIAN MARWOOD (forward): Championship winner with Arsenal in 1989 before signing for United in a £350,000 transfer in September 1990. Has also played for Hull and Sheffield Wednesday and has been capped once by England. Born Seaham Harbour 5.2.60.

JOHN PEMBERTON (defender): Began at Rochdale before moving to Crewe. Signed for Crystal Palace in 1988 for £100,000 and moved to United for £300,000 in July 1990. Born Oldham 11.11.64.

MELVYN REES (goalkeeper): Cost £25,000 from West Bromwich Albion on transfer deadline day in March 1992. Began at Cardiff and also played for Watford with loan spells at Crewe, Southampton and Leyton Orient. Born Cardiff 25.1.67.

SIMON TRACEY (goalkeeper): Was first with Dave Bassett as an apprentice at Wimbledon, and was understudy to Dave Beasant before signing for United in October 1988 for £7,500. Born Woolwich 9.12.67.

Sheffield Wednesday

(The Owls)

Founded 1867

Hillsborough,
Sheffield S6 1SW

Telephone numbers
Ground: 0742 343122
Clubcall: 0898 121186
Ticket details: 0742 337233
Club shop: 0742 343342
Community programme:
0742 313262
Development office:
0742 337235
Club fax: 0742 337145

Sheffield Wednesday, formed in 1867 by members of a cricket club, celebrate their 125th anniversary and begin the Premier League era with their first appearance in Europe since 1964. Wednesday finished their 89th season in the Football League in their highest place for 31 years. Elected to the Football League in 1892, the club spent only one of their first 24 seasons outside Division One, their best spell in that phase coming between 1896 and 1907 when they won the FA Cup twice (they had lost heavily in the 1890 final) and captured successive League titles in 1903 and 1904, after bouncing straight back following relegation in 1899.

The period between the two world wars began with another relegation in 1920, but after being Division Two Champions in 1926 and dramatically beating the drop in 1928 after looking doomed, they topped Division One in 1929 and 1930. Wednesday also won the FA Cup in 1935, during a seven-year spell in which they finished outside the top three only once. However, 1937 saw them relegated again, and in the yo-yo years of the 1950s they were promoted four times (winning three Division Two titles) and relegated three times.

Harry Catterick's team finished First Division runners-up to Spurs in 1961, while Alan Brown's side reached the 1966 FA Cup final, losing 3–2 after leading Catterick's Everton 2–0. Relegated in 1970, Wednesday fell into Division Three for the first time, in 1975, before Jack Charlton led them back in 1980, and Howard Wilkinson ended their Division One exile in 1984.

Ron Atkinson's side went down on goal difference in 1990, but in 1991 promotion coincided with a League Cup triumph – Wednesday's first major honour in 56 years.

Wembley success atoned for FA Cup semi-final defeats of 1983 and 1986, and for four League Cup failures in the quarter-finals in the previous eight years. Though Wednesday collected no trophies in 1992, their achievement of finishing third was highly satisfying, coming as it did in Trevor Francis's first term as manager following Ron Atkinson's switch to Villa.

THE MANAGER

Trevor Francis

Date of birth: 19 April, 1954
Birthplace: Plymouth
Date of appointment: June 1991
Previous club: Queen's Park Rangers

RECORDS

Biggest wins:
League: 9–1 v Birmingham, Division One, Dec 1930
FA Cup: 12–0 v Halliwell, 1st round, Jan 1891
League Cup: 8–0 v Aldershot, 2nd round, 2nd leg, Oct 1989
Record defeat: 0–10 v Aston Villa, Division One, Oct 1912
Most appearances: Andrew Wilson, 545, League and Cup, 1900–20
Most goals (aggregate): Andrew Wilson, 216, League and Cup, 1900–20

Most goals in a season: Derek Dooley, 47, League and Cup, 1951–52
Most capped players:
Past – Ron Springett, 33, England
Present – Nigel Worthington, 37, Northern Ireland
Other leading internationals:
England: Ernest Blenkinsop, 26; Alf Strange, 20; Peter Swan, 19
Scotland: Andrew Wilson, 6
Wales: Peter Rodrigues, 16 (40)
Northern Ireland: Dave Clements, 13 (48)
Republic of Ireland: Eddie Gannon, 11 (14); John Sheridan, 9 (14)

PEN-PIX

VIV ANDERSON (defender): Experienced player who began his career as an apprentice with Nottingham Forest, making his debut in September 1974. An England international, he also had spells with Arsenal and Manchester United before joining Wednesday in January 1991 on a free transfer. Born Nottingham 29.8.56.

CHRIS BART-WILLIAMS (midfielder): Joined the club from Leyton Orient in November 1991 in a player exchange with Chris Turner, for which Orient also received £350,000. England Youth international who made 17 appearances for Wednesday last season. Born Freetown, Sierra Leone, 16.6.74.

TREVOR FRANCIS (forward): Player/manager who made 22 appearances last season, all as substitute. An England international, he started at Birmingham before spells with Nottingham Forest, Manchester City, Sampdoria, Atalanta, Glasgow Rangers and QPR. Had an unsuccessful spell as QPR manager before move to Wednesday in January 1990, becoming manager in June 1991. Born Plymouth 19.4.54.

Paul Williams

THE F.A. PREMIER LEAGUE

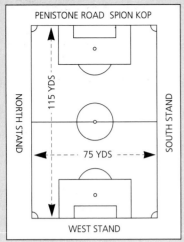

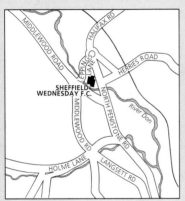

Ground capacity: 41,237
Number of seats: 23,470
Ground capacity (10 years ago): 50,174
Record attendance: 72,841 v Manchester City, FA Cup, 5th round, 17 March, 1923

Directions to ground
By car: **From north**, exit M1 Junction 34 following signs Sheffield A6109, take third exit at roundabout and in three-quarters-of-a-mile turn left into Herries Road South for ground.
From south and east, exit M1 Junction 31 or 33, take A57 to roundabout and exit into Prince of Wales Road; after five-and-three-quarter miles turn left into Herries Road South.
From west, take A57 until A6101 and turn left; after three-and-three-quarter miles turn left at T junction into Penistone Road for ground.
By train: Sheffield Midland Station
By bus: Penistone Road, Nos 42, 53, 79, 89. Middlewood Road, Nos 80, 81, 82, 83, 84, 85, 87, 88.

PHIL KING (defender): Began his career as an apprentice with Exeter, joining Torquay in July 1986. An England B international, he signed for Wednesday from Swindon for £400,000 in November 1989. Missed only three games last season. Born Bristol 28.12.67.
ROLAND NILSSON (defender): Joined Wednesday in December 1989 from Swedish club IFK Gothenburg for £375,000. Swedish international right-back who played in the European Championship finals. Born Helsingborg, Sweden, 27.11.63.
CARLTON PALMER (midfielder): A versatile player who played for England in the 1992 European Championship

Carlton Palmer

JOHN HARKES (defender): USA international who played in the 1990 World Cup finals. Signed from the US Soccer Federation in November 1990 for £90,000. Scored three goals last season. Can also play in midfield. Born New Jersey, USA, 8.3.67.
DAVID HIRST (forward): England international who started at Barnsley but after 28 League appearances and nine goals joined Wednesday for £200,000, in August 1986. Won a 1991 League Cup medal and was top-scorer last season with 20 goals. Born Barnsley 7.12.67.
GRAHAM HYDE (midfielder): Joined Wednesday from school as a trainee and signed professional forms in July 1991. Scored once in 17 appearances last season, making his debut at Manchester City in September 1991. Born Doncaster 10.11.70.

NIGEL JEMSON (forward): Scored the winning goal for Nottingham Forest in the 1990 League Cup final against Oldham. Started career with Preston, joining Forest in March 1988, and also had loan spells at Bolton and Preston. An England Under-21 international, he joined Wednesday in September 1991 for £800,000. Born Preston 10.8.69.
DAVID JOHNSON (forward): A product of Wednesday's youth policy, who signed trainee forms in July 1987 before turning professional in July 1989. Six first-team appearances last season. Born Sheffield 29.10.70.

finals. Started as an apprentice with WBA, joining Wednesday for £750,000 in February 1989. Born Oldbury 5.12.65.

NIGEL PEARSON (defender): Club captain, who lifted the Rumbelows Cup for Wednesday in 1991. Started his career with Shrewsbury before joining Wednesday in October 1987 for £250,000. Two goals last season. Born Nottingham 21.8.63.

KEVIN PRESSMAN (goalkeeper): An England Under-21 international who joined Wednesday, his only club, in November 1985. Had a spell on loan at Stoke towards the end of last season. Born Fareham 6.11.67.

JOHN SHERIDAN (midfielder): Scored the winner for Wednesday in 1991 Rumbelows Cup final against Manchester United. Republic of Ireland international who began with Leeds, joining Nottingham Forest in August 1989 for £650,000 – three months later he joined Wednesday for £500,000. Born Stretford 1.10.64.

PETER SHIRTLIFF (defender): Played for Wednesday in 1991 League Cup final win over Manchester United. In his second spell at the club, having started as an apprentice, before moving to Charlton in August 1986. Returned in £500,000 deal in July 1989. Born Sheffield 6.4.61.

CHRIS WADDLE (forward): England international (62 caps, 1985–91) signed for £1 million from French Champions Marseille. Won three French title medals and played in the 1991 European Cup final defeat by Red Star Belgrade after signing from Tottenham for £4.5 million in July 1989. Began his League career at Newcastle. Born Hepworth 14.12.60.

PAUL WARHURST (defender): Trevor Francis's first signing for Wednesday, when he paid Oldham £750,000 equalling the then club record fee. An England Under-21 international, he began his career with Manchester City before moving to Oldham. Born Stockport 26.9.69.

GORDON WATSON (forward): England Under-21 striker who joined from Charlton in February 1991 for £250,000. Began as an apprentice with Charlton, signing professional forms in May 1989. Born Sidcup 20.3.71.

PAUL WILLIAMS (forward): England B and Under-21 player who moved to Wednesday in August 1990 from Charlton for £600,000. Started with non-League Woodford Town and had a loan spell with Brentford. Scored 10 goals last season. Born London 16.8.65.

DANNY WILSON (midfielder): Northern Ireland international and League Cup winner with Luton in 1988. Previous clubs include Wigan, Bury, Chester, Nottingham Forest, Brighton and Luton. Cost Wednesday £200,000 in August 1990. Born Wigan 1.1.60.

CHRIS WOODS (goalkeeper): England international who became the youngest goalkeeper ever to appear in a Wembley final when he played for Nottingham Forest in the 1978 League Cup final, aged 18. Joined Wednesday for a club record £1.2 million from Glasgow Rangers in August 1991. Previously with Norwich and QPR. Born Boston 14.11.59.

NIGEL WORTHINGTON (midfielder): Versatile Northern Ireland international who joined the club from Notts County in February 1984 for £125,000, and has made more than 300 appearances. Born Ballymena 4.11.61.

SHEFFIELD WEDNESDAY: 10-YEAR RECORD

	Div	P	W	D	L	F	A	Pts	Pos	FA Cup	Lge Cup
1982–83	2	42	16	15	11	60	47	63	6	SF	QF
1983–84	2	42	26	10	6	72	34	88	2 (P)	QF	QF
1984–85	1	42	17	14	11	58	45	65	8	5	QF
1985–86	1	42	21	10	11	63	54	75	5	SF	3
1986–87	1	42	13	13	16	58	59	52	13	QF	3
1987–88	1	40	15	8	17	52	66	53	11	3	QF
1988–89	1	38	10	12	16	34	51	42	15	4	2
1989–90	1	38	11	10	17	35	51	43	18 (R)	4	3
1990–91	2	46	22	16	8	80	51	82	3 (P)	5	W
1991–92	1	42	21	12	9	62	49	75	3	4	3

Leading League scorers in last 10 seasons

		League hat-tricks
1982–83	Bannister 10	—
1983–84	Varadi 17	—
1984–85	Varadi 16	Varadi (1)*
1985–86	Marwood 13	Shutt (1)
1986–87	Chapman 19	—
1987–88	Chapman 19	—
1988–89	Hirst 7	—
1989–90	Hirst 14	—
1990–91	Hirst 24	Hirst (1 x 4)
1991–92	Hirst 18	Palmer (1)

Note: Blair scored a hat-trick of penalties v Luton in the League Cup, 20 Nov, 1984.

Southampton

(The Saints)

Founded 1885

The Dell, Milton Road,
Southampton SO9 4XX

Telephone numbers
Ground: 0703 220505
Clubcall: 0898 121178
Clubcall ticket information:
0890 121593
Ticket details: 0703 228575
Access/Visa ticket booking line:
0703 337171
Club shop: 0703 236400
Supporters' club: 0703 336450
Club fax: 0703 330360

Southampton, formed in 1885, had the distinction of reaching two FA Cup finals long before they graduated from the Southern League to the Football League in 1920. They lost to Bury in 1900 and to Sheffield United (in a replay) in 1902, but had to wait another 74 years to win the trophy and the first major honour in their history.

After gaining admission to the League, Southampton won the Third Division (South) title on goal average within two years, but thereafter became a solid Second Division outfit and did not reach Division One for the first time until 1966. Yet they were desperately close to promotion for three years running between 1948 and 1950. In 1949 they stumbled after leading Division Two by eight points with seven games left (it was the days of two points for a win), while in 1950 they lost out on goal average. In fact, they fell into Division Three for seven years before Ted Bates led them back in 1960, and finally guided them into Division One in 1966. In 1974, at the start of the Lawrie McMenemy era, they slumped to relegation following a mere three wins in their last 22 games.

However, McMenemy's side won the 1976 FA Cup final, beating Manchester United, and in 1978 they returned to the top grade, where they have remained. A year after promotion they reached the League Cup final, which they lost to Forest, but the peak of McMenemy's 11-and-a-half years was probably 1984, when his side finished Division One runners-up to Liverpool and fell in the FA Cup semi-final after being drawn away in every round.

Chris Nicholl led the Saints to an FA Cup semi-final in 1986 and they reached one semi-final and three quarter-finals in the League Cup, but their League form remained generally modest. Last season, when Ian Branfoot took over, Southampton fought a rearguard action to achieve safety with their lowest position since promotion, though they went to the FA Cup quarter-final and the Zenith Data Systems final.

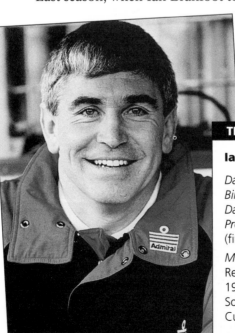

THE MANAGER

Ian Branfoot

Date of birth: 26 Jan, 1947
Birthplace: Gateshead
Date of appointment: June 1991
Previous clubs: Reading, Crystal Palace (first team coach)

Managerial honours:
Reading: Division Three Champions 1986; Simod Cup winners 1988
Southampton: Zenith Data Systems Cup finalists 1992

Southampton

RECORDS

Biggest wins
League: 9–3 v Wolverhampton Wanderers, Division Two, Sept 1965; 8–2 v Coventry City, Division One, April 1984
FA Cup: 7–1 v Ipswich Town, 3rd round, Jan 1961
Record defeats: 0–8 v Tottenham Hotspur, Division Two, March 1936; v Everton, Division One, Nov 1971
Most appearances: Terry Paine, 809, League and Cup, 1956–74
Most goals (aggregate): Mick Channon, 227, League and Cup, 1966–77 and 1979–82
Most goals in a season: Derek Reeves, 44, League and Cup, 1959–60
Most capped players:
Past – Peter Shilton, 49 (125), England
Present – Iain Dowie, 5 (12), Northern Ireland
Other leading internationals:
England: Mick Channon, 45 (46); Terry Paine, 19; Dave Watson, 18 (65)
Scotland: Jack Robertson, 1 (16); Ian Black, 1
Wales: Ron Davies, 23 (29)
Northern Ireland: Chris Nicholl, 37 (51)
Republic of Ireland: Tony Byrne, 14

Matthew Le Tissier

THE F.A. PREMIER LEAGUE

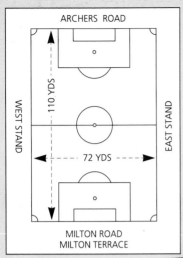

ARCHERS ROAD

WEST STAND

110 YDS

72 YDS

EAST STAND

MILTON ROAD
MILTON TERRACE

Ground capacity: 21,989
Number of seats: 8,714
Ground capacity (10 years ago):
25,000
Record attendance: 31,044 v
Manchester United, Division One,
10 Oct, 1969

Directions to ground

By car: M3/A33, follow signs for
city centre along The Avenue, turn
right at traffic lights into
Northlands Road.
By train: Southampton Central
station.
By bus: Nos 5, 25 from city centre.

PEN-PIX

MICKY ADAMS (defender): A former
England Youth international who
began his career with Gillingham
before moving on to Coventry and
Leeds. Signed for Southampton for
£250,000 in March 1989. Born
Sheffield 8.11.61.

IAN ANDREWS (goalkeeper): Reserve
team goalkeeper who signed from
Celtic in February 1990 for £200,000.
Started with Leicester and went on
loan to Swindon and Leeds. A former
England Under-21 international. Born
Nottingham 1.12.64.

Terry Hurlock

FRANCIS BENALI (defender): Local player who won England Schoolboy caps and firmly established himself at the end of the season. Born Southampton 30.12.68.

GLENN COCKERILL (midfielder): Seasoned player starting his 17th season as a professional. Signed from Sheffield United for £225,000 in October 1985, having previously played for Lincoln and Swindon. Born Grimsby 25.8.59.

KERRY DIXON (forward): Signed from Chelsea for £575,000 in July 1992. England international with eight caps. Formerly with Reading, Tottenham and Dunstable. Born Luton 24.7.61

JASON DODD (defender): England Under-21 right-back who signed from Bath City in April 1989. Born Bath 2.11.70.

IAIN DOWIE (forward): Former Luton and West Ham forward who was rejected by Southampton as a schoolboy. Northern Ireland international who used to work for British Aerospace and gained a degree in mechanical engineering. Signed from West Ham for £500,000 in August 1991. Born Hatfield 9.1.65.

TIM FLOWERS (goalkeeper): England Under-21 goalkeeper who signed from Wolves in 1986 for £75,000. Fractured cheekbone on home debut v Arsenal, November 1986. Born Kenilworth 3.2.67.

STUART GRAY (midfielder): Versatile player, equally at home in defence. Former clubs are Nottingham Forest, Bolton (loan), Barnsley and Aston Villa, where he was club captain before joining Southampton for £200,000 in September 1991. Born Withernsea 19.4.60.

RICHARD HALL (defender): Former county squash player who started at Scunthorpe before moving to Southampton for £200,000 in February 1991. Born Ipswich 14.3.72.

TERRY HURLOCK (midfielder): Former Brentford, Reading and Millwall player who was signed from Glasgow Rangers for £400,000 in September 1991. An England B international. Born Hackney 22.9.58.

SOUTHAMPTON: 10-YEAR RECORD

	Div	P	W	D	L	F	A	Pts	Pos	FA Cup	Lge Cup
1982–83	1	42	15	12	15	54	58	57	12	3	4
1983–84	1	42	22	11	9	66	38	77	2	SF	3
1984–85	1	42	19	11	12	56	47	68	5	5	4
1985–86	1	42	12	10	20	51	62	46	14	SF	4
1986–87	1	42	14	10	18	69	68	52	12	3	SF
1987–88	1	40	12	14	14	49	53	50	12	4	2
1988–89	1	38	10	15	13	52	66	45	13	3	QF
1989–90	1	38	15	10	13	71	63	55	7	5	QF
1990–91	1	38	12	9	17	58	69	45	14	5	QF
1991–92	1	42	14	10	18	39	55	52	16	QF	4

Leading League scorers in last 10 seasons

1982–83	Wallace 12
1983–84	Moran 21
1984–85	Jordan 12
1985–86	Armstrong 10
1986–87	Clarke 20
1987–88	Clarke 16
1988–89	Rod Wallace 12
1989–90	Le Tissier 20
1990–91	Le Tissier 19
1991–92	Shearer 13

League hat-tricks

Morgan (1)
Moran (1), Wallace (1)
Moran (1)
Moran (1)
Clarke (2), Hobson (1), Le Tissier (1)
Shearer (1)
—
Le Tissier (2)
—
—

JEFF KENNA (defender): Sturdily built Dubliner who has represented the Republic of Ireland Under-21. Made ten appearances last season. Born Dublin 27.8.70.

MATTHEW LE TISSIER (forward): England Youth and B international signed from Vale Recreation in Guernsey in 1986. The club's penalty-taker, who is valued in the £2 million bracket. Born Guernsey 14.10.68.

NEIL MADDISON (midfielder): Made his Southampton debut in October 1988, but has subsequently been plagued by injuries, making just one appearance as a substitute last season. Born Darlington 2.10.69.

PAUL MOODY (forward): Striker signed from non-League Waterlooville in July 1991. Made his Saints debut against Tottenham. Born 13.6.67.

KEVIN MOORE (defender): Spent nearly 11 years with Grimsby before moving to Oldham in the 1986–87 season and then Southampton in August 1987 for £125,000. Born Grimsby 29.4.58.

ALAN SHEARER (forward): Predatory marksman who scored on his England debut against France at Wembley in February 1992. Youngest player, at 17, to score a Division One hat-trick, in the 4–2 win over Arsenal in April 1988. Born Newcastle 13.8.70.

STEVE WOOD (defender): An accomplished player who enjoyed eight seasons at Reading before moving to Millwall in June 1987. Cost Southampton £400,000 in October 1991. Born Bracknell 2.2.63.

Tottenham Hotspur
(Spurs)
Founded 1882

748 High Road,
Tottenham,
London N17 0AP

Telephone numbers
Ground: 081-808 6666
Clubcall: 0898 100500
Ticket details: 081-808 8080
Fax-a-seat: 081-880 3428
Dial-a-seat: 081-808 3030
Club shop: 081-801 1669
Supporters' club: 081-880 3408
Mail order: 081-808 5959
Club fax: 081-885 1951

*F*rom 1908 Tottenham's 73 seasons in the Football League include only 16 outside Division One, with 13 of them between 1928 and 1950 and just one in the last 42 years. Formed in 1882, Spurs boast more FA Cup triumphs than any other club. The first of eight wins came in 1901 when, as members of the Southern League, they beat Sheffield United in a famous final replay at Bolton. Their only defeat in nine finals (seven at Wembley since 1961) was against Coventry in 1987.

Spurs gained First Division status within a year of joining the League. But in their first 20 years, though winning the FA Cup in 1921 and being Division One runners-up in 1922, they suffered two falls – in 1919 they were not spared relegation despite enlargement of the table, and then they went down unexpectedly in the famous 1928 scramble. They rose again in 1933, but fell back in 1935.

Arthur Rowe's great era as manager began with a Division Two title triumph by nine points in 1950, and a year later they were Division One Champions for the first time, then runners-up twice in the 1950s. Bill Nicholson had taken over by the time of the epic League and Cup double of 1961, when they won the title with 66 points, eight more than nearest rivals Sheffield Wednesday. Spurs won the FA Cup again in 1962 and 1967, and the European Cup Winners' Cup in 1963, when they last finished second in Division One.

In the 1970s they added two League Cup triumphs to their record (1971 and 1973), and in 1972 won the first of two UEFA Cup finals in three seasons, losing in 1974. In 1977 they began a year in Division Two, gaining prompt promotion on goal average. The 1980s brought further FA Cup successes (in replay victories in 1981 and 1982) and a penalty shoot-out triumph in the UEFA Cup in 1984. But they also lost twice at Wembley – in the 1982 League Cup final and the 1987 FA Cup final. Although Spurs chalked up their eighth FA Cup win in 1991 and reached the League Cup semi-final last season, 1991–92 saw them finish in their lowest League position since gaining promotion.

FIRST TEAM COACH

Doug Livermore

Date of birth: 27 Dec, 1947
Birthplace: Liverpool
Date of appointment: May 1992

Tottenham Hotspur

THE F.A. PREMIER LEAGUE

RECORDS

Biggest wins:
League: 9–0 v Bristol Rovers, Division Two, Oct 1977
FA Cup: 13–2 v Crewe Alexandra, 4th round, Feb 1960
Record defeat: 0–7 v Liverpool, Division One, Sept 1978
Most appearances: Steve Perryman, 855, League and Cup, 1969–86
Most goals (aggregate): Jimmy Greaves, 266, League and Cup, 1961–70
Most goals in a season: Clive Allen, 49, League and Cup, 1986–87

Most capped players:
Past – Pat Jennings, 74 (119), Northern Ireland
Present – Gary Mabbutt, 16, England
Other leading internationals:
England: Glenn Hoddle, 44 (53); Jimmy Greaves, 42 (57); Chris Waddle, 36 (62)
Scotland: Bill Brown, 24 (28)
Wales: Cliff Jones, 41 (59)
Northern Ireland: Danny Blanchflower, 43 (56)
Republic of Ireland: Chris Hughton, 51 (53)

PEN-PIX

Gary Mabbutt

PAUL ALLEN (midfielder): Former West Ham player who signed for Tottenham in 1985 for £400,000. Youngest player to appear in an FA Cup final, for West Ham in 1980, and a 1991 FA Cup winner with Tottenham. Cousin of striker Clive Allen. Born Aveley 28.8.62.

DARREN ANDERTON (forward): A £2.15 million signing from Portsmouth in June 1992. Scored five goals in the FA Cup last season to help Portsmouth reach the semi-final. Former England Youth international. Born Southampton 3.3.72.

DEAN AUSTIN (defender): Signed from Southend in May 1992 for a tribunal-set fee of £375,000 with a possible £150,000 to come. Joined Southend from non-League St Albans in March 1990. Born Hemel Hempstead 26.4.70.

PETER BEADLE (forward): Ex-Gillingham striker who cost £300,000 in June 1992, having joined Gillingham as a trainee and signed professional forms in May 1990. Scored seven goals last season. Born London 13.5.72.

GUDNI BERGSSON (defender): Icelandic international who joined Spurs in January 1989, following a trial period. Started with his local club Valur Reykjavik. Made his Spurs debut in December 1988 against Luton. Born Reykjavik 21.7.65.

JASON CUNDY (defender): Joined Tottenham on loan from Chelsea in March 1992 until the end of that season and signed for £750,000 in May. England Under-21 international who spent three seasons at Stamford Bridge. Born Wimbledon 12.11.69.

GORDON DURIE (forward): A £2.2 million signing in May 1991, formerly with East Fife, Hibernian and Chelsea. Part of Scotland's 1992 European Championship squad. Scored 11 goals for Spurs last season. Born Paisley 6.12.65.

JUSTIN EDINBURGH (defender): FA Cup winner with Spurs in 1991, who signed from Southend in July 1990 for £150,000 after a loan spell. Born Brentwood 18.12.69.

TERRY FENWICK (defender): England international (20 caps) signed from QPR for £550,000 in December 1987. Started at Crystal Palace and had a spell on loan with Leicester. Born Camden, Co. Durham, 17.11.59.

ANDY GRAY (midfielder): England international who cost £700,000 (plus two £100,000 payments if Spurs avoid relegation in next two seasons) from Crystal Palace in May 1992. His other clubs are Aston Villa and QPR. Born Lambeth 22.2.64.

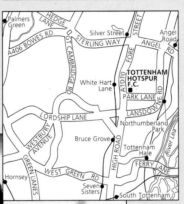

PAXTON ROAD NORTH STAND

WEST STAND HIGH ROAD

110 YDS

73 YDS

EAST STAND

PARK LANE SOUTH STAND

Vinny Samways

Ground capacity: 33,500
Number of seats: 26,093
Ground capacity (10 years ago): 48,200
Record attendance: 75,038 v Sunderland, FA Cup, 6th round, 5 March, 1938

Directions to ground

By car: **From all directions**, take A406 North Circular to Edmonton and at traffic lights follow signs for Tottenham (A1010) into Fore Street for ground. From Waltham Cross or Tottenham Hale, use north-south route (A1055) to Tottenham (Northumberland Park Area).

By train: Eastern Region Railway stations – White Hart Lane or Northumberland Park.

By bus: 76 serving Northumberland Park to Shoreditch, 149 Edmonton to Liverpool Street, 171 Forest Hill to Bruce Grove, W3 Finsbury Park to Northumberland Park, 243 Ilford to Wood Green, 259 Edmonton to King's Cross, 123 Ilford to Wood Green, 279 Waltham Cross to Smithfield, 359 Edmonton to King's Cross.

By tube: Manor House (Piccadilly Line), Seven Sisters (Victoria Line). Both stations link with bus routes 259, 359, 279 and (from Seven Sisters only) 149.

IAN HENDON (defender): England Youth and Under-21 international who made Spurs debut in March 1991, having joined the club as a trainee in 1988. 1990 FA Youth Cup winner. Born Ilford 5.12.71.

JOHN HENDRY (forward): Scottish-born player who was with Dundee and Forfar Athletic (loan) before moving to White Hart Lane in July 1990. Made six appearances last season. Born Glasgow 6.1.70.

SCOTT HOUGHTON (midfielder): Pupil at FA School of Excellence before signing for Spurs as trainee in 1988. The England Youth and Under-19 international made his League debut in April 1991 while on loan to Ipswich. Born Hitchin 22.10.71.

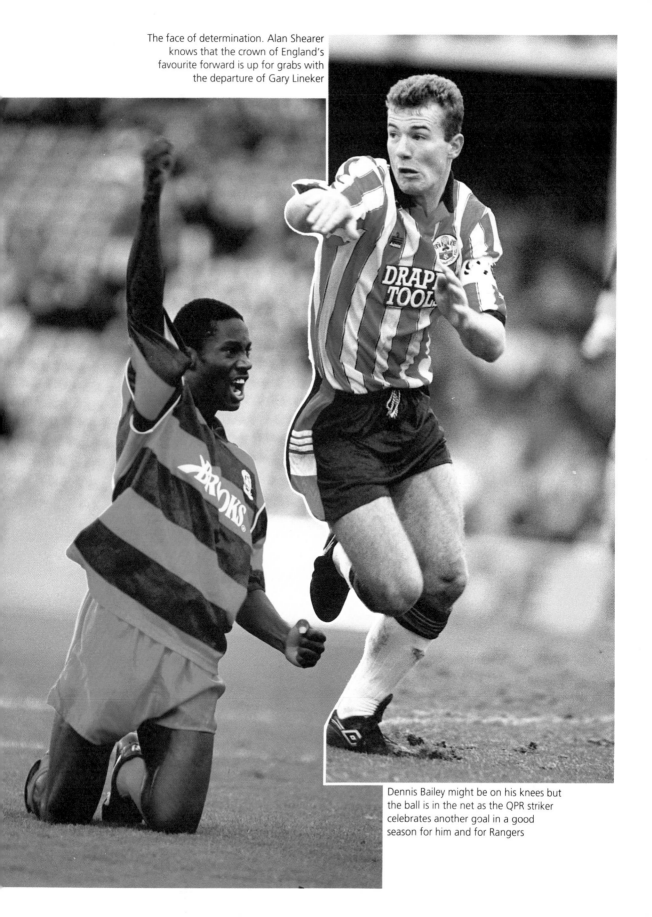

The face of determination. Alan Shearer knows that the crown of England's favourite forward is up for grabs with the departure of Gary Lineker

Dennis Bailey might be on his knees but the ball is in the net as the QPR striker celebrates another goal in a good season for him and for Rangers

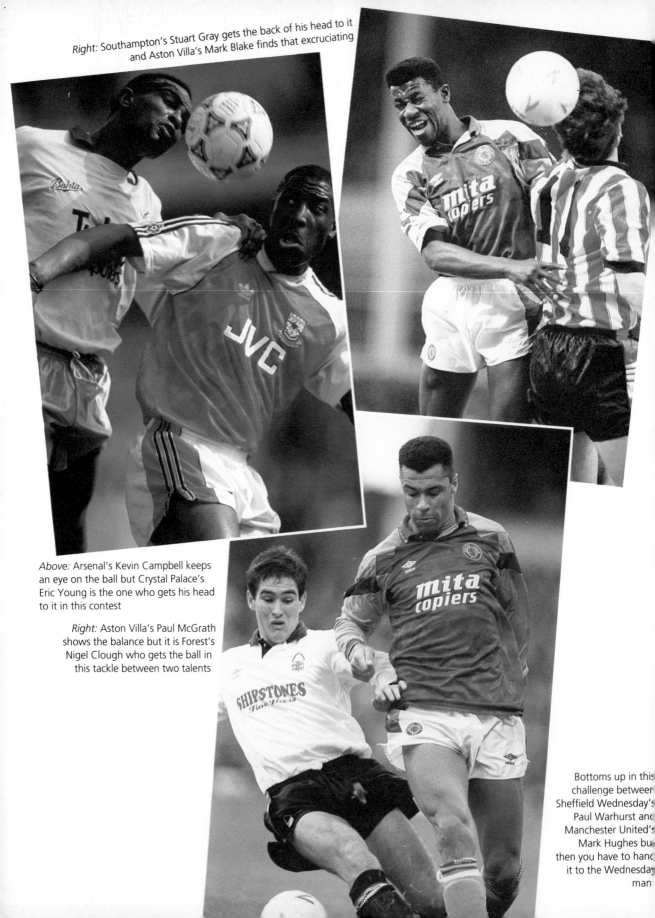

Right: Southampton's Stuart Gray gets the back of his head to it and Aston Villa's Mark Blake finds that excruciating

Above: Arsenal's Kevin Campbell keeps an eye on the ball but Crystal Palace's Eric Young is the one who gets his head to it in this contest

Right: Aston Villa's Paul McGrath shows the balance but it is Forest's Nigel Clough who gets the ball in this tackle between two talents

Bottoms up in this challenge between Sheffield Wednesday's Paul Warhurst and Manchester United's Mark Hughes but then you have to hand it to the Wednesday man

Left: When I run I'm ready for take-off, Sheffie
United's Dane Whitehouse tells Sheffield
Wednesday's Roland Nilsson

This is my bicycle kick, Blackburn's Simon
Garner tells Plymouth Argyle's Ryan Cross

Anyone got a comb? Chelsea's Paul Elliott shows a dishevelled
head of hair to Sheffield United's Kevin Gage

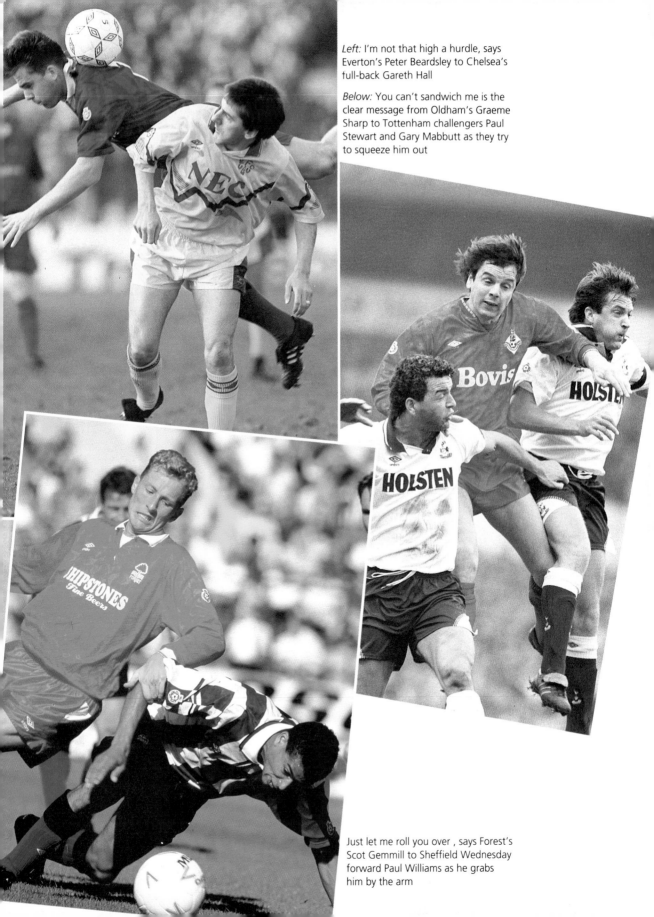

Left: I'm not that high a hurdle, says Everton's Peter Beardsley to Chelsea's full-back Gareth Hall

Below: You can't sandwich me is the clear message from Oldham's Graeme Sharp to Tottenham challengers Paul Stewart and Gary Mabbutt as they try to squeeze him out

Just let me roll you over , says Forest's Scot Gemmill to Sheffield Wednesday forward Paul Williams as he grabs him by the arm

Left: Ballet with a ball. Wimbledon's John Scales climbs with arms perfectly straight to outjump Manchester United's Brian McClair

Below: Wimbledon's John Fashanu shows his old team-mate Keith Curle that he is not only a penalty-area finisher

That's the way to the Premier League. Simon Milton celebrates his Ipswich goal that gave his team a 1–0 win over Bristol Rovers

Norwich City's John Polston demonstrates how good it feels to score when you are a defender during his side's 4–3 win over Crystal Palace

Top of the list. Howard Wilkinson shows how it feels to be named Manager of the Year

DAVID HOWELLS (midfielder): England Youth player, joined Spurs on YTS scheme in July 1984. Member of 1991 FA Cup-winning side. Made 42 appearances last season, scoring twice. Born Guildford 15.12.67.

GARY MABBUTT (defender): Club captain and England international, signed from Bristol Rovers in July 1982 for £150,000. UEFA Cup winner 1984 and FA Cup winner 1991. Scored three goals in 1991–92 season. Born Bristol 23.8.61.

JEFFREY MINTON (midfielder): Joined Tottenham from school, signing trainee forms in January 1988. Scored on his first-team debut against Everton in May (Gary Lineker's farewell White Hart Lane appearance). Born Hackney 28.12.73.

PAUL MORAN (forward): Former YTS player at Spurs in 1984, signed professional forms in 1985. Has had spells on loan at Portsmouth, Leicester, Newcastle and Southend. Spurs debut versus Everton in May 1987. Born Enfield 22.5.68.

NAYIM – full name: Mohamed Ali Amar (midfielder): Moroccan-born Spanish Under-21 international who followed Terry Venables from Barcelona in November 1989 for £300,000. FA Cup winner 1991. Born Ceuta 5.11.66.

NEIL RUDDOCK (defender): Former England Youth and Under-21 international who signed for Tottenham from Southampton for £750,000 in July 1992. Spent three seasons at White Hart Lane from 1985–88, making nine League appearances, before joining Millwall. Signed for Southampton from Millwall for £250,000 in February 1989. Born London 9.5.68.

VINNY SAMWAYS (midfielder): A 1991 FA Cup winner with Spurs, his only club, which he joined in November 1985. Was a regular last season, scoring twice in 43 games. An England Under-21 international. Born Bethnal Green 27.10.68.

STEVE SEDGLEY (defender): England Under-21 international who cost Spurs £750,000 from Coventry

TOTTENHAM HOTSPUR: 10–YEAR RECORD

	Div	P	W	D	L	F	A	Pts	Pos	FA Cup	Lge Cup
1982–83	1	42	20	9	13	65	50	69	4	5	QF
1983–84	1	42	17	10	15	64	65	61	8	4	3
1984–85	1	42	23	8	11	78	51	77	3	4	4
1985–86	1	42	19	8	15	74	52	65	10	5	4
1986–87	1	42	21	8	13	68	43	71	3	F	SF
1987–88	1	40	12	11	17	38	48	47	13	4	3
1988–89	1	38	15	12	11	60	46	57	6	3	4
1989–90	1	38	19	6	13	59	47	63	3	3	QF
1990–91	1	38	11	16	11	51	50	49	10	W	QF
1991–92	1	42	15	7	20	58	63	52	15	3	SF

Leading League scorers in last 10 seasons

		League hat-tricks
1982–83	Archibald 11	Brooke (1)
1983–84	Archibald 21	—
1984–85	Falco 22	—
1985–86	Falco 18	Falco (1), Galvin (1)
1986–87	Allen 33	Allen (2)
1987–88	Allen 11	—
1988–89	Waddle 14	Stewart (1)
1989–90	Lineker 24	Lineker (2)
1990–91	Lineker 15	Gascoigne (1), Walsh (1)
1991–92	Lineker 28	Durie (1), Lineker (1 x 4, 1 x 3)

in July 1989. Played in the 1991 FA Cup triumph. Originally a midfielder. Born Enfield 26.5.68.

PAUL STEWART (midfielder): England international who started his career with Blackpool before moving to Manchester City in March 1987. The former striker joined Spurs in June 1988 for £1.7 million and was an FA Cup winner in 1991. Born Manchester 7.10.64.

ERIK THORSTVEDT (goalkeeper): Norwegian international who moved to Spurs in December 1988 for £400,000 from IFK Gothenburg. A 1987 trialist with Arsenal after a spell with Borussia Moenchengladbach, he was a Wembley winner in the 1991 FA Cup final with Spurs. Born Stavanger 28.10.62.

DAVID TUTTLE (defender): Another to emerge through Spurs' vibrant

youth policy. Signed professional forms in February 1990, his debut coming the following December against Chelsea. Four appearances last season. Born Reading 6.2.72.

PAT VAN DEN HAUWE (defender): Belgian-born Welsh international signed from Everton in August 1989 for £575,000. At Goodison Park he won League Championship (1985, 1987) and European Cup Winners' Cup (1985) medals, and an FA Cup medal in 1991 with Spurs. Born Dendermonde 16.12.60.

IAN WALKER (goalkeeper): An England Under-21 international who joined Spurs from FA School of Excellence in 1988. Had spells on loan at Oxford and Ipswich before making Spurs debut in April 1991 at Norwich. Made 22 appearances last season. Born Watford 31.10.71.

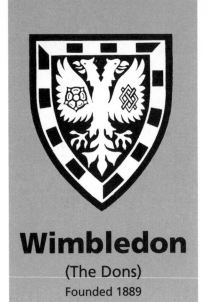

Wimbledon
(The Dons)
Founded 1889

Selhurst Park,
London SE25 6PU

Telephone numbers
Ground: 081-771 2233
Clubcall: 0898 121175
Ticket details: 081-771 8841
Club shop: 081-653 5584
Club fax: 081-768 0640

Wimbledon, launched as Wimbledon Old Centrals in 1889, did not adopt professionalism until 1964, and first caught national attention with their FA Cup exploits under Allen Batsford in 1975 – they won 1–0 at First Division Burnley in the third round and drew at Leeds at the next stage before losing the replay.

The Dons gained election to Division Four in 1977. Dario Gradi led them to promotion in 1979, but they were promptly relegated. They bounced straight back in 1981 at the start of the Dave Bassett era. Bassett's side suffered another early fall in 1982, and Wimbledon's dramatic climb to the top did not begin until 1983, when they were Division Four Champions. A year later they reached Division Two, and by 1986 were in Division One after only nine seasons in the League. Bassett's side confounded the critics – and there were plenty – by finishing sixth and reaching the FA Cup quarter-final in that first Division One term.

Bobby Gould maintained their League progress in his first season in charge (they finished seventh) and led Wimbledon to their first honour when a famous penalty save by David Beasant and a lone goal from Lawrie Sanchez clinched an FA Cup final triumph at Wembley in 1988, Wimbledon's success denying Liverpool the double.

Gould next saw them slip to 12th, then finish eighth. Having made the top seven in 1991 under Ray Harford, they slide to 13th in 1992 – their lowest position in six terms at the top. Peter Withe (from October) endured a long run with only one win, then Joe Kinnear (from late January) pulled them round with seven wins and five draws in 17 games following Harford's early-season departure in the first months of the post-Plough Lane era.

THE MANAGER

Joe Kinnear

Date of birth: 27 Dec, 1946
Birthplace: Dublin
Date of appointment: May 1992

Wimbledon

Largest wins:
League: 6–0 v Newport County,
Division Three, Sept 1983
FA Cup: 7–2 v Windsor & Eton, 1st
Round, Nov 1980
Record defeat: 0–8 v Everton,
League Cup, 2nd round, Aug 1978
Most appearances: Alan Cork, 430,
League and Cup, 1977–92
Most goals (aggregate): Alan Cork,
145, League and Cup, 1977–92
Most goals in a season: Alan Cork,
33, League and Cup, 1983–84
Most capped players:
Past – Glyn Hodges, 5 (16), Wales
Present – Terry Phelan, 7, Republic
of Ireland
Other leading internationals:
England: John Fashanu, 2
Northern Ireland: Lawrie Sanchez, 3

John Fashanu

THE F.A. PREMIER LEAGUE

Ground capacity: 30,312
Number of seats: 15,712
Ground capacity (10 years ago): 15,000 (at Plough Lane)
Record attendance: 18,000 v HMS Victory, FA Amateur Cup, 3rd round, 1935 (at Plough Lane)

Directions to ground

By car: **From north,** M1/A1 to North Circular (A406) to Chiswick; take South Circular (A205) to Wandsworth, take A3 to A214 and follow signs to Streatham to A23. Turn left on to B273 (1 mile), follow to end, turn left into High Street and into Whitehorse Lane.
From east, A232 (Croydon Road) to Shirley, join A215 (Norwood Road), after two-and-a-quarter miles turn left into Whitehorse Lane.
From south, A23, follow signs for Crystal Palace (B266) through Thornton Heath into Whitehorse Lane.
From west, M4 to Chiswick (then as north).
By train: (BR) Selhurst, Thornton Heath, Norwood Junction.
By bus: No 60 to Whitehorse Lane, Nos 50 or 250 to Thornton Heath High St.

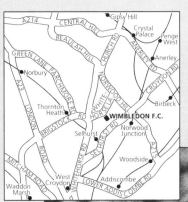

Warren Barton

WARREN BARTON (defender): England B international signed from Maidstone United for £300,000 in June 1990. Can play at right-back or in midfield and was ever-present last season. Born London 19.3.69.

DEAN BLACKWELL (defender): A product of Wimbledon's youth system who was troubled with injury last season. Has played for Plymouth on loan and represented England at Under-21 level. Born London 5.12.69.

ANDY CLARKE (forward): A £300,000 signing from Barnet in February 1990, after being chased by a clutch of top clubs. Scored on full League debut at Manchester United in April 1991. Used mainly as substitute last season. Born London 22.7.67.

GERALD DOBBS (midfielder): Given League debut in 3–0 win against Nottingham Forest in April 1992, he finished the season with four senior appearances. Born London 24.1.71.

ROBBIE EARLE (midfielder): The club's record signing at £775,000 from Port Vale in July 1991. Scored 14 League goals in first season for Wimbledon and earned call-up to full England squad. Born Newcastle-under-Lyme 27.1.65.

GARY ELKINS (defender): England Youth international who cost £20,000 from Fulham in August 1990. His seven years at Fulham included a loan spell with Exeter City in 1989. Born Wallingford 4.5.66.

CARLTON FAIRWEATHER (forward): Winger who played only five matches last season because of injury. Joined Wimbledon from non-League Tooting and Mitcham for £13,000 in 1984. Born London 22.9.61.

JOHN FASHANU (forward): England international, club captain and part-time television presenter. A £125,000 signing from Millwall in 1986 (then a club record). Joint third-leading scorer in the First Division last season with 18 goals. Other clubs: Cambridge, Norwich and Lincoln City, with a loan spell at Crystal Palace. Born Kensington 18.9.62.

SCOTT FITZGERALD (defender): Former apprentice who established a regular place last season. Partnered John Scales in centre of defence. Born London 13.8.69.

DEAN HOLDSWORTH (forward): Had a prolific season for Brentford in 1991–92, scoring 38 goals. Loaned to Wimbledon for the start of the 1992–93 season with a view to a permanent move. Started as a trainee at Watford, for whom he played three years of first-team football. Born Walthamstow 8.11.68.

ROGER JOSEPH (defender): England B international who signed from Brentford for £150,000 in August 1988. Previously with non-League Southall. Born Paddington 24.12.65.

BRIAN McALLISTER (defender): Has yet to establish a regular place in defence in the face of fierce competition. Played a handful of matches last season after making first-team breakthrough in 1989-90, and appeared for Plymouth on loan. Born Glasgow 30.11.70.

PAUL McGEE (forward): Signed for £125,000 having played just three games for Colchester, and that only a month after arriving in England from Bohemians. A regular on the left side of the Dons' attack. Born Dublin 17.5.68.

PAUL MILLER (forward): Made a come-back last season after 15 months out with knee ligament injury and finished the season as Fashanu's partner up front. Had spells on loan with Newport County and Bristol City. Born Bisley 31.1.68.

AIDAN NEWHOUSE (forward): England Youth international who cost £250,000 from Chester City in February 1990. Appearances limited last season and scored only once. Born Wallasey 23.5.72.

TERRY PHELAN (defender): Republic of Ireland left-back, began his career

with Leeds United before joining Swansea. Cost Wimbledon £100,000 in 1987 and played in the FA Cup final defeat of Liverpool in his first season. Born Manchester 16.3.67.

VAUGHAN RYAN (midfielder): Product of Wimbledon youth system, who was in and out of the side last season after being sent off against Crystal Palace in August. Had a spell on loan to Sheffield United in 1989. Born Westminster 2.9.68.

LAWRIE SANCHEZ (midfielder): Scored the winner in the 1988 FA Cup final defeat of Liverpool. A bargain £29,000 signing from Reading in 1984. Northern Ireland international and former club captain who struggled with injury last season. Born Lambeth 22.10.59.

JOHN SCALES (defender): Can play in defence or midfield. Signed from

Bristol Rovers for £70,000 in 1987 after failing to make a first-team breakthrough at Leeds United. Won FA Cup-winners' medal in 1988. Born Harrogate 4.7.66.

HANS SEGERS (goalkeeper): Dutch goalkeeper signed from Nottingham Forest for £125,000 shortly after Wimbledon's FA Cup triumph. Began career with PSV Eindhoven in Holland and came to England in 1984. Had loan spells with Stoke City, Sheffield United and Dunfermline. Born Eindhoven, Holland, 30.10.61.

NEIL SULLIVAN (goalkeeper): Loaned to Crystal Palace for last game of the season against QPR in May 1992 after injury to Nigel Martyn. Had previously made only two League appearances for Wimbledon. Former apprentice. Born Sutton 24.2.70.

WIMBLEDON: 10–YEAR RECORD

	Div	P	W	D	L	F	A	Pts	Pos	FA Cup	Lge Cup
1982–83	4	46	29	11	6	96	45	98	1 (P)	1	1
1983–84	3	46	26	9	11	97	76	87	2 (P)	2	4
1984–85	2	42	16	10	16	71	75	58	12	5	1
1985–86	2	42	21	13	8	58	37	76	3 (P)	3	3
1986–87	1	42	19	9	14	57	50	66	6	QF	2
1987–88	1	40	14	15	11	58	47	57	7	W	4
1988–89	1	38	14	9	15	50	46	51	12	QF	4
1989–90	1	38	13	16	9	47	40	55	8	3	4
1990–91	1	38	14	14	10	53	46	56	7	4	2
1991–92	1	42	13	14	15	53	53	53	13	3	2

Leading League scorers in last 10 seasons

		League hat-tricks
1982–83	Leslie 23	Cork (1), Evans (1)
1983–84	Cork 29	Cork (1)
1984–85	Evans 14	Fishenden (1)
1985–86	Cork 11	Hodges (1)
1986–87	Fashanu 11	Sayer (1)
1987–88	Fashanu 14	—
1988–89	Fashanu 12	Miller (1)
1989–90	Fashanu 11	—
1990–91	Fashanu 20	—
1991–92	Fashanu 18	—

Date	Comp	Opponents	Venue	Res	Scorers	Attendance
17 Aug	L	Queen's Park Rangers	H	1–1	Merson	38,099
20 Aug	L	Everton	A	1–3	Winterburn	31,200
24 Aug	L	Aston Villa	A	1–3	Smith	29,684
27 Aug	L	Luton Town	H	2–0	Smith, Merson	25,898
31 Aug	L	Manchester City	H	2–1	Smith, Limpar	35,009
3 Sept	L	Leeds United	A	2–2	Smith 2	29,396
7 Sept	L	Coventry City	H	1–2	Adams	28,142
14 Sept	L	Crystal Palace	A	4–1	Campbell 2, Smith, Thomas	24,228
18 Sept	EC 1/1	Austria Vienna	H	6–1	Smith 4, Limpar, Linighan	24,124
21 Sept	L	Sheffield United	H	5–2	Dixon [pen], Smith, Rocastle, Groves, Thomas	30,244
25 Sept	RC 2/1	Leicester City	A	1–1	Wright	20,679
28 Sept	L	Southampton	A	4–0	Wright 3, Rocastle	18,050
2 Oct	EC 1/2	Austria Vienna	A	0–1		10,000
5 Oct	L	Chelsea	H	3–2	Dixon [pen], Wright, Campbell	42,075
8 Oct	RC 2/2	Leicester City	H	2–0	Wright, Merson	28,580
19 Oct	L	Manchester United	A	1–1	Rocastle	46,594
23 Oct	EC 2/1	Benfica	A	1–1	Campbell	80,000
26 Oct	L	Notts County	H	2–0	Smith, Wright	30,011
30 Oct	RC 3	Coventry City	A	0–1		15,337
2 Nov	L	West Ham United	H	0–1		33,539
6 Nov	EC 2/2	Benfica	H	*1–3	Pates	35,815
16 Nov	L	Oldham Athletic	A	1–1	Wright	15,681
23 Nov	L	Sheffield Wednesday	A	1–1	Bould	32,174
1 Dec	L	Tottenham Hotspur	H	2–0	Wright, Campbell	38,892
8 Dec	L	Nottingham Forest	A	2–3	Smith, Merson	22,095
21 Dec	L	Everton	H	4–2	Wright 4	29,684
26 Dec	L	Luton Town	A	0–1		12,655
28 Dec	L	Manchester City	A	0–1		32,325
1 Jan	L	Wimbledon	H	1–1	Merson	26,839
4 Jan	FAC 3	Wrexham	A	1–2	Smith	13,343
11 Jan	L	Aston Villa	H	0–0		31,413
18 Jan	L	Queen's Park Rangers	A	0–0		20,497
28 Jan	L	Liverpool	A	0–2		33,753
1 Feb	L	Manchester United	H	1–1	Rocastle	41,703
8 Feb	L	Notts County	A	1–0	Smith	11,221
11 Feb	L	Norwich City	H	1–1	Merson	22,352
15 Feb	L	Sheffield Wednesday	H	7–1	Limpar 2, Smith, Merson, Wright, Campbell 2	26,805
22 Feb	L	Tottenham Hotspur	A	1–1	Wright	33,124
10 March	L	Oldham Athletic	H	2–1	Wright, Merson	22,096
14 March	L	West Ham United	A	2–0	Wright 2	22,640
22 March	L	Leeds United	H	1–1	Merson	27,844
28 March	L	Wimbledon	A	3–1	Campbell, Wright, Parlour	11,299
31 March	L	Nottingham Forest	H	3–3	Dixon [pen], Adams, Merson	27,036
4 April	L	Coventry City	A	1–0	Campbell	14,133
8 April	L	Norwich City	A	3–1	Wright 2 [1 pen], Campbell	12,971
11 April	L	Crystal Palace	H	4–1	Merson 3, Campbell	36,014
18 April	L	Sheffield United	A	1–1	Campbell	25,034
20 April	L	Liverpool	H	4–1	Wright 2, Limpar, Hillier	38,517
25 April	L	Chelsea	A	1–1	Dixon	26,003
2 May	L	Southampton	H	5–1	Wright 3 [1 pen], Campbell, Smith	37,702

Squad members who made first team appearances in 1991–92:
Seaman
Dixon
Winterburn
Hillier
O'Leary
Adams
Campbell
Davis
Smith
Merson
Limpar
Rocastle
Groves
Linighan
Thomas
Pates
Wright
Bould
Carter
Parlour
Lydersen
Morrow
Heaney

* after extra time

Date	Comp	Opponents	Venue	Res	Scorers	Attendance
17 Aug	L	Sheffield Wednesday	A	3–2	Staunton, Regis, Atkinson	36,749
21 Aug	L	Manchester United	H	0–1		39,995
24 Aug	L	Arsenal	H	3–1	Staunton [pen], Penrice, Daley	29,684
28 Aug	L	West Ham United	A	1–3	Daley	23,644
31 Aug	L	Southampton	A	1–1	Richardson	16,161
4 Sept	L	Crystal Palace	H	0–1		20,740
7 Sept	L	Tottenham Hotspur	H	0–0		33,096
14 Sept	L	Liverpool	A	1–1	Richardson	38,400
17 Sept	L	Chelsea	A	0–2		17,182
21 Sept	L	Nottingham Forest	H	3–1	Richardson, Yorke, Blake	28,506
25 Sept	RC 2/1	Grimsby Town	A	0–0		13,835
28 Sept	L	Coventry City	A	0–1		17,851
5 Oct	L	Luton Town	H	4–0	Richardson, Yorke, Regis, Mortimer	18,722
9 Oct	RC 2/2	Grimsby Town	H	*1–1	Teale	15,338
19 Oct	L	Everton	A	2–0	Regis, Daley	27,688
23 Oct	ZDS 2	Coventry City	A	2–0	Yorke, Olney	6,447
26 Oct	L	Wimbledon	H	2–1	Yorke, Olney	16,928
2 Nov	L	Queen's Park Rangers	A	1–0	Yorke	10,642
16 Nov	L	Notts County	H	1–0	Yorke	23,020
19 Nov	ZDS 3	Nottingham Forest	H	0–2		7,859
24 Nov	L	Leeds United	H	1–4	Yorke	23,713
30 Nov	L	Oldham Athletic	A	2–3	Atkinson, Blake	15,370
7 Dec	L	Manchester City	H	3–1	Yorke, Regis, Daley	26,265
14 Dec	L	Sheffield United	A	0–2		18,401
26 Dec	L	West Ham United	H	3–1	Richardson, Yorke, Daley	31,959
28 Dec	L	Southampton	H	2–1	Yorke, Regis	23,094
1 Jan	L	Norwich City	A	1–2	Regis	15,318
5 Jan	FAC 3	Tottenham Hotspur	H	0–0		29,316
11 Jan	L	Arsenal	A	0–0		31,413
14 Jan	FAC 3 R	Tottenham Hotspur	A	1–0	Yorke	25,462
18 Jan	L	Sheffield Wednesday	H	0–1		28,036
22 Jan	L	Manchester United	A	0–1		45,002
2 Feb	L	Everton	H	0–0		17,451
4 Feb	FAC 4	Derby County	A	4–3	Yorke 3, Parker	22,452
8 Feb	L	Wimbledon	A	0–2		5,534
16 Feb	FAC 5	Swindon Town	A	2–1	Yorke, Froggatt	16,402
22 Feb	L	Oldham Athletic	H	1–0	Regis	20,509
29 Feb	L	Manchester City	A	0–2		28,268
3 March	L	Leeds United	A	0–0		28,896
8 March	FAC 6	Liverpool	A	0–1		29,109
10 March	L	Notts County	A	0–0		8,389
14 March	L	Queen's Park Rangers	H	0–1		19,630
21 March	L	Crystal Palace	A	0–0		15,368
28 March	L	Norwich City	H	1–0	Staunton	16,985
31 March	L	Sheffield United	H	1–1	Regis	15,745
4 April	L	Tottenham Hotspur	A	5–2	Richardson, Yorke, Regis, Olney, Daley	26,370
11 April	L	Liverpool	H	1–0	Daley	35,755
18 April	L	Nottingham Forest	A	0–2		22,800
20 April	L	Chelsea	H	3–1	Staunton, McGrath, Parker	19,269
25 April	L	Luton Town	A	0–2		11,178
2 May	L	Coventry City	H	2–0	Regis, Yorke	31,984

Squad members who made first team appearances in 1991–92:

Spink
Mountfield
Staunton
Richardson
McGrath
Teale
Yorke
Regis
Atkinson
Cowans
Mortimer
Penrice
Olney
Ehiogu
Price
Daley
Kubicki
Ormondroyd
Blake
Sealey
Small
McLoughlin
Carruthers
Beinlich
Cox
Parker
Froggatt
Nielsen
Breukreitz
Barrett
Bosnich

* after extra time

BLACKBURN ROVERS: RESULTS 1991–92

Date	Comp	Opponents	Venue	Res	Scorers	Attendance
17 Aug	L	Portsmouth	H	1–1	Moran	11,118
20 Aug	RC 1/1	Hull City	H	1–1	Buckley [og]	6,300
24 Aug	L	Bristol City	A	0–1		11,217
27 Aug	RC 1/2	Hull City	A	0–1		3,227
31 Aug	L	Ipswich Town	H	1–2	Speedie	8,898
4 Sept	L	Derby County	A	2–0	Speedie, Wilcox	12,078
7 Sept	L	Sunderland	A	1–1	Speedie	17,043
14 Sept	L	Port Vale	H	1–0	Speedie	10,225
17 Sept	L	Watford	H	1–0	Richardson	9,542
21 Sept	L	Leicester City	A	0–3		13,278
28 Sept	L	Tranmere Rovers	H	0–0		11,449
1 Oct	ZDS 1	Port Vale	A	0–1		2,355
5 Oct	L	Millwall	A	3–1	Speedie, Garner, Rose	8,036
12 Oct	L	Plymouth Argyle	H	5–2	Moran, Speedie 2 [1 pen], Garner 2	10,830
19 Oct	L	Swindon Town	A	1–2	Speedie	10,717
26 Oct	L	Grimsby Town	H	2–1	Atkins, Garner	11,096
2 Nov	L	Brighton & Hove Albion	H	1–0	Livingstone [pen]	9,877
5 Nov	L	Southend United	A	0–3		4,860
9 Nov	L	Charlton Athletic	A	2–0	Speedie, Sellars	7,114
16 Nov	L	Barnsley	H	3–0	Speedie, Wilcox, Newell	13,797
23 Nov	L	Newcastle United	A	0–0		23,639
30 Nov	L	Middlesbrough	H	2–1	Atkins, Newell [pen]	15,541
7 Dec	L	Oxford United	A	3–1	Garner, Sellars, Cowans	5,924
14 Dec	L	Bristol Rovers	H	3–1	Atkins 2, Sellars	12,295
26 Dec	L	Wolverhampton Wanderers	A	0–0		18,277
28 Dec	L	Ipswich Town	A	1–2	Wright	17,675
1 Jan	L	Cambridge United	H	2–1	Speedie, Reid	15,001
5 Jan	FAC 3	Kettering Town	H	4–1	Cowans, Speedie, Newell 2	13,821
11 Jan	L	Bristol City	H	4–0	Newell 2, Speedie, Scott [og]	12,964
18 Jan	L	Portsmouth	A	2–2	Speedie 2	20,106
1 Feb	L	Swindon Town	H	2–1	Speedie, Hendry	14,887
4 Feb	FAC 4	Notts County	A	1–2	Newell	12,173
8 Feb	L	Grimsby Town	A	3–2	Sellars, Wilcox, Price	10,014
11 Feb	L	Derby County	H	2–0	Atkins, Price	15,350
15 Feb	L	Newcastle United	H	3–1	Speedie 3	19,551
22 Feb	L	Middlesbrough	A	0–0		19,353
25 Feb	L	Cambridge United	A	1–2	Hendry	7,857
29 Feb	L	Oxford United	H	1–1	Sellars [pen]	13,917
7 March	L	Bristol Rovers	A	0–3		6,313
10 March	L	Southend United	H	2–2	Speedie, Price	14,404
14 March	L	Brighton & Hove Albion	A	3–0	Wegerle, Hendry, Speedie	10,845
21 March	L	Charlton Athletic	H	0–2		14,844
28 March	L	Barnsley	A	1–2	Shearer	13,346
31 March	L	Port Vale	A	0–2		10,384
11 April	L	Watford	A	1–2	Wegerle .	10,552
14 April	L	Wolverhampton Wanderers	H	1–2	Sellars	14,114
18 April	L	Leicester City	H	0–1		18.075
20 April	L	Tranmere Rovers	A	2–2	Wilcox, Newell [pen]	13,705
25 April	L	Millwall	H	2–1	Atkins, Newell	12,820
29 April	L	Sunderland	H	2–2	Hendry, Sellars	15,079
2 May	L	Plymouth Argyle	A	3–1	Speedie 3	17,500
10 May	PLAY–OFF 1/1	Derby County	H	4–2	Speedie 2, Newell, Sellars	19,677
13 May	PLAY–OFF 1/2	Derby County	A	1–2	Moran	22,920
25 May	P/OFF FINAL	Leicester City	Wembley	1–0	Newell [pen]	68,147

Squad members who made first team appearances in 1991–92:
Mimms
Atkins
Sulley
Agnew
Moran
Dobson
Irvine
Richardson
Livingstone
Speedie
Sellars
Garner
Gayle
Reid
Shepstone
May
Munro
Skinner
Wilcox
Duxbury
Johnrose
Brown
Hill
Rose
Bach
Wright
Hendry
Newell
Cowans
Beardsmore
Price
Sherwood
Wegerle
Shearer
Dickins

Date	Comp	Opponents	Venue	Res	Scorers	Attendance	Squad members who made first team appearances in 1991–92:
17 Aug	L	Wimbledon	H	2–2	Elliott, Allon	22,574	Beasant
21 Aug	L	Oldham Athletic	A	0–3		14,997	Clarke
24 Aug	L	Tottenham Hotspur	A	3–1	Townsend, Dixon, Wilson	34,645	Boyd
28 Aug	L	Notts County	H	2–2	Elliott, Allon	15,847	Townsend
31 Aug	L	Luton Town	H	4–1	Townsend, Wise, Dixon, Le Saux	17,457	Elliott
3 Sept	L	Sheffield United	A	1–0	Wise	17,400	Monkou
7 Sept	L	West Ham United	A	1–1	Dixon	18,875	Wise
14 Sept	L	Leeds United	H	0–1		23,439	Dickens
18 Sept	L	Aston Villa	H	2–0	Townsend, Jones	17,182	Dixon
21 Sept	L	Queen's Park Rangers	A	2–2	Townsend, Wise	19,579	Wilson
25 Sept	RC 2/1	Tranmere Rovers	H	1–1	Townsend	11,311	Le Saux
28 Sept	L	Everton	H	2–2	Wise, Wilson	19,038	Allon
5 Oct	L	Arsenal	A	2–3	Wilson, Le Saux	42,075	Sinclair
9 Oct	RC 2/2	Tranmere Rovers	A	*1–3	Wise	11,165	Hitchcock
19 Oct	L	Liverpool	H	2–2	Myers, Jones	30,230	Johnsen
22 Oct	ZDS 2	Swindon Town	H	1–0	Jones	5,784	Myers
26 Oct	L	Crystal Palace	A	0–0		21,841	Jones
2 Nov	L	Coventry City	A	1–0	Le Saux	11,343	Matthew
16 Nov	L	Norwich City	H	0–3		15,755	Pearce
23 Nov	L	Southampton	A	0–1		14,933	Cundy
26 Nov	ZDS 3	Ipswich Town	H	**2–2	Allon, Jones	6,325	Burley
30 Nov	L	Nottingham Forest	H	1–0	Dixon	19,420	Stuart
7 Dec	L	Sheffield Wednesday	A	0–3		27,383	Lee
10 Dec	ZDS 4	Crystal Palace	A	1–0	Dixon	8,416	Allen
15 Dec	L	Manchester United	H	1–3	Allen	23,130	Hall
21 Dec	L	Oldham Athletic	H	4–2	Elliott, Wise [pen], Allen 2	13,136	Gilkes
26 Dec	L	Notts County	A	0–2		11,867	Cascarino
28 Dec	L	Luton Town	A	0–2		10,738	Barnard
1 Jan	L	Manchester City	H	1–1	Allen	18,196	Newton
5 Jan	FAC 3	Hull City	A	2–0	Wise, Jones	13,580	
11 Jan	L	Tottenham Hotspur	H	2–0	Wise, Allen	28,628	
18 Jan	L	Wimbledon	A	2–1	Townsend, Allen	8,413	
21 Jan	ZDS SAF1	Southampton	A	0–2		8,726	
26 Jan	FAC 4	Everton	H	1–0	Allen	21,152	
29 Jan	ZDS SAF2	Southampton	H	1–3	Wise [pen]	9,781	
1 Feb	L	Liverpool	A	2–1	Wise, Jones	38,681	
8 Feb	L	Crystal Palace	H	1–1	Cascarino	17,810	
12 Feb	L	Southampton	H	1–1	Townsend	7,148	
15 Feb	FAC 5	Sheffield United	H	1–0	Stuart	34,447	
22 Feb	L	Nottingham Forest	A	1–1	Allen	24,095	
26 Feb	L	Manchester United	A.	1–1	Donaghy [og]	44,872	
29 Feb	L	Sheffield Wednesday	H	0–3		17,538	
9 March	FAC 6	Sunderland	H	1–1	Allen	33,948	
11 March	L	Norwich City	A	1–0	Dixon	13,403	
14 March	L	Coventry City	H	0–1		10,972	
18 March	FAC 6 R	Sunderland	A	1–2	Wise	26,039	
21 March	L	Sheffield United	H	1–2	Cundy	11,247	
28 March	L	Manchester City	A	0–0		23,633	
4 April	L	West Ham United	H	2–1	Wise, Cascarino	20,684	
11 April	L	Leeds United	A	0–3		31,363	
18 April	L	Queen's Park Rangers	H	2–1	Clarke, Wise	18,952	
20 April	L	Aston Villa	A	1–3	Sinclair	19,269	
25 April	L	Arsenal	H	1–1	Wise	26,003	
2 May	L	Everton	A	1–2	Newton	20,163	

* after extra time
** Chelsea won on penalties after extra time

Date	Comp	Opponents	Venue	Res	Scorers	Attendance
17 Aug	L	Manchester City	H	0–1		18,013
21 Aug	L	Luton Town	H	5–0	Gallacher 2, Rosario, Smith, Furlong	10,084
24 Aug	L	Queen's Park Rangers	A	1–1	Gynn	9,393
28 Aug	L	Sheffield United	H	3–1	Smith [pen], Rosario, Furlong	12,601
31 Aug	L	Wimbledon	H	0–1		9,469
3 Sept	L	Oldham Athletic	A	1–2	Furlong	12,996
7 Sept	L	Arsenal	A	2–1	Ndlovu, Dixon [og]	28,142
14 Sept	L	Notts County	H	1–0	Furlong	10,635
18 Sept	L	Leeds United	H	0–0		15,488
21 Sept	L	Everton	A	0–3		20,542
25 Sept	RC 2/1	Rochdale	H	4–0	Rosario 2, McGrath, Gallacher	5,982
28 Sept	L	Aston Villa	H	1–0	Ndlovu	17,851
5 Oct	L	West Ham United	A	1–0	Gallacher	21,187
8 Oct	RC 2/2	Rochdale	A	0–1		2,288
19 Oct	L	Crystal Palace	H	1–2	Gynn [pen]	10,591
23 Oct	ZDS 2	Aston Villa	H	0–2		6,447
26 Oct	L	Liverpool	A	0–1		33,336
30 Oct	RC 3	Arsenal	H	1–0	Gallacher	15,337
2 Nov	L	Chelsea	H	0–1		11,343
16 Nov	L	Nottingham Forest	A	0–1		21,154
23 Nov	L	Norwich City	A	2–3	Gallacher 2	12,056
30 Nov	L	Southampton	H	2–0	Gallacher, Pearce	8,585
4 Dec	RC 4	Tottenham Hotspur	H	1–2	Furlong	20,095
7 Dec	L	Manchester United	A	0–4		42,549
20 Dec	L	Luton Town	A	0–1		7,533
26 Dec	L	Sheffield United	A	3–1	Robson, Billing, Flynn	19,638
28 Dec	L	Wimbledon	A	1–1	Robson	3,270
1 Jan	L	Tottenham Hotspur	H	1–2	Rosario	19,639
4 Jan	FAC 3	Cambridge United	H	1–1	Borrows [pen]	11,428
11 Jan	L	Queen's Park Rangers	H	2–2	Rosario, Gallacher	11,999
14 Jan	FAC 3 R	Cambridge United	A	0–1		9,864
18 Jan	L	Manchester City	A	0–1		23,005
1 Feb	L	Crystal Palace	A	1–0	Smith	13,818
8 Feb	L	Liverpool	H	0–0		21,540
22 Feb	L	Southampton	A	0–0		13,719
29 Feb	L	Manchester United	H	0–0		23,967
4 March	L	Norwich City	H	0–0		8,459
7 March	L	Sheffield Wednesday	A	1–1	Gallacher	23,959
11 March	L	Nottingham Forest	H	0–2		11,158
14 March	L	Chelsea	A	1–0	Robson	10,972
21 March	L	Oldham Athletic	H	1–1	Pearce	12,840
28 March	L	Tottenham Hotspur	A	3–4	Flynn, Smith, McGrath	22,744
4 April	L	Arsenal	H	0–1		14,133
8 April	L	Sheffield Wednesday	H	0–0		13,293
11 April	L	Notts County	A	0–1		6,655
18 April	L	Everton	H	0–1		14,669
20 April	L	Leeds United	A	0–2		26,582
25 April	L	West Ham United	H	1–0	Gynn	15,392
2 May	L	Aston Villa	A	0–2		31,984

Squad members who made first team appearances in 1991–92:

Ogrizovic
Borrows
Edwards
McGrath
Pearce
Peake
Woods
Gynn
Rosario
Smith
Gallacher
Furlong
Robson
Atherton
Ndlovu
Billing
Emerson
Drinkell
Hurst
Baker
Greenman
Butcher
Booty
Middleton
Sansom
Flynn
Heald
Sealey

CRYSTAL PALACE: RESULTS 1991–92

Date	Comp	Opponents	Venue	Res	Scorers	Attendance
24 Aug	L	Manchester City	A	2–3	Thomas, Bright	28,028
27 Aug	L	Wimbledon	H	3–2	Gray, Bright, Wright	16,340
31 Aug	L	Sheffield United	H	2–1	Thomas, Wright	15,507
4 Sept	L	Aston Villa	A	1–0	Wright	20,740
7 Sept	L	Everton	A	2–2	Gray, Bright	21,065
14 Sept	L	Arsenal	H	1–4	Bright	24,228
17 Sept	L	West Ham United	H	2–3	Salako, Wright	21,373
21 Sept	L	Oldham Athletic	A	3–2	Salako, Bright, Wright	13,391
25 Sept	RC 2/1	Hartlepool	A	1–1	Bright	6,697
28 Sept	L	Queen's Park Rangers	H	2–2	Bright, Collymore	15,372
1 Oct	L	Leeds United	H	1–0	Bright	18,298
5 Oct	L	Sheffield Wednesday	A	1–4	Bright	26,230
8 Oct	RC 2/2	Hartlepool	H	6–1	Gray [pen], Bright 2, Thorn, Collymore, Gabbiadini	9,153
19 Oct	L	Coventry City	A	2–1	Bright, Gabbiadini	10,591
22 Oct	ZDS 2	Southend United	H	*4–2	Gray, Thomas, Bright, McGoldrick	7,185
26 Oct	L	Chelsea	H	0–0		21,841
29 Oct	RC 3	Birmingham City	A	1–1	Gray	17,270
2 Nov	L	Liverpool	A	2–1	Thomas, Gabbiadini	34,321
16 Nov	L	Southampton	H	1–0	Thomas	15,806
19 Nov	RC 3 R	Birmingham City	H	*1–1	Thomas	10,698
23 Nov	L	Nottingham Forest	A	1–5	Thomas	22,387
26 Nov	DS 3	Queen's Park Rangers	A	3–2	Thomas, Young, Gabbiadini	4,492
30 Nov	L	Manchester United	H	1–3	Mortimer	29,017
3 Dec	RC 3 R	Birmingham City	H	2–1	Gray [pen], Thorn	11,384
7 Dec	L	Norwich City	A	3–3	McGoldrick, Osborn, Newman [og]	12,667
10 Dec	ZDS 4	Chelsea	H	0–1		8,416
17 Dec	RC 4	Swindon Town	A	1–0	Gray	10,044
22 Dec	L	Tottenham Hotspur	H	1–2	Fenwick [og]	22,491
26 Dec	L	Wimbledon	A	1–1	Gabbiadini	15,009
28 Dec	L	Sheffield United	A	1–1	Gabbiadini	17,969
1 Jan	L	Notts County	H	1–0	Gabbiadini	14,202
4 Jan	FAC 3	Leicester City	A	0–1		19,613
8 Jan	RC 5	Nottingham Forest	H	1–1	Walker [og]	14,941
11 Jan	L	Manchester City	H	1–1	Bright	14,766
18 Jan	L	Leeds United	A	1–1	Thomas	27,717
1 Feb	L	Coventry City	H	0–1		13,818
5 Feb	RC 5 R	Nottingham Forest	A	2–4	Bright, Whyte	18,918
8 Feb	L	Chelsea	A	1–1	Whyte	17,810
16 Feb	L	Tottenham Hotspur	A	1–0	McGoldrick	19,834
22 Feb	L	Manchester United	A	0–2		46,347
25 Feb	L	Luton Town	H	1–1	Bright	12,109
29 Feb	L	Norwich City	H	3–4	Bright 2, Osborn	14,021
3 March	L	Nottingham Forest	H	0–0		12,680
7 March	L	Luton Town	A	1–1	McGoldrick	8,951
11 March	L	Southampton	A	0–1		12,926
14 March	L	Liverpool	H	1–0	Young	23,680
21 March	L	Aston Villa	H	0–0		15,368
28 March	L	Notts County	A	3–2	Bright, Mortimer, Coleman	7,674
4 April	L	Everton	H	2–1	Bright [pen], Coleman	14,338
11 April	L	Arsenal	A	1–4	Coleman	36,016
18 April	L	Oldham Athletic	H	0–0		12,267
20 April	L	West Ham United	A	2–0	Bright, Coleman	17,710
25 April	L	Sheffield Wednesday	H	1–1	Bright	21,573
2 May	L	Queen's Park Rangers	A	0–1		14,903

Squad members who made first team appearances in 1991–92:

Martyn
Humphrey
Bodin
Gray
Shaw
Sinnott
Salako
Thomas
Bright
Wright
McGoldrick
Pardew
Thorn
Suckling
Southgate
Young
Collymore
Osborn
Gabbiadini
Rodger
Gordon
Mortimer
Coleman
Whyte
Moralee
Hedman
Barnes

* after extra time

EVERTON: RESULTS 1991–92

Date	Comp	Opponents	Venue	Res	Scorers	Attendance
17 Aug	L	Nottingham Forest	A	1–2	Pearce [og]	24,422
20 Aug	L	Arsenal	H	3–1	Ward 2, Cottee	31,200
24 Aug	L	Manchester United	H	0–0		36,085
28 Aug	L	Sheffield Wednesday	A	1–2	Watson	28,690
31 Aug	L	Liverpool	A	1–3	Newell	39,072
3 Sept	L	Norwich City	H	1–1	Ward	19,197
7 Sept	L	Crystal Palace	H	2–2	Beardsley, Warzycha	21,065
14 Sept	L	Sheffield United	A	1–2	Beardsley	19,817
17 Sept	L	Manchester City	A	1–0	Beardsley	27,509
21 Sept	L	Coventry City	H	3–0	Beardsley 3 [1 pen]	20,542
24 Sept	RC 2/1	Watford	H	1–0	Beardsley	8,284
28 Sept	L	Chelsea	A	2–2	Ebbrell, Beardsley	19,038
1 Oct	ZDS 2	Oldham Athletic	H	3–2	Newell, Watson, Cottee	4,588
5 Oct	L	Tottenham Hotspur	H	3–1	Cottee 3 [1 pen]	29,505
8 Oct	RC 2/2	Watford	A	1–2	Beardsley, Newell	11,651
19 Oct	L	Aston Villa	H	0–2		27,688
26 Oct	L	Queen's Park Rangers	A	1–3	Cottee	10,002
30 Oct	RC 3	Wolverhampton Wanderers	H	4–1	Beagrie 2, Beardsley, Cottee	19,065
2 Nov	L	Luton Town	A	1–0	Warzycha	8,002
16 Nov	L	Wimbledon	H	2–0	Cottee [pen], Watson	18,762
23 Nov	L	Notts County	H	1–0	Cottee	24,230
27 Nov	ZDS 3	Leicester City	A	1–2	Beardsley	13,242
30 Nov	L	Leeds United	A	0–1		30,043
4 Dec	RC 4	Leeds United	H	1–4	Atteveld	25,467
7 Dec	L	West Ham United	H	4–0	Beardsley, Cottee, Johnston, Beagrie	21,563
14 Dec	L	Oldham Athletic	A	2–2	Sheedy, Nevin	14,955
21 Dec	L	Arsenal	A	2–4	Johnston, Warzycha	29,684
26 Dec	L	Sheffield Wednesday	H	0–1		30,788
28 Dec	L	Liverpool	H	1–1	Johnston	37,681
1 Jan	L	Southampton	A	2–1	Beardsley, Ward	16,546
4 Jan	FAC 3	Southend United	H	1–0	Beardsley	22,606
11 Jan	L	Manchester United	A	0–1		46,619
19 Jan	L	Nottingham Forest	H	1–0	Watson	17,717
26 Jan	FAC 4	Chelsea	A	0–1		21,152
2 Feb	L	Aston Villa	A	0–0		17,451
8 Feb	L	Queen's Park Rangers	H	0–0		18,212
23 Feb	L	Leeds United	H	1–1	Jackson	19,248
29 Feb	L	West Ham United	A	2–0	Johnston, Ablett	20,976
7 March	L	Oldham Athletic	H	2–1	Beardsley 2	21,014
10 March	L	Wimbledon	A	0–0		3,569
14 March	L	Luton Town	H	1–1	Johnston	16,707
17 March	L	Notts County	A	0–0		7,480
21 March	L	Norwich City	A	3–4	Johnston 2, Beardsley	11,900
1 April	L	Southampton	H	0–1		15,201
4 April	L	Crystal Palace	A	0–2		14,338
11 April	L	Sheffield United	H	0–2		18,285
18 April	L	Coventry City	A	1–0	Beagrie	14,669
20 April	L	Manchester City	H	1–2	Nevin	21,101
25 April	L	Tottenham Hotspur	A	3–3	Beardsley 2, Unsworth	34,630
2 May	L	Chelsea	H	2–1	Beardsley [pen], Beagrie	20,163

Squad members who made first team appearances in 1991–92:

Southall
Harper
Ebbrell
Ratcliffe
Watson
Keown
Warzycha
Sheedy
Beardsley
Cottee
Ward
Nevin
McDonald
Newell
Hinchcliffe
Atteveld
Youds
Jackson
Beagrie
Johnston
Ablett
Barlow
Jenkins
Unsworth

IPSWICH TOWN: RESULTS 1991–92

Date	Comp	Opponents	Venue	Res	Scorers	Attendance
17 Aug	L	Bristol Rovers	A	3–3	Stockwell, Goddard, Dozzell	6,444
20 Aug	L	Port Vale	H	2–1	Thompson [pen], Kiwomya	8,937
24 Aug	L	Middlesbrough	H	2–1	Goddard, Dozzell	9,822
31 Aug	L	Blackburn Rovers	A	2–1	Goddard, Kiwomya	8,898
3 Sept	L	Swindon Town	H	1–4	Kiwomya	11,002
7 Sept	L	Southend United	H	1–0	Thompson [pen]	12,732
14 Sept	L	Barnsley	A	0–1		6,786
17 Sept	L	Newcastle United	A	1–1	Kiwomya	16,336
21 Sept	L	Bristol City	H	4–2	Thompson, Goddard, Kiwomya, Linighan	9,692
24 Sept	RC 2/1	Derby County	A	0–0		10,215
28 Sept	L	Grimsby Town	A	2–1	Johnson, Lowe	6,621
2 Oct	ZDS 1	Bristol Rovers	A	3–1	Lowe 2, Dozzell	1,490
5 Oct	L	Oxford United	H	2–1	Whitton, Milton	9,922
8 Oct	RC 2/2	Derby County	H	0–2		8,982
12 Oct	L	Brighton & Hove Albion	A	2–2	Dozzell, Milton	9,010
19 Oct	L	Millwall	H	0–0		11,175
22 Oct	ZDS 2	Luton Town	H	*1–1	Lowe	5,750
26 Oct	L	Portsmouth	A	1–1	Milton	8,007
30 Oct	L	Charlton Athletic	A	1–1	Whitton	6,939
2 Nov	L	Leicester City	A	2–2	Johnson, Wark	11,331
5 Nov	L	Sunderland	H	0–1		9,768
9 Nov	L	Cambridge United	H	1–2	Stockwell	20,586
16 Nov	L	Derby County	A	0–1		12,493
23 Nov	L	Wolverhampton Wanderers	A	2–1	Dozzell, Linighan	11,915
26 Nov	ZDS 3	Chelsea	A	**2–2	Kiwomya 2	6,325
30 Nov	L	Tranmere Rovers	H	4–0	Wark [pen], Milton, Linighan, Thompson	11,072
7 Dec	L	Plymouth Argyle	A	0–1		4,986
20 Dec	L	Swindon Town	A	0–0		7,404
26 Dec	L	Charlton Athletic	H	2–0	Kiwomya 2	13,826
28 Dec	L	Blackburn Rovers	H	2–1	Dozzell, Johnson	17,675
1 Jan	L	Port Vale	A	2–1	Kiwomya 2	8,075
5 Jan	FAC 3	Hartlepool	H	1–1	Dozzell	12,507
11 Jan	L	Middlesbrough	A	0–1		15,104
15 Jan	FAC 3 R	Hartlepool	A	2–0	Dozzell, Milton	8,500
18 Jan	L	Bristol Rovers	H	1–0	Milton	10,435
1 Feb	L	Millwall	A	3–2	Thompson, Dozzell, Kiwomya	8,847
5 Feb	FAC 4	Bournemouth	H	3–0	Dozzell, Kiwomya, Whitton	17,193
8 Feb	L	Portsmouth	H	5–2	Dozzell 2, Kiwomya 2, Awford [og]	13,494
15 Feb	FAC 5	Liverpool	H	0–0		26,140
21 Feb	L	Tranmere Rovers	A	1–0	Milton	9,161
26 Feb	FAC 5 R	Liverpool	A	†2–3	Johnson, Dozzell	27,355
29 Feb	L	Plymouth Argyle	H	2–0	Kiwomya, Whitton	12,852
7 March	L	Watford Town	A	1–0	Whitton	9,199
14 March	L	Leicester City	H	0–0		16,174
17 March	L	Watford	H	1–2	Dozzell	12,484
21 March	L	Cambridge United	A	1–1	Milton	9,766
28 March	L	Derby County	H	2–1	Dozzell 2	15,305
31 March	L	Barnsley	H	2–0	Kiwomya 2	14,148
4 April	L	Southend United	A	2–1	Thompson, Whelan	10,003
7 April	L	Wolverhampton Wanderers	H	2–1	Whelan, Whitton [pen]	17,379
11 April	L	Newcastle United	H	3–2	Whitton [pen], Wark, Kiwomya	20,673
14 April	L	Sunderland	A	0–3		22,131
18 April	L	Bristol City	A	1–2	Whitton [pen]	16,941
21 April	L	Grimsby Town	H	0–0		22,393
25 April	L	Oxford United	A	1–1	Johnson	10,525
2 May	L	Brighton & Hove Albion	H	3–1	Whitton 2 [pens], Johnson	26,803

Squad members who made first team appearances in 1991–92:

Forrest
Yallop
Thompson
Zondervan
Gayle
Humes
Stockwell
Goddard
Johnson
Dozzell
Kiwomya
Lowe
Whitton
Linighan
Milton
Wark
Whelan
Gregory
Edmonson
Palmer
Moncur
Youds
Pennyfather

* Ipswich won on penalties after extra time

** Ipswich lost on penalties after extra time

† after extra time

LEEDS UNITED: RESULTS 1991–92

Date	Comp	Opponents	Venue	Res	Scorers	Attendance
20 Aug	L	Nottingham Forest	H	1–0	McAllister	29,457
24 Aug	L	Sheffield Wednesday	H	1–1	Hodge	30,260
28 Aug	L	Southampton	A	4–0	Speed 2, Strachan 2 [pens]	15,862
31 Aug	L	Manchester United	A	1–1	Chapman	43,778
3 Sept	L	Arsenal	H	2–2	Strachan [pen], Chapman	29,396
7 Sept	L	Manchester City	H	3–0	Dorigo, Batty, Strachan [pen]	29,986
14 Sept	L	Chelsea	A	1–0	Shutt	23,439
18 Sept	L	Coventry City	A	0–0		15,488
21 Sept	L	Liverpool	H	1–0	Hodge	32,912
24 Sept	RC 2/1	Scunthorpe United	A	0–0		8,392
28 Sept	L	Norwich City	A	2–2	Speed, Dorigo	15,828
1 Oct	L	Crystal Palace	A	0–1		18,298
5 Oct	L	Sheffield United	H	4–3	Sterland 2 [1 pen], Hodge 2	28,362
8 Oct	RC 2/2	Scunthorpe United	H	3–0	Sterland [pen], Chapman, Speed	14,558
19 Oct	L	Notts County	A	4–2	Chapman, McAllister, Hodge, Whyte	12,964
22 Oct	ZDS 2	Nottingham Forest	H	1–3	Wallace	6,145
26 Oct	L	Oldham Athletic	H	1–0	Kilcline [og]	28,199
29 Oct	RC 3	Tranmere Rovers	H	3–1	Chapman 2, Shutt	18,266
2 Nov	L	Wimbledon	A	0–0		7,025
16 Nov	L	Queen's Park Rangers	H	2–0	Wallace, Sterland	27,087
24 Nov	L	Aston Villa	A	4–1	Chapman 2, Wallace, Sterland	23,713
30 Nov	L	Everton	H	1–0	Wallace	30,043
4 Dec	RC 4	Everton	A	4–1	Wallace 2, Chapman, Speed	25,467
7 Dec	L	Luton Town	A	2–0	Wallace, Speed	11,550
14 Dec	L	Tottenham Hotspur	H	1–1	Speed	31,404
22 Dec	L	Nottingham Forest	A	0–0		27,170
26 Dec	L	Southampton	H	3–3	Hodge 2, Speed	29,053
29 Dec	L	Manchester United	H	1–1	Sterland [pen]	32,638
1 Jan	L	West Ham United	A	3–1	Chapman 2, McAllister	21,766
8 Jan	RC 5	Manchester United	H	1–3	Speed	28,886
12 Jan	L	Sheffield Wednesday	A	6–1	Chapman 3, Dorigo, Whitlow, Wallace	32,228
15 Jan	FAC 3	Manchester United	H	0–1		31,819
18 Jan	L	Crystal Palace	H	1–1	Fairclough	27,717
1 Feb	L	Notts County	H	3–0	Sterland, Wallace, Batty	27,224
8 Feb	L	Oldham Athletic	A	0–2		18,409
23 Feb	L	Everton	A	1–1	Keown [og]	19,248
29 Feb	L	Luton Town	H	2–0	Chapman, Cantona	28,231
3 March	L	Aston Villa	H	0–0		28,896
7 March	L	Tottenham Hotspur	A	3–1	Wallace, McAllister, Newsome	27,622
11 March	L	Queen's Park Rangers	A	1–4	Speed	14,641
14 March	L	Wimbledon	H	5–1	Chapman 3, Wallace, Cantona	26,760
22 March	L	Arsenal	A	1–1	Chapman	27,844
28 March	L	West Ham United	H	0–0		31,101
4 April	L	Manchester City	A	0–4		30,239
11 April	L	Chelsea	H	3–0	Wallace, Chapman, Cantona	31,363
18 April	L	Liverpool	A	0–0		37,186
20 April	L	Coventry City	H	2–0	Fairclough, McAllister [pen]	26,582
26 April	L	Sheffield United	A	3–2	Wallace, Newsome, Gayle [og]	32,000
2 May	L	Norwich City	H	1–0	Wallace	32,673

Squad members who made first team appearances in 1991–92:

Lukic
McClelland
Dorigo
Batty
Fairclough
Whyte
Strachan
Wallace, Rod
Chapman
McAllister
Speed
Sterland
Hodge
Wetherall
Shutt
Varadi
Whitlow
Kelly
Williams
Kamara
Newsome
Grayson
Snodin
Dawson
Cantona
Agana

Date	Comp	Opponents	Venue	Res	Scorers	Attendance
17 Aug	L	Oldham Athletic	H	2–1	Houghton, Barnes	38,841
21 Aug	L	Manchester City	A	1–2	McManaman	37,322
24 Aug	L	Luton Town	A	0–0		11,132
27 Aug	L	Queen's Park Rangers	H	1–0	Saunders	32,700
31 Aug	L	Everton	H	3–1	Burrows, Saunders, Houghton	39,072
7 Sept	L	Notts County	A	2–1	Walters [pen], Rosenthal	16,051
14 Sept	L	Aston Villa	H	1–1	Walters [pen]	38,400
18 Sept	UEFA 1/1	Kuusysi Lahti	H	6–1	Saunders 4, Houghton 2	17,131
21 Sept	L	Leeds United	A	0–1		32,912
25 Sept	RC 2/1	Stoke City	H	2–2	Rush 2	18,389
28 Sept	L	Sheffield Wednesday	H	1–1	Houghton	37,071
2 Oct	UEFA 1/2	Kuusysi Lahti	A	0–1		8,800
6 Oct	L	Manchester United	A	0–0		44,997
9 Oct	RC 2/2	Stoke City	A	3–2	Saunders, McManaman, Walters	22,335
19 Oct	L	Chelsea	A	2–2	McManaman, Elliott [og]	30,230
23 Oct	UEFA 2/1	Auxerre	A	0–2		20,000
26 Oct	L	Coventry City	H	1–0	Houghton	33,336
29 Oct	RC 3	Port Vale	H	2–2	McManaman, Rush	21,553
2 Nov	L	Crystal Palace	H	1–2	Hysen	34,321
6 Nov	UEFA 2/2	Auxerre	H	3–0	Walters, Marsh, Molby [pen]	23,094
17 Nov	L	West Ham United	A	0–0		23,569
20 Nov	RC 3 R	Port Vale	A	4–1	Saunders, Houghton, McManaman, Walters	18,725
23 Nov	L	Wimbledon	A	0–0		13,373
27 Nov	UEFA 3/1	FC Tirol	A	2–0	Saunders 2	13,500
30 Nov	L	Norwich City	H	2–1	Houghton, Molby	34,881
3 Dec	RC 4	Peterborough	A	0–1		14,114
7 Dec	L	Southampton	A	1–1	Redknapp	19,053
11 Dec	UEFA 3/2	FC Tirol	H	4–0	Saunders 3, Venison	16,007
14 Dec	L	Nottingham Forest	H	2–0	McMahon, Molby	35,285
18 Dec	L	Tottenham Hotspur	A	2–1	Saunders, Houghton	27,434
21 Dec	L	Manchester City	H	2–2	Nicol, Saunders	36,743
26 Dec	L	Queen's Park Rangers	A	0–0		21,693
28 Dec	L	Everton	A	1–1	Tanner	37,681
1 Jan	L	Sheffield United	H	2–1	Saunders, Houghton	35,933
6 Jan	FAC 3	Crewe Alexandra	A	4–0	McManaman, Barnes 3 [1 pen]	7,400
11 Jan	L	Luton Town	H	2–1	Saunders, McManaman	35,095
18 Jan	L	Oldham Athletic	A	3–2	Saunders, McManaman, Thomas	18,952
24 Jan	L	Arsenal	H	2–0	Houghton, Molby [pen]	33,753
1 Feb	L	Chelsea	H	1–2	Rosenthal	38,681
5 Feb	FAC 4	Bristol Rovers	A	1–1	Saunders	9,464
8 Feb	L	Coventry City	A	0–0		21,540
11 Feb	FAC 4 R	Bristol Rovers	H	2–1	Saunders, McManaman	30,142
16 Feb	FAC 5	Ipswich Town	A	0–0		26,140
22 Feb	L	Norwich City	A	0–3		20,411
26 Feb	FAC 5 R	Ipswich Town	H	*3–2	Houghton, McManaman, Molby	27,355
29 Feb	L	Southampton	H	0–0		34,449
4 March	UEFA QF 1	Genoa	A	0–2		39,000
8 March	FAC 6	Aston Villa	H	1–0	Thomas	29,109
11 March	L	West Ham United	H	1–0	Saunders	30,821
14 March	L	Crystal Palace	A	0–1		23,680
18 March	UEFA QF 2	Genoa	H	1–2	Rush	38,840
21 March	L	Tottenham Hotspur	H	2–1	Saunders 2	36,968
28 March	L	Sheffield United	A	0–2		26,943
31 March	L	Notts County	H	4–0	Rush, McManaman, Venison, Thomas	25,457
5 April	FAC SF 1	Portsmouth	Highbury	*1–1	Whelan	41,869
8 April	L	Wimbledon	H	2–3	Thomas, Rosenthal	26,134
11 April	L	Aston Villa	A	0–1		35,755
13 April	FAC SF 2	Portsmouth	Villa Park	**0–0		40,077
18 April	L	Leeds United	H	0–0		37,186
20 April	L	Arsenal	A	0–4		38,517
22 April	L	Nottingham Forest	A	1–1	Rush	23,787
26 April	L	Manchester United	H	2–0	Rush, Thomas	38,669
2 May	L	Sheffield Wednesday	A	0–0		34,861
9 May	FAC F	Sunderland	Wembley	2–0	Thomas, Rush	79,544

Squad members who made first team appearances in 1991–92:

Grobbelaar
Ablett
Burrows
Nicol
Whelan
Wright
Saunders
Houghton
McManaman
Barnes
McMahon
Walters
Marsh
Tanner
Rosenthal
Harkness
Rush
Hooper
Jones, R
Carter
Redknapp
Jones, B
Hysen
Molby
Venison
Thomas
Kozma
Hutchison

* after extra time
** Liverpool won on penalties after extra time

MANCHESTER CITY: RESULTS 1991–92

Date	Comp	Opponents	Venue	Res	Scorers	Attendance
17 Aug	L	Coventry City	A	1–0	Quinn	18,013
21 Aug	L	Liverpool	H	2–1	White 2	37,322
24 Aug	L	Crystal Palace	H	3–2	White, Brennan [2 pens]	28,028
28 Aug	L	Norwich City	A	0–0		15,376
31 Aug	L	Arsenal	A	1–2	Brightwell	35,009
4 Sept	L	Nottingham Forest	H	2–1	Hill, Quinn	29,146
7 Sept	L	Leeds United	A	0–3		28,986
14 Sept	L	Sheffield Wednesday	H	0–1		29,453
17 Sept	L	Everton	H	0–1		27,509
21 Sept	L	West Ham United	A	2–1	Hendry, Redmond [pen]	25,588
25 Sept	RC 2/1	Chester City	H	3–1	Quinn 2, White	10,987
28 Sept	L	Oldham Athletic	H	1–2	White	31,271
6 Oct	L	Notts County	A	3–1	Sheron, Allen 2 [1 pen]	11,878
8 Oct	RC 2/2	Chester City	A	3–0	Brennan, Sheron, Allen	4,146
19 Oct	L	Tottenham Hotspur	A	1–0	Quinn	30,102
23 Oct	ZDS 2	Sheffield Wednesday	A	2–3	Hendry 2	7,951
26 Oct	L	Sheffield United	H	3–2	Quinn, Sheron, Hughes	25,495
29 Oct	RC 3	Queen's Park Rangers	H	0–0		15,512
2 Nov	L	Southampton	A	3–0	Quinn, Sheron, Gittens [og]	13,933
16 Nov	L	Manchester United	H	0–0		38,180
20 Nov	RC 3 R	Queen's Park Rangers	A	3–1	Quinn, Heath, Wilkins [og]	11,003
23 Nov	L	Luton Town	A	2–2	Curle, Quinn	10,031
30 Nov	L	Wimbledon	H	0–0		22,429
3 Dec	RC 4	Middlesbrough	A	1–2	White	17,256
7 Dec	L	Aston Villa	A	1–3	White	26,265
14 Dec	L	Queen's Park Rangers	H	2–2	Curle, White	21,437
21 Dec	L	Liverpool	A	2–2	White 2	36,743
26 Dec	L	Norwich City	H	2–1	Quinn, White	28,164
28 Dec	L	Arsenal	H	1–0	White	32,325
1 Jan	L	Chelsea	A	1–1	Sheron	18,196
4 Jan	FAC 3	Middlesbrough	A	1–2	Reid	21,174
11 Jan	L	Crystal Palace	A	1–1	Curle [pen]	14,766
18 Jan	L	Coventry City	H	1–0	White	23,005
1 Feb	L	Tottenham Hotspur	H	1–0	White	30,123
8 Feb	L	Sheffield United	A	2–4	Hill, Curle [pen]	22,000
15 Feb	L	Luton Town	H	4–0	Hill, White 2, Heath	22,137
22 Feb	L	Wimbledon	A	1–2	White	5,802
29 Feb	L	Aston Villa	H	2–0	Quinn, White	28,268
7 March	L	Queen's Park Rangers	A	0–4		10,779
15 March	L	Southampton	H	0–1		24,265
21 March	L	Nottingham Forest	A	0–2		21,115
28 March	L	Chelsea	H	0–0		23,633
4 April	L	Leeds United	H	4–0	Hill, Quinn, Brennan, Sheron	30,239
7 April	L	Manchester United	A	1–1	Curle [pen]	46,781
11 April	L	Sheffield Wednesday	H	0–2		32,138
18 April	L	West Ham United	H	2–0	Pointon, Clarke	25,601
20 April	L	Everton	A	2–1	Quinn 2	21,101
25 April	L	Notts County	H	2–0	Quinn, Simpson	23,426
2 May	L	Oldham Athletic	A	5–2	White 3, Sheron, Mike	18,588

Squad members who made first team appearances in 1991–92:

Margetson
Hill
Brightwell, I
Curle
Hendry
Pointon
Redmond
Reid
Quinn
White
Brennan
Coton
Heath
Megson
Sheron
Hughes
Dibble
Hoekman
Allen
Quigley
Mauge
McMahon
Brightwell, D
Simpson
Clarke
Vonk
Mike

MANCHESTER UNITED: RESULTS 1991–92

Date	Comp	Opponents	Venue	Res	Scorers	Attendance
17 Aug	L	Notts County	H	2–0	Robson, Hughes	46,278
21 Aug	L	Aston Villa	A	1–0	Bruce	39,995
24 Aug	L	Everton	A	0–0		36,085
28 Aug	L	Oldham Athletic	H	1–0	McClair	42,078
31 Aug	L	Leeds United	H	1–1	Robson	43,778
3 Sept	L	Wimbledon	A	2–1	Blackmore, Pallister	13,824
7 Sept	L	Norwich City	H	3–0	Irwin, McClair, Giggs	44,946
14 Sept	L	Southampton	A	1–0	Hughes	19,264
18 Sept	ECWC 1/1	Athinaikos	A	0–0		11,000
21 Sept	L	Luton Town	H	5–0	Bruce, Ince, McClair 2, Hughes	46,491
25 Sept	RC 2/1	Cambridge United	H	3–0	McClair, Bruce, Giggs	30,934
28 Sept	L	Tottenham Hotspur	A	2–1	Robson, Hughes	35,087
2 Oct	ECWC 1/2	Athinaikos	H	*2–0	McClair, Hughes	35,023
6 Oct	L	Liverpool	H	0–0		44,997
9 Oct	RC 2/2	Cambridge United	A	1–1	McClair	9,248
19 Oct	L	Arsenal	H	1–1	Bruce	46,594
23 Oct	ECWC 2/1	Atletico Madrid	A	0–3		52,000
26 Oct	L	Sheffield Wednesday	A	2–3	McClair 2	38,260
30 Oct	RC 3	Portsmouth	H	3–1	Robins 2, Robson	29,543
2 Nov	L	Sheffield United	H	2–0	Hughes, Hoyland [og]	42,942
6 Nov	ECWC 2/2	Atletico Madrid	H	1–1	Hughes	39,654
16 Nov	L	Manchester City	A	0–0		38,180
19 Nov	ESC	Red Star Belgrade	H	1–0	McClair	22,110
23 Nov	L	West Ham United	H	2–1	Robson, Giggs	47,185
30 Nov	L	Crystal Palace	A	3–1	McClair, Kanchelskis, Webb	29,017
4 Dec	RC 4	Oldham Athletic	H	2–0	McClair, Kanchelskis	38,550
7 Dec	L	Coventry City	H	4–0	Bruce, McClair, Hughes, Webb	42,549
15 Dec	L	Chelsea	A	3–1	Irwin, Bruce [pen], McClair	23,120
26 Dec	L	Oldham Athletic	A	6–3	Irwin 2, McClair 2, Kanchelskis, Giggs	18,947
29 Dec	L	Leeds United	A	1–1	Webb	32,638
1 Jan	L	Queen's Park Rangers	H	1–4	McClair	38,554
8 Jan	RC 5	Leeds United	A	3–1	Blackmore, Kanchelskis, Giggs	28,886
11 Jan	L	Everton	H	1–0	Kanchelskis	46,619
15 Jan	FAC 3	Leeds United	A	1–0	Hughes	31,819
18 Jan	L	Notts County	A	1–1	Blackmore [pen]	21,055
22 Jan	L	Aston Villa	H	1–0	Hughes	45,022
27 Jan	FAC 4	Southampton	A	0–0		19,506
1 Feb	L	Arsenal	A	1–1	McClair	41,703
5 Feb	FAC 4 R	Southampton	H	**2–2	McClair, Kanchelskis	33,414
8 Feb	L	Sheffield Wednesday	H	1–1	McClair	47,074
22 Feb	L	Crystal Palace	H	2–0	Hughes 2	46,347
26 Feb	L	Chelsea	H	1–1	Hughes	44,872
29 Feb	L	Coventry City	A	0–0		23,967
4 March	RC SF/1	Middlesbrough	A	0–0		25,572
11 March	RC SF/2	Middlesbrough	H	*2–1	Giggs, Sharpe	45,875
14 March	L	Sheffield United	A	2–1	Blackmore, McClair	30,183
18 March	L	Nottingham Forest	A	0–1		28,062
21 March	L	Wimbledon	H	0–0		45,428
28 March	L	Queen's Park Rangers	A	0–0		22,630
31 March	L	Norwich City	A	3–1	Ince 2, McClair	17,489
7 April	L	Manchester City	H	1–1	Giggs	46,781
12 April	RC F	Nottingham Forest	Wembley	1–0	McClair	76,810
16 April	L	Southampton	H	1–0	Kanchelskis	43,972
18 April	L	Luton Town	A	1–1	Sharpe	13,410
20 April	L	Nottingham Forest	H	1–2	McClair	47,576
22 April	L	West Ham United	A	0–1		24,197
26 April	L	Liverpool	A	0–2		38,669
2 May	L	Tottenham Hotspur	H	3–1	Hughes 2, McClair	44,595

Squad members who made first team appearances in 1991–92:

Schmeichel
Irwin
Blackmore
Bruce
Ferguson
Parker
Robson
Ince
McClair
Hughes
Kanchelskis
Giggs
Pallister
Donaghy
Webb
Phelan
Robins
Beardsmore
Wallace
Walsh
Martin
Wilkinson
Sharpe

* after extra time
** Manchester United lost on penalties after extra time

Date	Comp	Opponents	Venue	Res	Scorers	Attendance
17 Aug	L	Millwall	H	1–0	Mustoe	16,234
21 Aug	L	Derby County	A	0–2		12,805
24 Aug	L	Ipswich Town	A	1–2	Wilkinson	9,822
27 Aug	L	Newcastle United	H	3–0	Falconer, Proctor, Wilkinson	16,970
31 Aug	L	Portsmouth	H	2–0	Falconer, Slaven	12,320
4 Sept	L	Oxford United	A	2–1	Slaven 2	4,229
7 Sept	L	Watford	A	2–1	Wilkinson, Falconer	8,715
14 Sept	L	Leicester City	H	3–0	Wilkinson 2, Slaven	16,633
17 Sept	L	Tranmere Rovers	H	1–0	Falconer	16,550
21 Sept	L	Plymouth Argyle	A	1–1	Wilkinson	5,280
24 Sept	RC 2/1	Bournemouth	H	1–1	Wilkinson	10,577
28 Sept	L	Sunderland	H	2–1	Wilkinson, Slaven	19,424
6 Oct	L	Bristol Rovers	A	1–2	Yates [og]	4,936
8 Oct	RC 2/2	Bournemouth	A	*2–1	Parkinson [pen], Hendrie	5,528
12 Oct	L	Wolverhampton Wanderers	H	0–0		15,253
19 Oct	L	Grimsby Town	A	0–1		10,265
22 Oct	ZDS 2	Derby County	H	*4–2	Phillips, Wilkinson 2, Slaven	6,385
26 Oct	L	Port Vale	H	1–0	Kernaghan	11,403
29 Oct	RC 3	Barnsley	H	1–0	Wilkinson	9,381
2 Nov	L	Southend United	H	1–1	Ripley	9,664
5 Nov	L	Barnsley	A	1–2	Slaven	6,525
9 Nov	L	Brighton & Hove Albion	A	1–1	Slaven [pen]	8,270
16 Nov	L	Charlton Athletic	H	2–0	Mohan, Slaven	13,093
23 Nov	L	Bristol City	H	3–1	Slaven 2, Payton	12,928
26 Nov	ZDS 3	Tranmere Rovers	H	0–1		6,952
30 Nov	L	Blackburn Rovers	A	1–2	Slaven [pen]	15,541
3 Dec	RC 4	Manchester City	A	2–1	Mustoe, Wilkinson	15,286
7 Dec	L	Swindon Town	H	2–2	Wilkinson, Slaven	13,300
26 Dec	L	Newcastle United	A	1–0	Wilkinson	26,563
28 Dec	L	Portsmouth	A	0–4		12,324
1 Jan	L	Derby County	H	1–1	Mohan	16,288
5 Jan	FAC 3	Manchester City	H	2–1	Kernaghan, Wilkinson	21,174
8 Jan	RC 5	Peterborough United	A	0–0		15,302
11 Jan	L	Ipswich Town	H	1–0	Payton	15,104
18 Jan	L	Millwall	A	0–2		8,125
4 Feb	FAC 4	Sheffield Wednesday	A	2–1	Hendrie, Wilkinson	29,772
8 Feb	L	Port Vale	A	2–1	Mustoe, Hendrie	7,019
12 Feb	RC 5 R	Peterborough United	H	1–0	Ripley	21,973
15 Feb	FAC 5	Portsmouth	A	1–1	Kernaghan	18,138
22 Feb	L	Blackburn Rovers	H	0–0		19,353
26 Feb	FAC 5 R	Portsmouth	A	2–4	Wilkinson 2	19,479
29 Feb	L	Swindon Town	A	1–0	Kernaghan	10,379
4 March	RC SF 1	Manchester United	H	0–0		25,572
7 March	L	Cambridge United	H	1–1	Wilkinson	14,686
11 March	RC SF 2	Manchester United	A	*1–2	Slaven	45,875
14 March	L	Southend United	A	1–0	Slaven [pen]	7,272
17 March	L	Cambridge United	A	0–0		7,318
21 March	L	Brighton & Hove Albion	H	4–0	Hendrie, Slaven 3 [1 pen]	13,054
28 March	L	Charlton Athletic	A	0–0		8,250
1 April	L	Leicester City	A	1–2	Pollock	19,325
4 April	L	Watford	H	1–2	Wilkinson	13,669
7 April	L	Bristol City	A	1–1	Hendrie	12,814
10 April	L	Tranmere Rovers	A	2–1	Proctor, Phillips	8,842
13 April	L	Barnsley	H	0–1		12,743
15 April	L	Oxford United	H	2–1	Ripley, Payton	11,928
18 April	L	Plymouth Argyle	H	2–1	Ripley, Falconer	15,086
20 April	L	Sunderland United	A	0–1		25,093
25 April	L	Bristol Rovers	H	2–1	Wilkinson 2	14,057
28 April	L	Grimsby Town	H	2–0	Wilkinson, Phillips [pen]	18,570
2 May	L	Wolverhampton Wanderers	A	2–1	Slaven, Wilkinson	19,132

Squad members who made first team appearances in 1991–92:

Pears
Parkinson
Phillips
Mowbray
Kernaghan
Falconer
Mustoe
Proctor
Wilkinson
Ripley
Hendrie
Slaven
Fleming
Hewitt
Shannon
Pollock
Arnold
Marwood
Young
Mohan
Payton
Peake
Gittens
Ironside

* after extra time

Date	Comp	Opponents	Venue	Res	Scorers	Attendance
17 Aug	L	Sheffield United	H	2–2	Fleck 2	16,380
21 Aug	L	Queen's Park Rangers	A	2–0	Gordon, Newman	10,626
24 Aug	L	Oldham Athletic	A	2–2	Crook, Newman	13,548
28 Aug	L	Manchester City	H	0–0		15,376
31 Aug	L	Tottenham Hotspur	H	0–1		19,460
3 Sept	L	Everton	A	1–1	Phillips	19,197
7 Sept	L	Manchester United	A	0–3		44,946
14 Sept	L	West Ham United	H	2–1	Gordon, Fox	15,348
18 Sept	L	Sheffield Wednesday	H	1–0	Fleck [pen]	12,503
21 Sept	L	Notts County	A	2–2	Bowen [pen], Ullathorne	9,488
25 Sept	RC 2/1	Charlton Athletic	A	2–0	Gordon, Newman	2,886
28 Sept	L	Leeds United	H	2–2	Gordon 2	15,828
5 Oct	L	Wimbledon	A	1–3	Beckford	3,531
9 Oct	RC 2/2	Charlton Athletic	H	3–0	Fleck 2, Beckford	5,507
19 Oct	L	Southampton	A	0–0		12,516
23 Oct	ZDS 2	Queen's Park Rangers	H	1–2	Beckford	4,436
26 Oct	L	Luton Town	H	1–0	Newman	10,514
30 Oct	RC 3	Brentford	H	4–1	Fleck, Beckford 2, Millen [og]	7,394
2 Nov	L	Nottingham Forest	H	0–0		13,014
16 Nov	L	Chelsea	A	3–0	Bowen, Fleck 2	15,755
23 Nov	L	Coventry City	H	3–2	Bowen, Fleck, Sutton	12,056
30 Nov	L	Liverpool	A	1–2	Beckford	34,881
4 Dec	RC 4	West Ham United	H	2–1	Fleck 2 [1 pen]	16,321
7 Dec	L	Crystal Palace	H	3–3	Newman, Beckford, Thorn [og]	12,667
21 Dec	L	Queen's Park Rangers	H	0–1		11,436
26 Dec	L	Manchester City	A	1–2	Newman	28,164
28 Dec	L	Tottenham Hotspur	A	0–3		27,969
1 Jan	L	Aston Villa	H	2–1	Fleck [pen], Ullathorne	15,318
4 Jan	FAC 3	Barnsley	H	1–0	Fleck [pen]	12,189
8 Jan	RC 5	Tottenham Hotspur	A	1–2	Fleck	29,471
11 Jan	L	Oldham Athletic	H	1–2	Beckford	10,986
18 Jan	L	Sheffield United	A	0–1		17,549
1 Feb	L	Southampton	H	2–1	Fleck, Ullathorne	10,660
5 Feb	FAC 4	Millwall	H	2–1	Bowen, Fleck	16,500
8 Feb	L	Luton Town	A	0–2		8,554
11 Feb	L	Arsenal	A	1–1	Fox	22,352
15 Feb	FAC 5	Notts County	H	3–0	Phillips, Sutton 2	14,511
22 Feb	L	Liverpool	H	3–0	Fleck 2, Woodthorpe	20,411
29 Feb	L	Crystal Palace	A	4–3	Newman, Goss, Polston, Sutton	14,201
4 March	L	Coventry City	A	0–0		8,459
7 March	FAC 6	Southampton	A	0–0		20,088
11 March	L	Chelsea	H	0–1		13,430
14 March	L	Nottingham Forest	A	0–2		20,721
18 March	FAC 6 R	Southampton	H	*2–1	Newman, Sutton	21,017
21 March	L	Everton	H	4–3	Beckford 3, Newman	11,900
28 March	L	Aston Villa	A	0–1		16,985
31 March	L	Manchester United	H	1–3	Power	17,489
5 April	FAC SF	Sunderland	Hillsborough	0–1		40,462
8 April	L	Arsenal	H	1–3	Butterworth	12,971
11 April	L	West Ham United	A	0–4		16,896
18 April	L	Notts County	H	0–1		12,100
20 April	L	Sheffield Wednesday	A	0–2		27,362
25 April	L	Wimbledon	H	1–1	Fleck	11,061
2 May	L	Leeds United	A	0–1		32,673

Squad members who made first team appearances in 1991–92:

Gunn
Culverhouse
Bowen
Butterworth
Blades
Crook
Gordon
Fleck
Newman
Beckford
Phillips
Fox
Goss
Ullathorne
Woodthorpe
Ball
Mortensen
Polston
Sherwood
Sutton
Sutch
Walton
Power
Smith
Johnson

* after extra time

Date	Comp	Opponents	Venue	Res	Scorers	Attendance
17 Aug	L	Everton	H	2–1	Clough, Jemson	24,422
20 Aug	L	Leeds United	A	0–1		29,457
24 Aug	L	Notts County	A	4–0	Charles, Keane, Crosby, Sheringham	21,044
28 Aug	L	Tottenham Hotspur	H	1–3	Clough	24,018
31 Aug	L	Oldham Athletic	H	3–1	Pearce, Keane, Gemmill	23,244
4 Sept	L	Manchester City	A	1–2	Sheringham	29,146
7 Sept	L	Sheffield Wednesday	A	1–2	Crosby	31,289
14 Sept	L	Wimbledon	H	4–2	Keane 2, Black, Elkins [og]	19,707
21 Sept	L	Aston Villa	A	1–3	Teale [og]	28,506
25 Sept	RC 2/1	Bolton Wanderers	H	4–0	Keane, Black, Gaynor 2	19,936
28 Sept	L	West Ham United	H	2–2	Sheringham, Wassall	25,613
5 Oct	L	Queen's Park Rangers	A	2–0	Sheringham 2	13,508
8 Oct	RC 2/2	Bolton Wanderers	A	5–2	Keane 2, Sheringham, Black, Gaynor	5,469
19 Oct	L	Sheffield United	A	2–4	Chettle, Parker	23,030
22 Oct	ZDS 2	Leeds United	A	3–1	Crosby, Sheringham 2 [1 pen]	6,145
26 Oct	L	Southampton	H	1–3	Black	20,026
30 Oct	RC 3	Bristol Rovers	H	2–0	Gemmill, Glover	17,529
2 Nov	L	Norwich City	A	0–0		13,014
16 Nov	L	Coventry City	H	1–0	Sheringham	21,154
19 Nov	ZDS 3	Aston Villa	A	2–0	Pearce, Woan	7,859
23 Nov	L	Crystal Palace	H	5–1	Pearce, Gemmill, Sheringham 2 [1 pen], Woan	22,387
30 Nov	L	Chelsea	A	0–1		19,420
4 Dec	RC 4	Southampton	H	0–0		17,939
8 Dec	L	Arsenal	H	3–2	Gemmill, Sheringham, Woan	22,095
10 Dec	ZDS 4	Tranmere Rovers	A	2–0	Keane 2	8,034
14 Dec	L	Liverpool	A	0–2		35,285
17 Dec	RC 4 R	Southampton	A	1–0	Gemmill	10,861
22 Dec	L	Leeds United	H	0–0		27,170
26 Dec	L	Tottenham Hotspur	A	2–1	Pearce, Clough	31,079
28 Dec	L	Oldham Athletic	A	1–2	Pearce	16,496
1 Jan	L	Luton Town	H	1–1	Walker	23,809
4 Jan	FAC 3	Wolverhampton Wanderers	H	1–0	Clough	27,068
8 Jan	RC 5	Crystal Palace	A	1–1	Clough	14,941
11 Jan	L	Notts County	H	1–1	Black	30,168
19 Jan	L	Everton	A	1–1	Gemmill	17,717
26 Jan	FAC 4	Hereford United	H	2–0	Pearce, Sheringham	24,259
1 Feb	L	Sheffield United	H	2–5	Pearce [pen], Keane	22,412
5 Feb	RC 5 R	Crystal Palace	H	4–2	Pearce, Sheringham 3 [1 pen]	18,918
9 Feb	RC SF 1	Tottenham Hotspur	H	1–1	Sheringham	21,402
12 Feb	ZDS SAF 1	Leicester City	A	1–1	Gemmill	19,537
15 Feb	FAC 5	Bristol City	H	4–1	Pearce, Clough, Sheringham [pen], Llewellyn [og]	24,615
22 Feb	L	Chelsea	H	1–1	Sheringham	24,095
26 Feb	ZDS SAF 2	Leicester City	H	2–1	Crosby, Wassall	21,562
1 March	RC SF 2	Tottenham Hotspur	A	*2–1	Keane, Glover	28,216
3 March	L	Crystal Palace	A	0–0		12,680
7 March	FAC 6	Portsmouth	A	0–1		25,402
11 March	L	Coventry City	A	2–0	Sheringham, Smith [og]	11,158
14 March	L	Norwich City	H	2–0	Keane, Gemmill	20,721
18 March	L	Manchester United	H	1–0	Clough	28,062
21 March	L	Manchester City	H	2–0	Keane, Crosby	21,115
29 March	ZDS F	Southampton	Wembley	*3–2	Gemmill 2, Black	67,688
31 March	L	Arsenal	A	3–3	Keane, Clough, Woan	27,036
2 April	L	Wimbledon	A	0–3		3,542
4 April	L	Sheffield Wednesday	H	0–2		26,105
8 April	L	Southampton	A	1–0	Tiler	14,905
12 April	RC F	Manchester United	Wembley	0–1		76,810
14 April	L	Luton Town	A	1–2	Black	8,014
18 April	L	Aston Villa	H	2–0	Gemmill, Sheringham	22,800
20 April	L	Manchester United	A	2–1	Gemmill, Woan	47,576
22 April	L	Liverpool	H	1–1	Sheringham [pen]	23,787
25 April	L	Queen's Park Rangers	H	1–1	Gemmill	22,228
2 May	L	West Ham United	A	0–3		20,629

Squad members who made first team appearances in 1991–92:

Crossley
Charles
Pearce
Walker
Tiler
Keane
Crosby
Gemmill
Clough
Sheringham
Jemson
Chettle
Laws
Black
Williams
Parker
Boardman
Gaynor
Woan
Wassall
Glover
Marriott
Wilson
Stone
Kaminsky
Orlygsson

* after extra time

OLDHAM ATHLETIC: RESULTS 1991–92

Date	Comp	Opponents	Venue	Res	Scorers	Attendance
17 Aug	L	Liverpool	A	1–2	Barrett	38,841
21 Aug	L	Chelsea	H	3–0	Marshall, Holden, Currie	14,997
24 Aug	L	Norwich City	H	2–2	Barrett, Marshall	13,548
28 Aug	L	Manchester United	A	0–1		42,078
31 Aug	L	Nottingham Forest	A	1–3	Marshall	23,244
3 Sept	L	Coventry City	H	2–1	Henry, Adams	12,996
7 Sept	L	Sheffield United	H	2–1	Snodin, Marshall	15,064
14 Sept	L	Luton Town	A	1–2	Marshall	9,005
21 Sept	L	Crystal Palace	H	2–3	Marshall, Holden	13,391
24 Sept	RC 2/1	Torquay United	H	7–1	Henry, Sharp, Milligan, Ritchie 4	7,250
28 Sept	L	Manchester City	A	2–1	Sharp 2	31,271
1 Oct	ZDS 2	Everton	A	2–3	Milligan, Holden	4,588
5 Oct	L	Southampton	H	1–1	Henry	13,133
9 Oct	RC 2/2	Torquay United	A	2–0	Jobson, Holden	1,955
19 Oct	L	West Ham United	H	2–2	McDonald, Breacker [og]	14,365
26 Oct	L	Leeds United	A	0–1		28,199
29 Oct	RC 3	Derby County	H	2–1	Sharp, Palmer	11,219
2 Nov	L	Notts County	A	0–2		7,634
16 Nov	L	Arsenal	H	1–1	Barlow	15,681
23 Nov	L	Queen's Park Rangers	A	3–1	Henry, Sharp, Palmer	8,947
30 Nov	L	Aston Villa	H	3–2	Sharp 2 [1 pen], Palmer	15,370
4 Dec	RC 4	Manchester United	A	0–2		38,550
7 Dec	L	Wimbledon	A	1–2	Marshall [pen]	4,011
14 Dec	L	Everton	H	2–2	Milligan, Palmer	14,955
21 Dec	L	Chelsea	A	2–4	Marshall 2	13,136
26 Dec	L	Manchester United	H	3–6	Bernard, Sharp, Milligan	18,947
28 Dec	L	Nottingham Forest	H	2–1	Bernard, Sharp	16,496
1 Jan	L	Sheffield Wednesday	A	1–1	Adams	32,679
5 Jan	FAC 3	Leyton Orient	H	1–1	Sharp	10,764
11 Jan	L	Norwich City	A	2–1	Bernard, Holden	10,986
14 Jan	FAC 3 R	Leyton Orient	A	*2–4	Adams, Palmer	10,056
18 Jan	L	Liverpool	H	2–3	Bernard, Adams	18,952
26 Jan	L	Tottenham Hotspur	A	0–0		20,843
1 Feb	L	West Ham United	A	0–1		19,012
8 Feb	L	Leeds United	H	2–0	Bernard, Barlow	18,409
15 Feb	L	Queen's Park Rangers	H	2–1	Jobson, Holden	13,092
22 Feb	L	Aston Villa	A	0–1		20,509
29 Feb	L	Wimbledon	A	0–1		12,166
7 March	L	Everton	A	1–2	Fleming	21,014
10 March	L	Arsenal	A	1–2	Ritchie	22,096
14 March	L	Notts County	H	4–3	Marshall, Holden, Ritchie 2	12,125
21 March	L	Coventry City	A	1–1	Henry	12,840
28 March	L	Sheffield Wednesday	H	3–0	Jobson, Sharp, Adams	15,897
4 April	L	Sheffield United	A	0–2		19,843
11 April	L	Luton Town	H	5–1	Sharp 4, Milligan	13,210
18 April	L	Crystal Palace	A	0–0		12,267
20 April	L	Tottenham Hotspur	H	1–0	Henry	15,443
25 April	L	Southampton	A	0–1		15,857
2 May	L	Manchester City	H	2–5	Henry, Moulden	18,588

Squad members who made first team appearances in 1991–92:
Hallworth
Halle
Snodin
Henry
Barrett
Jobson
Bernard
Marshall
Sharp
Milligan
Holden
Kane
Currie
Adams
Fleming
Kilcline
Ritchie
Keeley
Barlow
McDonald
Palmer
Moulden

* after extra time

Date	Comp	Opponents	Venue	Res	Scorers	Attendance
17 Aug	L	Arsenal	A	1–1	Bailey	38,099
21 Aug	L	Norwich City	H	0–2		10,626
24 Aug	L	Coventry City	H	1–1	Wegerle	9,393
27 Aug	L	Liverpool	A	0–1		32,700
31 Aug	L	Sheffield Wednesday	A	1–4	Bailey	25,022
4 Sept	L	West Ham United	H	0–0		16,616
7 Sept	L	Southampton	H	2–2	Barker, Thompson	9,237
14 Sept	L	Tottenham Hotspur	A	0–2		30,059
17 Sept	L	Luton Town	A	1–0	Barker	9,185
21 Sept	L	Chelsea	H	2–2	Peacock, Wilson	19,579
24 Sept	RC 2/1	Hull City	A	3–0	Barker 2, Thompson	4,979
28 Sept	L	Crystal Palace	A	2–2	Wegerle [pen], Barker	15,372
5 Oct	L	Nottingham Forest	H	0–2		13,508
9 Oct	RC 2/2	Hull City	H	5–1	Bardsley, Bailey 2, Thompson	5,251
19 Oct	L	Wimbledon	A	1–0	Bailey	4,630
22 Oct	ZDS 2	Norwich City	A	2–1	Sinton, Impey	4,436
26 Oct	L	Everton	H	3–1	Bailey, Barker 2	10,002
29 Oct	RC 3	Manchester City	A	0–0		15,512
2 Nov	L	Aston Villa	H	0–1		10,642
16 Nov	L	Leeds United	A	0–2		27,087
20 Nov	RC 3 R	Manchester City	H	1–3	Penrice	11,003
23 Nov	L	Oldham Athletic	H	1–3	Ferdinand	8,947
26 Nov	ZDS 3	Crystal Palace	H	2–3	Bardsley, Wilkins	4,492
30 Nov	L	Notts County	A	1–0	Ferdinand	7,901
7 Dec	L	Sheffield United	H	1–0	Wegerle	10,106
14 Dec	L	Manchester City	A	2–2	Bailey, Wegerle	21,437
21 Dec	L	Norwich City	A	1–0	Bailey	11,436
26 Dec	L	Liverpool	H	0–0		21,693
28 Dec	L	Sheffield Wednesday	H	1–1	Wilkins	12,990
1 Jan	L	Manchester United	A	4–1	Bailey 3, Sinton	38,554
4 Jan	FAC 3	Southampton	A	0–2		13,710
11 Jan	L	Coventry City	A	2–2	Penrice 2	11,999
18 Jan	L	Arsenal	H	0–0		20,497
1 Feb	L	Wimbledon	H	1–1	Penrice	9,149
8 Feb	L	Everton	A	0–0		18,212
15 Feb	L	Oldham Athletic	A	1–2	Wegerle	13,092
22 Feb	L	Notts County	H	1–1	Ferdinand	8,300
29 Feb	L	Sheffield United	A	0–0		17,958
7 March	L	Manchester City	H	4–0	Barker, Ferdinand 2, Wilson [pen]	10,779
11 March	L	Leeds United	H	4–1	Allen, Ferdinand, Sinton, Wilson [pen]	16,641
14 March	L	Aston Villa	A	1–0	Ferdinand	19,630
21 March	L	West Ham United	A	2–2	Allen 2	20,401
28 March	L	Manchester United	H	0–0		22,603
4 April	L	Southampton	A	1–2	Ferdinand	15,205
11 April	L	Tottenham Hotspur	H	1–2	Sinton	20,000
18 April	L	Chelsea	A	1–2	Allen	18,952
20 April	L	Luton Town	H	2–1	Ferdinand 2	10,479
25 April	L	Nottingham Forest	A	1–1	Allen	22,228
2 May	L	Crystal Palace	H	1–0	Humphrey [og]	14,903

Squad members who made first team appearances in 1991–92:

Stejskal
Bardsley
Brevett
Wiikins
Peacock
Maddix
Bailey
Barker
Allen
Ferdinand
Wegerle
Sinton
Holloway
Thompson
Wilson
McDonald
Roberts
Tillson
Iorfa
Walsh
Herrera
Ready
Impey
Penrice
Channing
McCarthy
Meaker

Date	Comp	Opponents	Venue	Res	Scorers	Attendance
17 Aug	L	Norwich City	A	2–2	Hill, Deane	16,380
20 Aug	L	West Ham United	H	1–1	Beesley	21,463
24 Aug	L	Southampton	H	0–2		18,029
28 Aug	L	Coventry City	A	1–3	Bryson	12,601
31 Aug	L	Crystal Palace	A	1–2	Hodges	15,507
3 Sept	L	Chelsea	H	0–1		17,400
7 Sept	L	Oldham Athletic	A	1–2	Deane	15,064
14 Sept	L	Everton	H	2–1	Hoyland, Bryson	19,817
17 Sept	L	Notts County	H	1–3	Agana	19,375
21 Sept	L	Arsenal	A	2–5	Agana, Mendonca	30,244
24 Sept	RC 2/1	Wigan Athletic	A	2–2	Deane 2	3,647
28 Sept	L	Wimbledon	A	0–0		16,062
5 Oct	L	Leeds United	A	3–4	Hoyland, Agana, Bradshaw	28,362
8 Oct	RC 2/2	Wigan Athletic	H	1–0	Hoyland	6,608
19 Oct	L	Nottingham Forest	H	4–2	Hoyland, Whitehouse, Agana, Bryson	23,080
22 Oct	ZDS 2	Notts County	H	*3–3	Whitehouse 2, Gayle	3,291
26 Oct	L	Manchester City	A	2–3	Gayle 2	25,495
29 Oct	RC 3	West Ham United	H	0–2		11,144
2 Nov	L	Manchester United	A	0–2		42,942
17 Nov	L	Sheffield Wednesday	H	2–0	Whitehouse, Deane	31,832
23 Nov	L	Tottenham Hotspur	A	1–0	Deane	28,168
30 Nov	L	Luton Town	H	1–1	Bryson	21,804
7 Dec	L	Queen's Park Rangers	A	0–1		10,106
14 Dec	L	Aston Villa	H	2–0	Ward, McGrath [og]	18,401
21 Dec	L	West Ham United	A	1–1	Deane	19,287
26 Dec	L	Coventry City	H	0–3		19,638
28 Dec	L	Crystal Palace	H	1–1	Hoyland	17,969
1 Jan	L	Liverpool	A	1–2	Deane	35,993
4 Jan	FAC 3	Luton Town	H	4–0	Whitehouse, Deane, Hodges, Lake	12,201
11 Jan	L	Southampton	A	4–2	Lake 2, Ward, Marwood	13,689
18 Jan	L	Norwich City	H	1–0	Bryson	17,549
26 Jan	FAC 4	Charlton Athletic	A	0–0		11,982
1 Feb	L	Nottingham Forest	A	5–2	Deane, Bryson, Lake, Gannon, Bradshaw	22,412
5 Feb	FAC 4 R	Charlton Athletic	H	3–1	Deane, Gayle, Bradshaw	19,000
8 Feb	L	Manchester City	H	4–2	Whitehouse, Deane, Lake, Gayle	22,000
15 Feb	FAC 5	Chelsea	A	0–1		34,447
22 Feb	L	Luton Town	A	1–2	Bryson	9,003
29 Feb	L	Queen's Park Rangers	H	0–0		17,958
11 March	L	Sheffield Wednesday	A	3–1	Whitehouse, Davison 2	40,327
14 March	L	Manchester United	H	1–2	Deane	30,183
21 March	L	Chelsea	A	2–1	Whitehouse 2	11,247
28 March	L	Liverpool	H	2–0	Deane 2	26,943
31 March	L	Aston Villa	A	1–1	Gage	15,745
4 April	L	Oldham Athletic	H	2–0	Whitehouse, Bryson	19,843
11 April	L	Everton	A	2–0	Bryson, Cork	18,285
14 April	L	Tottenham Hotspur	H	2–0	Deane 2	21,526
18 April	L	Arsenal	H	1–1	Davison	25,034
20 April	L	Notts County	A	3–1	Beesley, Hodges, Davison	12,605
26 April	L	Leeds United	H	2–3	Cork, Chapman [og]	32,000
2 May	L	Wimbledon	A	0–3		8,768

Squad members who made first team appearances in 1991–92:

Tracey
Pemberton
Cowan
Jones
Beesley
Hill
Hoyland
Whitehouse
Agana
Deane
Bryson
Booker
Hodges
Wilder
Wood
Littlejohn
Mendonca
Hartfield
Duffield
Lucas
Barnes
Lake
Gayle
Kite
Gannon
Bradshaw
Fickling
Ward
Clarke
Gage
Peel
Marwood
Rogers
Davison
Cork
Rees
Day
Reed

* Sheffield United lost on penalties after extra time

Date	Comp	Opponents	Venue	Res	Scorers	Attendance
17 Aug	L	Aston Villa	H	2–3	Wilson, Hirst	36,749
24 Aug	L	Leeds United	A	1–1	Hirst	30,260
28 Aug	L	Everton	H	2–1	Wilson, Anderson	28,690
31 Aug	L	Queen's Park Rangers	H	4–1	Palmer 3, Sheridan	25,022
3 Sept	L	Notts County	A	1–2	Pearson	12,297
7 Sept	L	Nottingham Forest	H	2–1	Williams, Francis	31,289
14 Sept	L	Manchester City	A	1–0	Williams	29,453
18 Sept	L	Norwich City	A	0–1		12,503
21 Sept	L	Southampton	H	2–0	Williams, Worthington	27,291
24 Sept	RC 2/1	Leyton Orient	A	0–0		6,231
28 Sept	L	Liverpool	A	1–1	Harkes	37,071
2 Oct	L	Wimbledon	A	1–2	Pearson	3,121
5 Oct	L	Crystal Palace	H	4–1	Palmer, Hirst 2, Worthington	26,230
9 Oct	RC 2/2	Leyton Orient	H	4–1	Williams, Francis 2, Anderson	14,398
19 Oct	L	Luton Town	A	2–2	Sheridan, Hirst	9,401
23 Oct	ZDS 2	Manchester City	H	3–2	Hirst, Hyde, Jemson	7,951
26 Oct	L	Manchester United	H	3–2	Hirst, Jemson 2	38.260
29 Oct	RC 3	Southampton	H	1–1	Hirst	17,627
2 Nov	L	Tottenham Hotspur	H	0–0		31,573
17 Nov	L	Sheffield United	A	0–2		31,832
20 Nov	RC 3 R	Southampton	A	0–1		10,801
23 Nov	L	Arsenal	H	1–1	Hirst	32,174
26 Nov	ZDS 3	Notts County	A	0–1		4,118
30 Nov	L	West Ham United	A	2–1	Harkes, Jemson	24,116
7 Dec	L	Chelsea	H	3–0	Hirst 2, Williams	27,383
21 Dec	L	Wimbledon	H	2–0	Sheridan 2 [1 pen]	20,574
26 Dec	L	Everton	A	1–0	Hirst	30,788
28 Dec	L	Queen's Park Rangers	A	1–1	Hirst	12,990
1 Jan	L	Oldham Athletic	H	1–1	Sharp [og]	32,679
4 Jan	FAC 3	Preston	A	2–0	Sheridan [pen], Bart–Williams	14,337
12 Jan	L	Leeds United	H	1–6	Sheridan	32,228
18 Jan	L	Aston Villa	A	1–0	Jemson	28,036
1 Feb	L	Luton Town	H	3–2	Hirst, Williams, Harkes	22,291
4 Feb	FAC 4	Middlesbrough	H	1–2	Hirst	29,772
8 Feb	L	Manchester United	A	1–1	Hirst	47,074
15 Feb	L	Arsenal	A	1–7	Worthington	26,805
22 Feb	L	West Ham United	H	2–1	Palmer, Anderson	26,150
29 Feb	L	Chelsea	A	3–0	Wilson, Williams, Worthington	17,538
7 March	L	Coventry City	H	1–1	Anderson	23,959
11 March	L	Sheffield United	H	1–3	King	40,327
14 March	L	Tottenham Hotspur	A	2–0	Hirst, Williams	23,027
21 March	L	Notts County	H	1–0	Harkes	23,910
28 March	L	Oldham Athletic	A	0–3		15,897
4 April	L	Nottingham Forest	A	2–0	Hirst, Williams	26,105
8 April	L	Coventry City	A	0–0		13,293
11 April	L	Manchester City	H	2–0	Hirst, Worthington	32,138
18 April	L	Southampton	A	1–0	Hirst	17,715
20 April	L	Norwich City	H	2–0	Nilsson	27,362
25 April	L	Crystal Palace	A	1–1	Williams	21,573
2 May	L	Liverpool	H	0–0		34,861

Squad members who made first team appearances in 1991–92:

Woods
Nilsson
King
Palmer
Pearson
Warhurst
Wilson
Sheridan
Hirst
Williams
Worthington
Harkes
Francis
Anderson
Mackenzie
Watson
Hyde
Jemson
Wood
Bart-Williams
Pressman
Shirtliff
Johnson

Date	Comp	Opponents	Venue	Res	Scorers	Attendance
17 Aug	L	Tottenham Hotspur	H	2–3	Hall, Shearer	18,581
20 Aug	L	Notts County	A	0–1		9,613
24 Aug	L	Sheffield United	A	2–0	Le Tissier, Shearer	18,029
28 Aug	L	Leeds United	H	0–4		15,862
31 Aug	L	Aston Villa	H	1–1	Shearer	16,161
4 Sept	L	Luton Town	A	1–2	Le Tissier [pen]	8,055
7 Sept	L	Queen's Park Rangers	A	2–2	Shearer, Dowie	9,237
14 Sept	L	Manchester United	H	0–1		19,264
18 Sept	L	Wimbledon	H	1–0	Cockerill	11,280
21 Sept	L	Sheffield Wednesday	A	0–2		27,291
24 Sept	RC 2/1	Scarborough	A	3–1	Cockerill, Shearer 2	2,302
28 Sept	L	Arsenal	H	0–4		18,050
5 Oct	L	Oldham Athletic	A	1–1	Shearer	13,133
9 Oct	RC 2/2	Scarborough	H	2–2	Le Tissier, Cockerill	4,036
19 Oct	L	Norwich City	H	0–0		12,516
22 Oct	ZDS 2	Bristol City	A	2–1	Le Tissier, Shearer	5,672
26 Oct	L	Nottingham Forest	A	3–1	Le Tissier 2 [1 pen], Shearer	20,026
30 Oct	RC 3	Sheffield Wednesday	A	1–1	Shearer	17,627
2 Nov	L	Manchester City	H	0–3		13,933
16 Nov	L	Crystal Palace	A	0–1		15,806
20 Nov	RC 3 R	Sheffield Wednesday	H	1–0	Horne	10,801
23 Nov	L	Chelsea	H	1–0	Shearer	14,933
26 Nov	ZDS 3	Plymouth Argyle	A	1–0	Le Tissier	5,578
30 Nov	L	Coventry City	A	0–2		8,585
4 Dec	RC 4	Nottingham Forest	A	0–0		17,939
7 Dec	L	Liverpool	H	1–1	Shearer	19,053
17 Dec	RC 4 R	Nottingham Forest	H	0–1		10,861
20 Dec	L	Notts County	H	1–1	Dowie	11,054
26 Dec	L	Leeds United	A	3–3	Shearer, Dowie 2	29,053
28 Dec	L	Aston Villa	A	1–2	Shearer	23,094
1 Jan	L	Everton	H	1–2	Adams	16,546
4 Jan	FAC 3	Queen's Park Rangers	H	2–0	Le Tissier, Wood	13,710
7 Jan	ZDS 4	West Ham United	H	2–1	Le Tissier, Shearer	6,861
11 Jan	L	Sheffield United	H	2–4	Hall, Le Tissier	13,689
18 Jan	L	Tottenham Hotspur	A	2–1	Adams, Dowie	23,191
21 Jan	ZDS SF/1	Chelsea	H	2–0	Shearer, Hurlock	8,726
27 Jan	FAC 4	Manchester United	H	0–0		19,506
29 Jan	ZDS SF/2	Chelsea	A	3–1	Le Tissier 3 [1 pen]	9,781
1 Feb	L	Norwich City	A	1–2	Cockerill	10,660
5 Feb	FAC 4 R	Manchester United	A	**2–2	Shearer, Gray	33,414
12 Feb	L	Chelsea	A	1–1	Horne	7,148
16 Feb	FAC 5	Bolton Wanderers	A	2–2	Hall 2	20,136
22 Feb	L	Coventry City	H	0–0		13,719
26 Feb	FAC 5 R	Bolton Wanderers	H	*3–2	Horne 2, Shearer	18,009
29 Feb	L	Liverpool	A	0–0		34,449
3 March	L	West Ham	H	1–0	Dowie	14,548
7 March	FAC 6	Norwich City	H	0–0		20,088
11 March	L	Crystal Palace	H	1–0	Le Tissier	12,926
15 March	L	Manchester City	H	1–0	Dowie	24,265
18 March	FAC 6 R	Norwich City	A	*1–2	Ruddock	21,017
21 March	L	Luton Town	H	2–1	Shearer, Dowie	15,313
29 March	ZDS F	Nottingham Forest	Wembley	*2–3	Le Tissier, Moore	67,688
1 April	L	Everton	A	1–0	Cockerill	15,201
4 April	L	Queen's Park Rangers	H	2–1	Shearer [pen], Dowie	15,205
8 April	L	Nottingham Forest	H	0–1		14,905
14 April	L	West Ham United	A	1–0	Adams	18,298
16 April	L	Manchester United	A	0–1		43,972
18 April	L	Sheffield Wednesday	H	0–1		17,715
20 April	L	Wimbledon	A	1–0	Hall	4,025
25 April	L	Oldham Athletic	H	1–0	Shearer	15,857
2 May	L	Arsenal	A	1–5	Cockerill	37,702

Squad members who made first team appearances in 1991–92:

Flowers
Dodd
Osman
Horne
Hall
Ruddock
Le Tissier
Cockerill
Shearer
Rideout
Adams
Moody
McLaughlin
Lee
Benali
Banger
Dowie
Gittens
Hurlock
Andrews
Gray
Wood
Moore
Davies
Kenna
Maddison
Gilkes
Powell
Widdrington
Bound

* after extra time
** Southampton won on penalties after extra time

Date	Comp	Opponents	Venue	Res	Scorers	Attendance
17 Aug	L	Southampton	A	3–2	Lineker 2, Durie	18,581
21 Aug	ECWC Prem/1	SV Stockerau	A	1–0	Durie	15,500
24 Aug	L	Chelsea	H	1–3	Lineker	34,645
28 Aug	L	Nottingham Forest	A	3–1	Lineker, Durie, Bergsson	24,018
31 Aug	L	Norwich City	A	1–0	Lineker	19,460
4 Sept	ECWC Prem/2	SV Stockerau	H	1–0	Mabbutt	28,072
7 Sept	L	Aston Villa	A	0–0		33,096
14 Sept	L	Queen's Park Rangers	H	2–0	Lineker 2	30,059
17 Sept	ECWC 1/1	Hajduk Split	A	0–1		7,000
21 Sept	L	Wimbledon	A	5–3	Lineker 4 [1 pen], Samways	11,927
25 Sept	RC 2/1	Swansea City	A	0–1		11,416
28 Sept	L	Manchester United	H	1–2	Durie	35,087
2 Oct	ECWC 1/2	Hajduk Split	H	2–0	Tuttle, Durie	24,297
5 Oct	L	Everton	A	1–3	Lineker	29,505
9 Oct	RC 2/2	Swansea City	H	5–1	Stewart, Samways, Lineker [pen], Allen, Brazil [og]	20,198
19 Oct	L	Manchester City	H	0–1		30,102
23 Oct	ECWC 2/1	Porto	H	3–1	Lineker 2, Durie	23,621
26 Oct	L	West Ham United	A	1–2	Lineker	23,946
29 Oct	RC 3	Grimsby Town	A	3–0	Howells, Durie, Lineker	17,017
2 Nov	L	Sheffield Wednesday	A	0–0		31,573
7 Nov	ECWC 2/2	Porto	H	0–0		55,000
16 Nov	L	Luton Town	H	4–1	Lineker 2, Houghton 2	27,543
23 Nov	L	Sheffield United	H	0–1		28,168
1 Dec	L	Arsenal	A	0–2		38,892
4 Dec	RC 4	Coventry City	A	2–1	Allen, Durie	20,095
7 Dec	L	Notts County	H	2–1	Mabbutt, Walsh	23,364
14 Dec	L	Leeds United	A	1–1	Howells	31,404
18 Dec	L	Liverpool	H	1–2	Walsh	27,434
22 Dec	L	Crystal Palace	A	2–1	Lineker, Walsh	22,491
26 Dec	L	Nottingham Forest	H	1–2	Stewart	31,079
28 Dec	L	Norwich City	H	3–0	Lineker, Allen, Nayim	27,969
1 Jan	L	Coventry City	A	2–1	Stewart, Lineker	19,639
5 Jan	FAC 3	Aston Villa	A	0–0		29,316
8 Jan	RC 5	Norwich City	H	2–1	Walsh, Lineker	29,471
11 Jan	L	Chelsea	A	0–2		28,268
13 Jan	FAC 3 R	Aston Villa	H	0–1		25,462
18 Jan	L	Southampton	H	1–2	Mabbutt	23,191
25 Jan	L	Oldham Athletic	H	0–0		20,843
1 Feb	L	Manchester City	A	0–1		30,123
9 Feb	RC SF/1	Nottingham Forest	A	1–1	Lineker [pen]	21,402
16 Feb	L	Crystal Palace	H	0–1		19,834
22 Feb	L	Arsenal	H	1–1	Stewart	33,124
1 March	RC SF/2	Nottingham Forest	H	*1–2	Lineker	28,216
4 March	ECWC 3/1	Feyenoord	A	0–1		48,000
7 March	L	Leeds United	H	1–3	Allen	27,622
11 March	L	Luton Town	A	0–0		11,494
14 March	L	Sheffield Wednesday	H	0–2		23,027
18 March	ECWC 3/2	Feyenoord	H	0–0		29,834
21 March	L	Liverpool	A	1–2	Stewart	36,968
28 March	L	Coventry City	H	4–3	Durie 3, Lineker	22,744
1 April	L	West Ham United	H	3–0	Lineker 3 [1 pen]	31,809
4 April	L	Aston Villa	H	2–5	Lineker, Teale [og]	26,370
7 April	L	Notts County	A	2–0	Lineker 2	9,205
11 April	L	Queen's Park Rangers	A	2–1	Gray, Wilson [og]	20,000
14 April	L	Sheffield United	A	0–2		21,526
18 April	L	Wimbledon	H	3–2	Lineker 2, Hendry	23,934
20 April	L	Oldham Athletic	A	0–1		15,443
25 April	L	Everton	H	3–3	Stewart, Allen, Minton	34,630
2 May	L	Manchester United	A	1–3	Lineker	44,545

Squad members who made first team appearances in 1991–92:

Thorstvedt
Fenwick
Van den Hauwe
Sedgley
Howells
Mabbutt
Stewart
Durie
Samways
Lineker
Allen
Nayim
Bergsson
Hendon
Walker
Hendry
Moran
Moncur
Houghton
Tuttle
Edinburgh
Walsh
Gray
Cundy
Minton

* after extra time

Date	Comp	Opponents	Venue	Res	Scorers	Attendance
17 Aug	L	Chelsea	A	2–2	Earle, Fashanu	22,574
24 Aug	L	West Ham United	H	2–0	Earle, Fashanu	10,081
27 Aug	L	Crystal Palace	A	2–3	Earle, Fashanu	16,340
31 Aug	L	Coventry City	A	1–0	Cork	9,469
3 Sept	L	Manchester United	H	1–2	Fashanu	13,824
7 Sept	L	Luton Town	H	3–0	Ryan 2, Clarke	3,231
14 Sept	L	Nottingham Forest	A	2–4	McGee, Fashanu [pen]	19,707
18 Sept	L	Southampton	A	0–1		11,280
21 Sept	L	Tottenham Hotspur	H	3–5	Fashanu [pen], Cork, Bennett	11,927
24 Sept	RC 2/1	Peterborough	H	1–2	McGee	2,081
28 Sept	L	Sheffield United	A	0–0		16,062
2 Oct	L	Sheffield Wednesday	H	2–1	Blackwell, Newhouse	3,121
5 Oct	L	Norwich City	H	3–1	Fitzgerald, Fashanu, Clarke	3,531
9 Oct	RC 2/2	Peterborough United	A	2–2	Fashanu [pen], Clarke	5,939
19 Oct	L	Queen's Park Rangers	H	0–1		4,630
23 Oct	ZDS 2	Brighton	A	2–3	Earle, Scales	2,796
26 Oct	L	Aston Villa	A	1–2	Fashanu	16,928
2 Nov	L	Leeds United	H	0–0		7,025
16 Nov	L	Everton	A	0–2		18,762
23 Nov	L	Liverpool	H	0–0		13,373
30 Nov	L	Manchester City	A	0–0		22,429
7 Dec	L	Oldham Athletic	H	2–1	Earle 2	4,011
21 Dec	L	Sheffield Wednesday	A	0–2		20,574
26 Dec	L	Crystal Palace	H	1–1	Barton	15,009
28 Dec	L	Coventry City	H	1–1	Earle	3,270
1 Jan	L	Arsenal	A	1–1	Miller	26,839
4 Jan	FAC 3	Bristol City	A	1–1	Fashanu	12,679
11 Jan	L	West Ham United	A	1–1	Sanchez	18,485
14 Jan	FAC 3 R	Bristol City	H	0–1		3,747
18 Jan	L	Chelsea	H	1–2		8,467
1 Feb	L	Queen's Park Rangers	A	1–1		9,194
8 Feb	L	Aston Villa	H	2–0	Phelan, Fashanu	5,534
22 Feb	L	Manchester City	H	2–1	Earle, Fashanu	5,802
25 Feb	L	Notts County	A	1–1	Fashanu [pen]	6,198
29 Feb	L	Oldham Athletic	A	1–0	McGee	12,166
7 March	L	Notts County	H	2–0	Earle, Fashanu	4,196
10 March	L	Everton	H	0–0		3,569
14 March	L	Leeds United	A	1–5	Miller	26,760
21 March	L	Manchester United	A	0–0		45,428
28 March	L	Arsenal	H	1–3	Earle	11,299
2 April	L	Nottingham Forest	H	3–0	Earle, Fashanu 2	3,542
4 April	L	Luton Town	A	1–2	Fashanu	7,754
8 April	L	Liverpool	A	3–2	Fashanu [pen], Clarke, Sanchez	26,134
18 April	L	Tottenham Hotspur	A	2–3	Earle, Sanchez	23,934
20 April	L	Southampton	H	0–1		4,025
25 April	L	Norwich City	A	1–1	Elkins	11,061
2 May	L	Sheffield United	H	3–0	Earle 2, Clarke	8,768

Squad members who made first team appearances in 1991–92:

Segers
Joseph
Phelan
Earle
Scales
Blackwell
Fitzgerald
Ryan
McGee
Fashanu
Barton
Cork
Clarke
Fairweather
Elkins
Newhouse
Ardley
Gibson
Kruszynski
Bennett
Anthrobus
Miller
Sanchez
McAllister
Dobbs
Hayes
Sullivan
Cosover
Castledine

		P	HOME					AWAY					Pts	Goal Diff
		P	W	D	L	F	A	W	D	L	F	A	Pts	Diff
BARCLAYS	Leeds United	42	13	8	0	38	13	9	8	4	36	24	82	37+
LEAGUE	Manchester United	42	12	7	2	34	13	9	8	4	29	30	78	30+
DIVISION 1	Sheffield Wednesday	42	13	5	3	39	24	8	7	6	23	25	75	13+
	Arsenal	42	12	7	2	51	22	7	8	6	30	24	72	35+
	Manchester City	42	13	4	4	32	14	7	6	8	29	34	70	13+
	Liverpool	42	13	5	3	34	17	3	11	7	13	23	64	7+
	Aston Villa	42	13	3	5	31	16	4	6	11	17	28	60	4+
	Nottingham Forest	42	10	7	4	36	27	6	4	11	24	31	59	2+
	Sheffield United	42	9	6	6	29	23	7	3	11	36	40	57	2+
	Crystal Palace	42	7	8	6	24	25	7	7	7	29	36	57	8–
	Queen's Park Rangers	42	6	10	5	25	21	6	8	7	23	26	54	1+
	Everton	42	8	8	5	28	19	5	6	10	24	32	53	1+
	Wimbledon	42	10	5	6	32	20	3	9	9	21	33	53	0
	Chelsea	42	7	8	6	31	30	6	6	9	19	30	53	10–
	Tottenham Hotspur	42	7	3	11	33	35	8	4	9	25	28	52	5–
	Southampton	42	7	5	9	17	28	7	5	9	22	27	52	16–
	Oldham Athletic	42	11	5	5	46	36	3	4	14	17	31	51	4–
	Norwich City	42	8	6	7	29	28	3	6	12	18	35	45	16–
	Coventry City	42	6	7	8	18	15	5	4	12	17	29	44	9–
	Luton Town	42	10	7	4	25	17	0	5	16	13	54	42	33–
	Notts County	42	7	5	9	24	29	3	5	13	16	33	40	22–
	West Ham United	42	6	6	9	22	24	3	5	13	15	35	38	22–
BARCLAYS	Ipswich Town	46	16	3	4	42	22	8	9	6	28	28	84	20+
LEAGUE	Middlesbrough	46	15	6	2	37	13	8	5	10	21	28	80	17+
DIVISION 2	Derby County	46	11	4	8	35	24	12	5	6	34	27	78	18+
	Leicester City	46	14	4	5	41	24	9	4	10	21	31	77	7+
	Cambridge United	46	10	9	4	34	19	9	8	6	31	28	74	18+
	* Blackburn Rovers	46	14	5	4	41	21	7	6	10	29	32	74	17+
	Charlton Athletic	46	9	7	7	25	23	11	4	8	29	25	71	6+
	Swindon Town	46	15	3	5	38	22	3	12	8	31	33	69	14+
	Portsmouth	46	15	6	2	41	12	4	6	13	24	39	69	14+
	Watford	46	9	5	9	25	23	9	6	8	26	25	65	3+
	Wolverhampton Wanderers	46	11	6	6	36	24	7	4	12	25	30	64	7+
	Southend United	46	11	5	7	37	26	6	6	11	26	37	62	0
	Bristol Rovers	46	11	9	3	43	29	5	5	13	17	34	62	3–
	Tranmere Rovers	46	9	9	5	37	32	5	10	8	19	24	61	0
	Millwall	46	10	4	9	32	32	7	6	10	32	39	61	7–
	Barnsley	46	11	4	8	27	25	5	7	11	19	32	59	11–
	Bristol City	46	10	8	5	30	24	3	7	13	25	47	54	16–
	Sunderland	46	10	8	5	36	23	4	3	16	25	42	53	4–
	Grimsby Town	46	7	5	11	25	28	7	6	10	22	34	53	15–
	Newcastle United	46	9	8	6	38	30	4	5	14	28	54	52	18–
	Oxford United	46	10	6	7	39	30	3	5	15	27	43	50	7–
	Plymouth Argyle	46	11	5	7	26	26	2	4	17	16	38	48	22–
	Brighton & Hove Albion	46	7	7	9	36	37	5	4	14	20	40	47	21–
	Port Vale	46	7	8	8	23	25	3	7	13	19	34	45	17–

* *Blackburn Rovers promoted via play-offs*

				HOME					AWAY						Goal
		P	W	D	L	F	A	W	D	L	F	A	Pts	Diff
BARCLAYS	Brentford	46	17	2	4	55	29	8	5	10	26	26	82	26+
LEAGUE	Birmingham City	46	15	6	2	42	22	8	6	9	27	30	81	17+
DIVISION 3	Huddersfield Town	46	15	4	4	36	15	7	8	8	23	23	78	21+
	Stoke City	46	14	5	4	45	24	7	9	7	24	25	77	20+
	Stockport County	46	15	5	3	47	19	7	5	11	28	32	76	24+
	* Peterborough United	46	13	7	3	38	20	7	7	9	27	38	74	7+
	West Bromwich Albion	46	12	6	5	45	25	7	8	8	19	24	71	15+
	AFC Bournemouth	46	13	4	6	33	18	7	7	9	19	30	71	4+
	Fulham	46	11	7	5	29	16	8	6	9	23	37	70	1–
	Leyton Orient	46	12	7	4	36	18	6	4	13	26	34	65	10+
	Hartlepool United	46	12	5	6	30	21	6	6	11	27	36	65	0
	Reading	46	9	8	6	33	27	7	5	11	26	35	61	3–
	Bolton Wanderers	46	10	9	4	26	19	4	8	11	31	37	59	1+
	Hull City	46	9	4	10	28	23	7	7	9	26	31	59	0
	Wigan Athletic	46	11	6	6	33	21	4	8	11	25	43	59	6–
	Bradford City	46	8	10	5	36	30	5	9	9	26	31	58	1+
	Preston North End	46	12	7	4	42	32	3	5	15	19	40	57	11–
	Chester City	46	10	6	7	34	29	4	8	11	22	30	56	3–
	Swansea City	46	10	9	4	35	24	4	5	14	20	41	56	10–
	Exeter City	46	11	7	5	34	25	3	4	16	23	55	53	23–
	Bury	46	8	7	8	31	31	5	5	13	24	43	51	19–
	Shrewsbury Town	46	7	7	9	30	31	5	4	14	23	37	47	15–
	Torquay United	46	13	3	7	29	19	0	5	18	13	49	47	26–
	Darlington	46	5	5	13	31	39	5	2	16	25	51	37	34–
BARCLAYS	Burnley	42	14	4	3	42	16	11	4	6	37	27	83	36+
LEAGUE	Rotherham United	42	12	6	3	38	16	10	5	6	32	21	77	33+
DIVISION 4	Mansfield Town	42	13	4	4	43	26	10	4	7	32	27	77	22+
	** Blackpool	42	17	3	1	48	13	5	7	9	23	32	76	26+
	Scunthorpe United	42	14	5	2	39	18	7	4	10	25	41	72	5+
	Crewe Alexandra	42	12	6	3	33	20	8	4	9	33	31	70	15+
	Barnet	42	16	1	4	48	23	5	5	11	33	38	69	20+
	Rochdale	42	12	6	3	34	22	6	7	8	23	31	67	4+
	Cardiff City	42	13	3	5	42	26	4	12	5	24	27	66	13+
	Lincoln City	42	9	5	7	21	24	8	6	7	29	20	62	6+
	Gillingham	42	12	5	4	41	19	3	7	11	22	34	57	10+
	Scarborough	42	12	5	4	39	28	3	7	11	25	40	57	4–
	Chesterfield	42	6	7	8	26	28	8	4	9	23	33	53	12–
	Wrexham	42	11	4	6	31	26	3	5	13	21	47	51	21–
	Walsall	42	5	10	6	28	26	7	3	11	20	32	49	10–
	Northampton Town	42	5	9	7	25	23	6	4	11	21	34	46	11–
	Hereford United	42	9	4	8	31	24	3	4	14	13	33	44	13–
	Maidstone United	42	6	9	6	24	22	2	9	10	21	34	42	11–
	York City	42	6	9	6	26	23	2	7	12	16	35	40	16–
	Halifax Town	42	7	5	9	23	35	3	3	15	11	40	38	41–
	Doncaster Rovers	42	6	2	13	21	35	3	6	12	19	30	35	25–
	Carlisle United	42	5	9	7	24	27	2	4	15	17	40	34	26–

    * *Peterborough United promoted via play-offs*
  ** *Blackpool promoted via play-offs*

Aldershot disbanded, all results removed
Colchester United promoted from GM Vauxhall Conference

DIVISION TWO

1st legs, 10 May
Blackburn Rovers 4 (Sellars, Newell, Speedie 2), Derby County 2 (Gabbiadini, Johnson). (Attendance 19,677)
Cambridge United 1 (O'Shea), Leicester City 1 (Russell). (Attendance 9,225)

2nd legs, 13 May
Derby County 2 (Comyn, McMinn), Blackburn Rovers 1 (Moran). (Attendance 22,920)
Leicester City 5 (Wright 2, Thompson, Russell, Ormondroyd), Cambridge United 0. (Attendance 21,024)

Final, 25 May at Wembley
Blackburn Rovers 1 (Newell [pen]), Leicester City 0. (Attendance 68,147)

DIVISION THREE

1st leg, 10 May
Stockport County 1 (Ward), Stoke City 0. (Attendance 7,537)

1st leg, 11 May
Peterborough United 2 (Charnley, Halsall), Huddersfield Town 2 (Onuora, Robinson og). (Attendance 11,751)

2nd leg, 13 May
Stoke City 1 (Stein), Stockport County 1 (Beaumont). (Attendance 16,170)

2nd leg, 14 May
Huddersfield Town 1 (Starbuck), Peterborough United 2 (Sterling, Cooper). (Attendance 16, 167)

Final, 24 May at Wembley
Peterborough United 2 (Charnley 2), Stockport County 1 (Francis). (Attendance 35, 087)

DIVISION FOUR

1st legs, 10 May
Barnet 1 (Carter), Blackpool 0. (Attendance 5,629)
Crewe Alexandra 2 (Hignett, Naylor), Scunthorpe United 2 (Helliwell 2). (Attendance 6,083)

2nd legs, 13 May
Blackpool 2 (Groves, Garner [pen]), Barnet 0. (Attendance 7,588)
Scunthorpe United 2 (Martin, Hamilton), Crewe Alexandra 0. (Attendance 7,938)

Final, 23 May at Wembley
Blackpool 1 (Bamber), Scunthorpe United 1 (Daws) after extra time. Blackpool won 4–3 on penalties. (Attendance 22,741)

1991–92 HONOURS

Division One:
Champions: Leeds United (£100,000)
Runners-up: Manchester United (£50,000)
UEFA Cup place: Sheffield Wednesday
Relegated: Luton Town, Notts County, West Ham United.

Division Two:
Champions: Ipswich Town (£50,000)
Runners-up: Middlesbrough (£25,000)
Promoted from play-offs: Blackburn Rovers
Relegated: Plymouth Argyle, Brighton & Hove Albion, Port Vale

Division Three:
Champions: Brentford (£25,000)
Runners-up: Birmingham City (£10,000)
Promoted from play-offs: Peterborough United
Relegated: Bury, Shrewsbury Town, Torquay United, Darlington

Division Four:
Champions: Burnley (£25,000)
Runners-up: Rotherham United (£10,000)
Third: Mansfield Town (£5,000)
Promoted from play-offs: Blackpool
Promoted from GM Vauxhall Conference: Colchester United

FA Cup winners: Liverpool.
Rumbelows Cup winners: Manchester United (£100,000).
Zenith Data Systems Cup winners: Nottingham Forest (£100,000).

FOOTBALL LEAGUE CHAMPIONS 1888–1992

Year	Team	Points	Year	Team	Points	League titles
1888–89	Preston	40	1946–47	Liverpool	57	Liverpool 18
1889–90	Preston	33	1947–48	Arsenal	59	Arsenal 10
1890–91	Everton	29	1948–49	Portsmouth	58	Everton 9
1891–92	Sunderland	42	1949–50	Portsmouth	53	Manchester United 7
1892–93	Sunderland	48	1950–51	Tottenham Hotspur	60	Aston Villa 7
1893–94	Aston Villa	44	1951–52	Manchester United	57	Sunderland 6
1894–95	Sunderland	47	1952–53	Arsenal	54	Newcastle United 4
1895–96	Aston Villa	45	1953–54	Wolverhampton Wanderers	57	Sheffield Wednesday 4
1896–97	Aston Villa	47	1954–55	Chelsea	52	Huddersfield 3
1897–98	Sheffield United	42	1955–56	Manchester United	60	Wolverhampton Wanderers 3
1898–99	Aston Villa	45	1956–57	Manchester United	64	Leeds United 3
1899–1900	Aston Villa	50	1957–58	Wolverhampton Wanderers	64	Blackburn Rovers 2
1900–01	Liverpool	45	1958–59	Wolverhampton Wanderers	61	Portsmouth 2
1901–02	Sunderland	44	1959–60	Burnley	55	Preston 2
1902–03	Sheffield Wednesday	42	1960–61	Tottenham Hotspur	66	Burnley 2
1903–04	Sheffield Wednesday	47	1961–62	Ipswich Town	56	Manchester City 2
1904–05	Newcastle United	48	1962–63	Everton	61	Tottenham Hotspur 2
1905–06	Liverpool	51	1963–64	Liverpool	57	Derby County 2
1906–07	Newcastle United	51	1964–65	Manchester United	61	Chelsea 1
1907–08	Manchester United	52	1965–66	Liverpool	61	Sheffield United 1
1908–09	Newcastle United	53	1966–67	Manchester United	60	West Bromwich Albion 1
1909–10	Aston Villa	53	1967–68	Manchester City	58	Ipswich Town 1
1910–11	Manchester United	52	1968–69	Leeds United	67	Nottingham Forest 1
1911–12	Blackburn Rovers	49	1969–70	Everton	66	
1912–13	Sunderland	54	1970–71	Arsenal	65	
1913–14	Blackburn Rovers	51	1971–72	Derby County	58	
1914–15	Everton	46	1972–73	Liverpool	60	
1919–20	West Bromwich Albion	60	1973–74	Leeds United	62	
1920–21	Burnley	59	1974–75	Derby County	53	
1921–22	Liverpool	57	1975–76	Liverpool	60	
1922–23	Liverpool	60	1976–77	Liverpool	57	
1923–24	Huddersfield	57	1977–78	Nottingham Forest	64	
1924–25	Huddersfield	58	1978–79	Liverpool	68	
1925–26	Huddersfield	57	1979–80	Liverpool	60	
1926–27	Newcastle United	56	1980–81	Aston Villa	60	
1927–28	Everton	53	1981–82	Liverpool	87	
1928–29	Sheffield Wednesday	52	1982–83	Liverpool	82	
1929–30	Sheffield Wednesday	60	1983–84	Liverpool	80	
1930–31	Arsenal	66	1984–85	Everton	90	
1931–32	Everton	56	1985–86	Liverpool	88	
1932–33	Arsenal	58	1986–87	Everton	86	
1933–34	Arsenal	59	1987–88	Liverpool	90	
1934–35	Arsenal	58	1988–89	Arsenal	76	
1935–36	Sunderland	56	1989–90	Liverpool	79	
1936–37	Manchester City	57	1990–91	Arsenal	83	
1937–38	Arsenal	52	1991–92	Leeds United	82	
1938–39	Everton	59				

Barclays Young Eagle of the Year 1992

Roy Keane, of Nottingham Forest, was elected the 1992 Barclays Young Eagle of the Year by a committee chaired by England manager Graham Taylor and including Jack Charlton, Jimmy Armfield, Stan Cullis, Trevor Cherry, Bill Nicholson, Bill Dodgin and Terry Yorath.

In naming the lad snapped up from Cobh Ramblers for £25,000 by Brian Clough, the England manager Taylor said: 'I saw Roy make his debut for Nottingham Forest at Anfield against Liverpool in August 1990. He ended up running last season's winner, Lee Sharpe, very close and he has now convinced me that he has earned this year's award for his consistency over a two-year period.

'Some youngsters, and sometimes even the more experienced players, excel for one season, but a lot of them then find it hard to build on that the following year. But that is what Roy Keane has done.

'Not only is he good from box to box and a good passer of the ball – he knows how to intercept and tackle, he scores goals and I don't think that you can ask for much more from a young player.'

Football Writers' Association Footballer of the Year 1948–92

1948 Stanley Matthews (Blackpool)
1949 Johnny Carey (Manchester United)
1950 Joe Mercer (Arsenal)
1951 Harry Johnston (Blackpool)
1952 Billy Wright (Wolverhampton Wanderers)
1953 Nat Lofthouse (Bolton Wanderers)
1954 Tom Finney (Preston North End)
1955 Don Revie (Manchester City)
1956 Bert Trautmann (Manchester City)
1957 Tom Finney (Preston North End)
1958 Danny Blanchflower (Tottenham Hotspur)
1959 Syd Owen (Luton Town)
1960 Bill Slater (Wolverhampton Wanderers)

1961 Danny Blanchflower (Tottenham Hotspur)
1962 Jimmy Adamson (Burnley)
1963 Stanley Matthews (Stoke City)
1964 Bobby Moore (West Ham United)
1965 Bobby Collins (Leeds United)
1966 Bobby Charlton (Manchester United)
1967 Jackie Charlton (Leeds United)
1968 George Best (Manchester United)
1969 Dave Mackay (Derby County) shared with Tony Book (Manchester City)
1970 Billy Bremner (Leeds United)
1971 Frank McLintock (Arsenal)
1972 Gordon Banks (Stoke City)
1973 Pat Jennings (Tottenham Hotspur)
1974 Ian Callaghan (Liverpool)
1975 Alan Mullery (Fulham)
1976 Kevin Keegan (Liverpool)
1977 Emlyn Hughes (Liverpool)
1978 Kenny Burns (Nottingham Forest)
1979 Kenny Dalglish (Liverpool)
1980 Terry McDermott (Liverpool)
1981 Frans Thijssen (Ipswich Town)
1982 Steve Perryman (Tottenham Hotspur)
1983 Kenny Dalglish (Liverpool)
1984 Ian Rush (Liverpool)
1985 Neville Southall (Everton)
1986 Gary Lineker (Everton)
1987 Clive Allen (Tottenham Hotspur)
1988 John Barnes (Liverpool)
1989 Steve Nicol (Liverpool)
1990 John Barnes (Liverpool)
1991 Gordon Strachan (Leeds United)
1992 Gary Lineker (Tottenham Hotspur).

PFA Footballer of the Year 1974–92

1974 Norman Hunter (Leeds United)
1975 Colin Todd (Derby County)
1976 Pat Jennings (Tottenham Hotspur)
1977 Andy Gray (Aston Villa)
1978 Peter Shilton (Nottingham Forest)
1979 Liam Brady (Arsenal)
1980 Terry McDermott (Liverpool)
1981 John Wark (Ipswich Town)
1982 Kevin Keegan (Southampton)
1983 Kenny Dalglish (Liverpool)
1984 Ian Rush (Liverpool)

1985 Peter Reid (Everton)
1986 Gary Lineker (Everton)
1987 Clive Allen (Tottenham Hotspur)
1988 John Barnes (Liverpool)
1989 Mark Hughes (Manchester United)
1990 David Platt (Aston Villa)
1991 Mark Hughes (Manchester United)
1992 Gary Pallister (Manchester United)

Young Player of the Year 1974–92

1974 Kevin Beattie (Ipswich Town)
1975 Mervyn Day (West Ham United)
1976 Peter Barnes (Manchester City)
1977 Andy Gray (Aston Villa)
1978 Tony Woodcock (Nottingham Forest)
1979 Cyrille Regis (West Bromwich Albion)
1980 Glenn Hoddle (Tottenham Hotspur)
1981 Gary Shaw (Aston Villa)
1982 Steve Moran (Southampton)
1983 Ian Rush (Liverpool)
1984 Paul Walsh (Luton Town)
1985 Mark Hughes (Manchester United)
1986 Tony Cottee (West Ham United)
1987 Tony Adams (Arsenal)
1988 Paul Gascoigne (Newcastle United)
1989 Paul Merson (Arsenal)
1990 Matthew Le Tissier (Southampton)
1991 Lee Sharpe (Manchester United)
1992 Ryan Giggs (Manchester United)

Year	Winners		Runners-up	Result
1872	Wanderers	v	Royal Engineers	1–0
1873	Wanderers	v	Oxford University	2–0
1874	Oxford University	v	Royal Engineers	2–0
1875	Royal Engineers	v	Old Etonians	2–0 after 1–1 draw
1876	Wanderers	v	Old Etonians	3–0 after 0–0 draw
1877	Wanderers	v	Oxford University	2–0 after extra time
1878	Wanderers*	v	Royal Engineers	3–1
1879	Old Etonians	v	Clapham Rovers	1–0
1880	Clapham Rovers	v	Oxford University	1–0
1881	Old Carthusians	v	Old Etonians	3–0
1882	Old Etonians	v	Blackburn Rovers	1–0
1883	Blackburn Olympic	v	Old Etonians	2–1 after extra time
1884	Blackburn Rovers	v	Queen`s Park, Glasgow	2–1
1885	Blackburn Rovers	v	Queen`s Park, Glasgow	2–0
1886	Blackburn Rovers**	v	West Bromwich Albion	2–0 after 0–0 draw
1887	Aston Villa	v	West Bromwich Albion	2–0
1888	West Bromwich Albion	v	Preston North End	2–1
1889	Preston North End	v	Wolverhampton Wanderers	3–0
1890	Blackburn Rovers	v	Sheffield Wednesday	6–1
1891	Blackburn Rovers	v	Notts County	3–1
1892	West Bromwich Albion	v	Aston Villa	3–0
1893	Wolverhampton Wanderers	v	Everton	1–0
1894	Notts County	v	Bolton Wanderers	4–1
1895	Aston Villa	v	West Bromwich Albion	1–0
1896	Sheffield Wednesday	v	Wolverhampton Wanderers	2–1
1897	Aston Villa	v	Everton	3–2
1898	Nottingham Forest	v	Derby County	3–1
1899	Sheffield United	v	Derby County	4–1
1900	Bury	v	Southampton	4–0
1901	Tottenham Hotspur	v	Sheffield United	3–1 after 2–2 draw
1902	Sheffield United	v	Southampton	2–1 after 1–1 draw
1903	Bury	v	Derby County	6–0
1904	Manchester City	v	Bolton Wanderers	1–0
1905	Aston Villa	v	Newcastle United	2–0
1906	Everton	v	Newcastle United	1–0
1907	Sheffield Wednesday	v	Everton	2–1
1908	Wolverhampton Wanderers	v	Newcastle United	3–1
1909	Manchester United	v	Bristol City	1–0
1910	Newcastle United	v	Barnsley	2–0 after 1–1 draw
1911	Bradford City	v	Newcastle United	1–0 after 0–0 draw
1912	Barnsley	v	West Bromwich Albion	1–0 after 0–0 draw
1913	Aston Villa	v	Sunderland	1–0
1914	Burnley	v	Liverpool	1–0
1915	Sheffield United	v	Chelsea	3–0
1920	Aston Villa	v	Huddersfield Town	1–0 after extra time
1921	Tottenham Hotspur	v	Wolverhampton Wanderers	1–0
1922	Huddersfield Town	v	Preston North End	1–0
1923	Bolton Wanderers	v	West Ham United	2–0
1924	Newcastle United	v	Aston Villa	2–0
1925	Sheffield United	v	Cardiff City	1–0
1926	Bolton Wanderers	v	Manchester City	1–0
1927	Cardiff City	v	Arsenal	1–0
1928	Blackburn Rovers	v	Huddersfield Town	3–1
1929	Bolton Wanderers	v	Portsmouth	2–0
1930	Arsenal	v	Huddersfield Town	2–0
1931	West Bromwich Albion	v	Birmingham	2–1

Venues:	
1872	Kennington Oval
1873	Lillie Bridge, London
1874–92	Kennington Oval
1886	Replay at Derby
1893	Fallowfield, Manchester
1894	Goodison Park, Liverpool
1895–1914	Crystal Palace
1901	Replay at Bolton
1910	Replay at Goodison Park, Liverpool
1911	Replay at Old Trafford, Manchester
1912	Replay at Bramall Lane, Sheffield
1915	Old Trafford, Manchester
1920–22	Stamford Bridge, London
1923 to date	Wembley Stadium

* Won outright but restored to the Association

** A special trophy was awarded for third consecutive win

FA CUP WINNERS: 1872–1992

Year	Winners		Runners-up	Result	Venues:	
1932	Newcastle United	v	Arsenal	2–1	1923 to date	Wembley Stadium
1933	Everton	v	Manchester City	3–0	1970	Replay at Old Trafford,
1934	Manchester City	v	Portsmouth	2–1		Manchester
1935	Sheffield Wednesday	v	West Bromwich Albion	4–2	1981	Replay at Wembley
1936	Arsenal	v	Sheffield United	1–0	1982	Replay at Wembley
1937	Sunderland	v	Preston North End	3–1	1983	Replay at Wembley
1938	Preston North End	v	Huddersfield Town	1–0 after extra time	1990	Replay at Wembley
1939	Portsmouth	v	Wolverhampton Wanderers	4–1		
1946	Derby County	v	Charlton Athletic	4–1 after extra time		
1947	Charlton Athletic	v	Burnley	1–0 after extra time		
1948	Manchester United	v	Blackpool	4–2		
1949	Wolverhampton Wanderers	v	Leicester City	3–1		
1950	Arsenal	v	Liverpool	2–0		
1951	Newcastle United	v	Blackpool	2–0		
1952	Newcastle United	v	Arsenal	1–0		
1953	Blackpool	v	Bolton Wanderers	4–3		
1954	West Bromwich Albion	v	Preston North End	3–2		
1955	Newcastle United	v	Manchester City	3–1		
1956	Manchester City	v	Birmingham City	3–1		
1957	Aston Villa	v	Manchester United	2–1		
1958	Bolton Wanderers	v	Manchester United	2–0		
1959	Nottingham Forest	v	Luton Town	2–1		
1960	Wolverhampton Wanderers	v	Blackburn Rovers	3–0		
1961	Tottenham Hotspur	v	Leicester City	2–0		
1962	Tottenham Hotspur	v	Burnley	3–1		
1963	Manchester United	v	Leicester City	3–1		
1964	West Ham United	v	Preston North End	3–2		
1965	Liverpool	v	Leeds United	2–1 after extra time		
1966	Everton	v	Sheffield Wednesday	3–2		
1967	Tottenham Hotspur	v	Chelsea	2–1		
1968	West Bromwich Albion	v	Everton	1–0 after extra time		
1969	Manchester City	v	Leicester City	1–0		
1970	Chelsea	v	Leeds United	2–1 after 2–2 draw, both games extra time		
1971	Arsenal	v	Liverpool	2–1 after extra time		
1972	Leeds United	v	Arsenal	1–0		
1973	Sunderland	v	Leeds United	1–0		
1974	Liverpool	v	Newcastle United	3–0		
1975	West Ham United	v	Fulham	2–0		
1976	Southampton	v	Manchester United	1–0		
1977	Manchester United	v	Liverpool	2–1		
1978	Ipswich Town	v	Arsenal	1–0		
1979	Arsenal	v	Manchester United	3–2		
1980	West Ham United	v	Arsenal	1–0		
1981	Tottenham Hotspur	v	Manchester City	3–2 after 1–1 draw, after extra time		
1982	Tottenham Hotspur	v	Queen's Park Rangers	1–0 after 1–1 draw, after extra time		
1983	Manchester United	v	Brighton & Hove Albion	4–0 after 2–2 draw, after extra time		
1984	Everton	v	Watford	2–0		
1985	Manchester United	v	Everton	1–0 after extra time		
1986	Liverpool	v	Everton	3–1		
1987	Coventry City	v	Tottenham Hotspur	3–2 after extra time		
1988	Wimbledon	v	Liverpool	1–0		
1989	Liverpool	v	Everton	3–2 after extra time		
1990	Manchester United	v	Crystal Palace	1–0 after 3–3 draw, after extra time		
1991	Tottenham Hotspur	v	Nottingham Forest	2–1 after extra time		
1992	Liverpool	v	Sunderland	2–0		

LEAGUE CUP FINALS: 1961–92

Two-legged finals until 1966; all finals after 1966 played at Wembley

Year	Winners		Runners-up	Result
1961	Aston Villa	v	Rotherham United	3–2 (0–2, 3–0 after extra time)
1962	Norwich City	v	Rochdale	4–0 (3–0, 1–0)
1963	Birmingham City	v	Aston Villa	3–1 (3–1, 0–0)
1964	Leicester City	v	Stoke City	4–3 (1–1, 3–2)
1965	Chelsea	v	Leicester City	3–2 (3–2, 0–0)
1966	West Bromwich Albion	v	West Ham United	5–3 (1–2, 4–1)
1967	Queen's Park Rangers	v	West Bromwich Albion	3–2
1968	Leeds United	v	Arsenal	1–0
1969	Swindon Town	v	Arsenal	3–1 after extra time
1970	Manchester City	v	West Bromwich Albion	2–1 after extra time
1971	Tottenham Hotspur	v	Aston Villa	2–0
1972	Stoke City	v	Chelsea	2–1
1973	Tottenham Hotspur	v	Norwich City	1–0
1974	Wolverhampton Wanderers	v	Manchester City	2–1
1975	Aston Villa	v	Norwich City	1–0
1976	Manchester City	v	Newcastle United	2–1
1977	Aston Villa	v	Everton	0–0
	Aston Villa	v	Everton	1–1 after extra time; replay at Hillsborough
	Aston Villa	v	Everton	3–2 after extra time; 2nd replay at Old Trafford
1978	Nottingham Forest	v	Liverpool	0–0
	Nottingham Forest	v	Liverpool	1–0 replay at Old Trafford
1979	Nottingham Forest	v	Southampton	3–2
1980	Wolverhampton Wanderers	v	Nottingham Forest	1–0
1981	Liverpool	v	West Ham United	1–1 after extra time
	Liverpool	v	West Ham United	2–1 replay at Villa Park

as Milk Cup

Year	Winners		Runners-up	Result
1982	Liverpool	v	Tottenham Hotspur	3–1 after extra time
1983	Liverpool	v	Manchester United	2–1 after extra time
1984	Liverpool	v	Everton	0–0 after extra time
	Liverpool	v	Everton	1–0 replay at Maine Road
1985	Norwich City	v	Sunderland	1–0
1986	Oxford United	v	Queen's Park Rangers	3–0

as Littlewoods Cup

Year	Winners		Runners-up	Result
1987	Arsenal	v	Liverpool	2–1
1988	Luton Town	v	Arsenal	3–2
1989	Nottingham Forest	v	Luton Town	3–1
1990	Nottingham Forest	v	Oldham Athletic	1–0

as Rumbelows Cup

Year	Winners		Runners-up	Result
1991	Sheffield Wednesday	v	Manchester United	1–0
1992	Manchester United	v	Nottingham Forest	1–0

ATTENDANCES: 1958–1992

Premier League gates (*In 10-year cycles plus last two seasons; in 000s*)

	1958–59	1968–69	1978–79	1988–89	1990–91	1991–92
Arsenal	45.2	38.4	36.4	35.6	36.9	31.9
Aston Villa	33.9	24.7	32.8	23.3	25.7	24.9
Blackburn Rovers	30.5	11.1	8.6	8.9	8.1	13.2
Chelsea	40.9	37.6	24.8	15.7	20.7	18.7
Coventry City	16.3	33.2	22.6	16.0	13.8	13.1
Crystal Palace	14.9	20.8	23.3	10.7	19.7	17.6
Everton	39.2	46.0	35.5	27.8	25.0	23.0
Ipswich Town	14.3	23.6	21.7	15.3	11.8	14.5
Leeds United	24.9	37.0	27.6	21.8	29.3	29.5
Liverpool	36.7	47.3	6.4	38.6	36.0	34.9
Manchester City	32.6	35.2	36.2	23.5	27.9	27.7
Manchester United	53.3	51.2	46.4	36.5	43.2	45.0
Middlesbrough	24.9	21.1	18.5	20.0	17.0	14.8
Norwich City	21.1	13.8	17.9	16.8	15.5	14.3
Nottingham Forest	28.7	26.4	29.6	20.8	22.1	22.6
Oldham Athletic	5.3	4.1	7.0	7.2	13.2	15.1
Queen's Park Rangers	9.2	21.6	16.3	12.3	13.5	13.6
Sheffield United	19.6	15.5	16.3	12.2	21.5	21.8
Sheffield Wednesday	27.0	26.9	10.9	20.0	26.6	29.6
Southampton	21.5	22.5	21.3	15.6	15.4	14.4
Tottenham Hotspur	40.4	37.5	34.9	24.5	30.6	27.8
Wimbledon	—	—	3.7	7.8	7.6	7.1

Figures courtesy of The Football Trust Digest of Football Statistics 1990–91

The attendance in the Barclays League rose for the sixth successive year and gates were at their highest average level for ten seasons.

Season	Gates	Matches	Average
1990–91	19,541,341	2,036	9,598
1991–92	20,493,233	2,064	9,929

Alcock, P E (S Merstham, Surrey)
Allison, D B (Lancaster)
Ashby, G R (Worcester)
Axcell, D J (Southend)
Bailey, M C (Impington, Cambridge)
Barratt, K P (Coventry)
Bell, S D (Huddersfield)
Bigger, R L (Croydon)
Bodenham, M J (Looe, Cornwall)
Borrett, I J (Harleston, Norfolk)
Brandwood, M J (Lichfield, Staffs)
Breen, K J (Liverpool)
Buksh, A N (London)
Burge, W K (Tonypandy)
Burns, W C (Scarborough)
Callow, V G (Solihull)
Carter, J M (Christchurch)
Coddington, B (Sheffield)
Cooper, K (Pontypridd)
Cooper, K A (Swindon)
Cruikshanks, I G (Hartlepool)
Danson, P S (Leicester)
Dawson, A (Jarrow)
Dilkes, L R (Mossley, Lancs)
Don, P (Hanworth Park, Middlesex)
Dunn, S W (Bristol)
Durkin, P A (Portland, Dorset)
Elleray, D R (Harrow)
Fitzharris, T (Bolton)
Flood, W A (Stockport)
Foakes, P L (Clacton-on-Sea)

Frampton, D G (Poole, Dorset)
Gallagher, D J (Banbury, Oxon)
Gifford, R B (Llanbradach, Mid Glam)
Groves, R G (Weston-Super-Mare)
Gunn, A (South Chailey, Sussex)
Hackett, K S (Sheffield)
Hamer, R L (Bristol)
Harrison, P W (Oldham)
Hart, R A (Darlington)
Hemley, I S (Amphill, Beds)
Hendrick, I A (Preston)
Hill, B (Kettering)
Holbrook, T J (Walsall)
James, M L (Horsham)
Jones, P (Loughborough)
Key, J M (Sheffield)
King, H W (Merthyr Tydfil)
Kirkby, J A (Sheffield)
Leach, K A (Wolverhampton)
Lewis, R S (Gt Bookham, Surrey)
Lloyd, J W (Wrexham)
Lodge, S J (Barnsley)
Lunt, T (Ashton-in-Makerfield, Lancs)
Lutpon, K A (Stockton-on-Tees)
Lynch, K M (Lincoln)
Martin, J E (Nr Alton, Hants)
Milford, R G (Bristol)
Morton, K (Bury St Edmunds)
Moules, J A (Erith, Kent)
Nixon, R F (West Kirby, Wirral)
Parker, E J (Preston)

Pawley, R K (Cambridge)
Peck, M G (Kendal)
Pierce, M E (Portsmouth)
Poll, G (Berkhamstead)
Pooley, G R (Bishop's Stortford)
Poulain, R (Huddersfield)
Redfern, K A (Whitley Bay)
Reed, M D (Birmingham)
Rushton, J (Stoke-on-Trent)
Scoble, P M (Portsmouth)
Shadwell, D (Bromsgrove)
Shepherd, R (Leeds)
Singh, G (Wolverhampton)
Smith, A W (Rubery, Birmingham)
Smith, J G (Stafford)
Taylor, P (Waltham Cross, Herts)
Trussell, C C (Liverpool)
Vanes, P W (Warley, West Midlands)
Ward, A W (London)
Watson, J L (Whitley Bay)
West, T E (Hull)
Wilkes, C R (Gloucester)
Wilkie, A B (Chester-le-Street)
Willard, G S (Worthing, W Sussex)
Winter, J T (Middlesbrough)
Wiseman, R M (Borehamwood, Herts)
Wolstenholme, E K (Blackburn)
Worrall, J B (Warrington)
Wright, P L (Northwich)

AMENDMENTS TO THE LAWS OF THE GAME

At its annual meeting in Newport, Wales, on 30 May 1992, the International Football Association Board made a number of amendments to the Laws of the Game which were subsequently enforced on 25 July 1992.

The Punishment section of Law IV (Players' Equipment) was lengthened in order to further assist referees with its application.

Law V (Referees): clause (e) misconduct or ungentlemanly conduct was altered to include specific reference to the yellow card, while clause (h) violent conduct, serious foul play, the use of foul or abusive language was altered to include specific reference to the red card, thereby making these cards mandatory at all levels of the game. (Previously these clauses made no mention of the cards.)

Furthermore, if a player is sent off for a second cautionable offence, the referee must show both the yellow and the red card simultaneously in one hand, in order to differentiate between a second cautionable offence and an offence requiring immediate expulsion.

A new paragraph was inserted into Law XII (Fouls and Misconduct), concerning the deliberate pass back to the goalkeeper. It is no longer permissible for the goalkeeper to touch the ball with his hands, from a pass which has been kicked to him (although it is permissible for a goalkeeper to handle a ball played with the head, chest or the knee, or by deflection). An infringement of this Law is punishable by an indirect free-kick taken from the place where the infringement occurred subject to the over-riding conditions of Law XIII (Free-kick).

A stricter implementation of Law XII decision 17 (Control of the ball by the goalkeeper) was also insisted upon; as was the rule regarding the wearing of cycling shorts. These must now be of the same colour as the team shorts, extending no farther than the top of the knee.

In order to help reduce time wasting, Law XIII (Free-kick) now allows a free-kick awarded to the defending team inside its goal-area, to be taken from any point within the goal-area. (Previously the free-kick had to be taken within the half of the goal-area in which it had been awarded.) Likewise, Law XVI (Goal-kick) was simplified to allow a goal-kick to be taken from any point within the goal area.

The Board also insisted that referees be much stricter when dealing with time-wasting tactics. In particular, the referee must caution the following: a player guilty of kicking the ball away after a free-kick has been given; a player encroaching from a 'wall', a player who stands in front of the ball when a free-kick has been given against his team.

August

Sat   1   Opening of Season
Sat   8   Tennents FA Charity Shield
Sat   15   FA Premier League and Football League
programmes begin
Sat   29   FA Cup Preliminary Round

September

Sat   5   FA Vase Extra Preliminary Round
Wed   9   England v Continental Opposition
Sat   12   FA Cup First Qualifying Round
FA Youth Cup Preliminary Round
Wed   16   European club competitions: First round, first leg
Sat   19   FA Trophy First Qualifying Round
Sat   26   FA Cup Second Qualifying Round
Wed   30   European club competitions: First Round, second leg

October

Sat   3   FA Vase Preliminary Round
FA Youth Cup First Qualifying Round
Sat   10   FA Cup Third Qualifying Round
Sun   11   FA Sunday Cup First Round
Wed   14   England v Norway (World Cup)
Sat   17   FA Trophy Second Qualifying Round
FA Youth Cup Second Qualifying Round
FA County Youth Cup First Round
Wed   21   European club competitions: Second Round, first leg
Sat   24   FA Cup Fourth Qualifying Round
Sat   31   FA Vase First Round

November

Wed   4   European club competitions: Second Round,
second leg
Sun   8   FA Sunday Cup Second Round
Sat   14   FA Cup First Round
FA Youth Cup First Round
Wed   18   England v Turkey (World Cup)
Sat   21   FA Vase Second Round
Wed   25   European Cup group matches;
UEFA Cup Third Round, first leg
Sat   28   FA Trophy Third Qualifying Round
FA County Youth Cup Second Round

December

Sat   5   FA Cup Second Round
Sun   6   FA Sunday Cup Third Round
Wed   9   European Cup group matches;
UEFA Cup Third Round, second leg
Sat   12   FA Vase Third Round
FA Youth Cup Second Round

January 1993

Sat   2   FA Cup Third Round
Sat   9   FA Trophy First Round
Sat   16   FA Vase Third Round
FA Youth Cup Third Round

Sun   17   FA Sunday Cup Fourth Round
Sat   23   FA Cup Fourth Round
Sat   30   FA Trophy Second Round

February

Sat   6   FA Vase Fifth Round
FA Youth Cup Fourth Round
Sat   13   FA Cup Fifth Round
Sun   14   FA Sunday Cup Fifth Round
Wed   17   England v San Marino (World Cup)
Sat   20   FA Trophy Third Round
FA County Youth Cup Fourth Round
Sat   27   FA Vase Sixth Round

March

Wed   3   European Cup group matches; ECWC & UEFA Cup
Quarter-final, first leg
Sat   6   FA Cup Sixth Round
FA Youth Cup Fifth Round
Sat   13   FA Trophy Fourth Round
Wed   17   European Cup group matches; ECWC & UEFA Cup
Quarter-final, second leg
Sat   20   FA Vase Semi-final, first leg
FA County Youth Cup Semi-final
Sun   21   FA Sunday Cup Semi-final
Sat   27   FA Vase Semi-final, second leg
Wed   31   Turkey v England (World Cup)

April

Sat   3   FA Trophy Semi-final, first leg
FA Youth Challenge Cup Semi-final
Sun   4   FA Cup Semi-finals
Wed   7   European Cup group matches; ECWC & UEFA Cup
Semi-final, first leg
Sat   10   FA Trophy Semi-final, second leg
Wed   21   European Cup group matches; ECWC & UEFA Cup
Semi-final, second leg
Wed   28   England v Holland (World Cup)

May

Sat   1   FA County Youth Cup Final
Sun   2   FA Sunday Cup Final
Wed   5   UEFA Cup Final first leg
Sat   8   FA Vase Final
FA Youth Cup Final
Sun   9   FA Trophy Final
Wed   12   European Cup Winners` Cup Final
Sat   15   FA Cup Final
Wed   19   UEFA Cup Final second leg
Wed   26   European Cup Final
Sat   29   Poland v England (World Cup)

June

Wed   2   Norway v England (World Cup)

ARSENAL

1963–64 FAIRS CUP
1st round v Staevnet Copenhagen (Denmark)
23 Sept   (a) W 7–1 (Strong 3, Baker 3,
                              MacLeod)
22 Oct   (h) L 2–3 (Skirton, Barnwell)
2nd round v Liege (Belgium)
13 Nov   (h) D 1–1 (Anderson)
18 Dec   (a) L 1–3 (McCullough)

1969–70 FAIRS CUP
1st round v Glentoran (Northern Ireland)
 9 Sept   (h) W 3–0 (Graham 2, Gould)
29 Sept   (a) L 0–1
2nd round v Sporting Lisbon (Portugal)
29 Oct   (a) D 0–0
26 Nov   (h) W 3–0 (Radford, Graham 2)
3rd round v Rouen (France)
17 Dec   (a) D 0–0
13 Jan   (h) W 1–0 (Sammels)
Quarter-final v Dynamo Bacau (Romania)
11 March   (a) W 2–0 (Sammels, Radford)
18 March   (h) W 7–1 (George 2, Sammels 2,
                              Radford 2, Graham)
Semi-final v Ajax Amsterdam (Holland)
 8 April   (h) W 3–0 (George 2 [1 pen],
                              Sammels)
15 April   (a) L 0–1
Final v Anderlecht (Belgium)
22 April   (a) L 1–3 (Kennedy)
28 April   (h) W 3–0 (Kelly, Radford,
                              Sammels)

1970–71 FAIRS CUP
1st round v Lazio (Italy)
16 Sept   (a) D 2–2 (Radford 2)
23 Sept   (h) W 2–0 (Radford, Armstrong)
2nd round v Sturm Graz (Austria)
21 Oct   (a) L 0–1
 4 Nov   (h) W 2–0 (Storey [pen], Kennedy)
3rd round v Beveren (Belgium)
 2 Dec   (h) W 4–0 (Graham, Kennedy 2,
                              Sammels)
16 Dec   (a) D 0–0
Quarter-final v FC Cologne (West Germany)
 9 March   (h) W 2–1 (McLintock, Storey)
23 March   (a) L 0–1
Lost on away goals

1971–72 EUROPEAN CUP
1st round v Stromsgodset (Norway)
15 Sept   (a) W 3–1 (Simpson, Marinello,
                              Kelly)
29 Sept   (h) W 4–0 (Kennedy, Radford 2,
                              Armstrong)
2nd round v Grasshoppers (Switzerland)
20 Oct   (a) W 2–0 (Kennedy, Graham)
 3 Nov   (h) W 3–0 (Kennedy, George,
                              Radford)
Quarter-final v Ajax (Holland)
 8 March   (a) L 1–2 (Kennedy)
22 March   (h) L 0–1

1978–79 UEFA CUP
1st round v Lokomotiv Leipzig (East Germany)
13 Sept   (h) W 3–0 (Stapleton 2,
                              Sunderland)
27 Sept   (a) W 4–1 (Brady [pen], Stapleton
                              2, Sunderland)
2nd round v Hajduk Split (Yugoslavia)
18 Oct   (a) L 1–2 (O'Leary)
 1 Nov   (h) W 1–0 (Young)
Won on away goals
3rd round v Red Star Belgrade (Yugoslavia)
22 Nov   (a) L 0–1
 6 Dec   (h) D 1–1 (Sunderland)

1979–80 EUROPEAN CUP WINNERS' CUP
1st round v Fenerbahce (Turkey)
19 Sept   (h) W 2–0 (Sunderland, Young)
 3 Oct   (a) D 0–0
2nd round v Magdeburg (East Germany)
24 Oct   (h) W 2–1 (Young, Sunderland)
 7 Nov   (a) D 2–2 (Price, Brady)
Quarter-final v Gothenburg (Sweden)
 5 March   (h) W 5–1 (Sunderland 2, Price,
                              Brady, Young)
19 March   (a) D 0–0
Semi-final v Juventus (Italy)
 9 April   (h) D 1–1 (og)
23 April   (a) W 1–0 (Vaessen)
Final v Valencia (Spain) In Brussels
14 May   D 0–0
Lost 4–5 on penalties

1981–82 UEFA CUP
1st round v Panathinaikos (Greece)
16 Sept   (a) W 2–0 (McDermott, Meade)
30 Sept   (h) W 1–0 (Talbot)
2nd round v Winterslag (Belgium)
20 Oct   (a) L 0–1
 3 Nov   (h) W 2–1 (Hollins, Rix)
Lost on away goals

1982–83 UEFA CUP
1st round v Moscow Spartak (USSR)
14 Sept   (a) L 2–3 (Robson, Chapman)
29 Sept   (h) L 2–5 (Chapman, og)

1991–92 EUROPEAN CUP
1st round v Austria Vienna (Austria)
18 Sept   (h) W 6–1 (Smith 4, Linighan,
                              Limpar)
 2 Oct   (a) L 0–1
2nd round v Benfica (Portugal)
23 Oct   (a) D 1–1 (Campbell)
 7 Nov   (h) L 1–3 (Pates)

ASTON VILLA

1975–76 UEFA CUP
1st round v Antwerp (Belgium)
17 Sept   (a) L 1–4 (Graydon)
 1 Oct   (h) L 0–1

1977–78 UEFA CUP
1st round v Fenerbahce (Turkey)
14 Sept   (h) W 4–0 (Gray, Deehan 2, Little)
28 Sept   (a) W 2–0 (Deehan, Little)

2nd round v Gornik Zabrze (Poland)
19 Oct   (h) W 2–0 (McNaught 2)
 2 Nov   (a) D 1–1 (Gray)
3rd round v Athletic Bilbao (Spain)
23 Nov   (h) W 2–0 (og, Deehan)
 7 Dec   (a) D 1–1 (Mortimer)
Quarter-final v Barcelona (Spain)
 1 March   (h) D 2–2 (McNaught, Deehan)
15 March   (a) L 1–2 (Little)

1981–82 EUROPEAN CUP
1st round v Valur (Iceland)
16 Sept   (h) W 5–0 (Morley, Withe 2,
                              Donovan 2)
30 Sept   (a) W 2–0 (Shaw 2)
2nd round v Dynamo Berlin (East Germany)
21 Oct   (a) W 2–1 (Morley 2)
 4 Nov   (h) L 0–1
Quarter-final v Dynamo Kiev (USSR)
 3 March   (a) D 0–0
17 March   (h) W 2–0 (Shaw, McNaught)
Semi-final v Anderlecht (Belgium)
 7 April   (h) W 1–0 (Morley)
21 April   (a) D 0–0
Final v Bayern Munich (West Germany)
In Rotterdam
26 May   W 1–0 (Withe)

1982–83 EUROPEAN CUP
1st round v Besiktas (Turkey)
15 Sept   (h) W 3–1 (Withe, Morley,
                              Mortimer)
29 Sept   (a) D 0–0
2nd round v Dinamo Bucharest (Romania)
20 Oct   (a) W 2–0 (Shaw 2)
 3 Nov   (h) W 4–2 (Shaw 3, Walters)
Quarter-final v Juventus (Italy)
 2 March   (h) L 1–2 (Cowans)
16 March   (a) L 1–3 (Withe)

1983–84 UEFA CUP
1st round v Vitoria Guimaraes (Portugal)
14 Sept   (a) L 0–1
28 Sept   (h) W 5–0 (Withe 3, Ormsby,
                              Gibson)
2nd round v Moscow Spartak (USSR)
19 Oct   (a) D 2–2 (Gibson, Walters)
 2 Nov   (h) L 1–2 (Withe)

1990–91 UEFA CUP
1st round v Banik Ostrava (Czechoslovakia)
19 Sept   (h) W 3–1 (Platt, Mountfield,
                              Olney)
 3 Oct   (a) W 2–1 (Mountfield, og)
2nd round v Inter–Milan (Italy)
24 Oct   (h) W 2–0 (Nielsen, Platt)
 7 Nov   (a) L 0–3

CHELSEA

1958–60 FAIRS CUP
1st round v Frem Copenhagen (Denmark) 1958
30 Sept   (a) W 3–1 (Harrison, Greaves, Nicholas)
 4 Nov   (h) W 4–1 (Greaves 2, P Sillett, og)
Quarter-final v Belgrade (Yugoslavia) 1959
29 April   (h) W 1–0 (Brabrook)
13 May   (a) L 1–4 (Brabrook)

1965–66 FAIRS CUP
1st round v Roma (Italy)
22 Sept   (h) W 4–1 (Venables 3, Graham)
 6 Oct   (a) D 0–0
2nd round v Wiener SK (Austria)
17 Nov   (a) L 0–1
 1 Dec   (h) W 2–0 (Murray, Osgood)
3rd round v AC Milan (Italy)
 9 Feb   (a) L 1–2 (Graham)
16 Feb   (h) W 2–1 (Graham, Osgood)
 2 March   (a) D 1–1 (Bridges)
Won on toss of coin
Quarter-final v Munich 1860 (West Germany)
15 March (a) D 2–2 (Tambling 2)
29 March (h) W 1–0 (Osgood)
Semi-final v Barcelona (Spain)
27 April   (a) L 0–2
11 May   (h) W 2–0 (og 2)
25 May   (n) L 0–5

1968–69 FAIRS CUP
1st round v Morton (Scotland)
18 Sept   (h) W 5–0 (Osgood, Birchenall, Cooke, Boyle, Hollins)
30 Sept   (a) W 4–3 (Baldwin, Birchenall, Houseman, Tambling)
2nd round v DWS Amsterdam (Holland)
23 Oct   (h) D 0–0
30 Oct   (a) D 0–0
Lost on toss of coin

1970–71 EUROPEAN CUP WINNERS' CUP
1st round v Aris Salonika (Greece)
16 Sept   (a) D 1–1 (Hutchinson)
30 Sept   (h) W 5–1 (Hutchinson 2, Hollins 2, Hinton)
2nd round v CSKA Sofia (Bulgaria)
21 Oct   (a) W 1–0 (Baldwin)
 4 Nov   (h) W 1–0 (Webb)
Quarter-final v FC Bruges (Belgium)
10 March (a) L 0–2
24 March (h) W 4–0 (Houseman, Osgood 2, Baldwin)
Semi-final v Manchester City
14 April   (h) W 1–0 (Smethurst)
28 April   (a) W 1–0 (Weller)
Final v Real Madrid (Spain) In Athens
19 May   D 1–1 (Osgood)
Final Replay v Real Madrid (Spain) in Athens
21 May   W 2–1 (Dempsey, Osgood)

1971–72 EUROPEAN CUP WINNERS' CUP
1st round v Jeunesse Hautcharage (Luxembourg)
15 Sept   (a) W 8–0 (Osgood 3, Houseman 2, Hollins, Webb, Baldwin)
29 Sept   (h) W 13–0 (Osgood 5, Hudson, Webb, Baldwin 3, Houseman, Hollins [pen], Harris)
2nd round v Atvidaberg (Sweden)
20 Oct   (a) D 0–0
 3 Nov   (h) D 1–1 (Hudson)
Lost on away goals

COVENTRY CITY

1970–71 FAIRS CUP
1st round v Trakia Plovdiv (Bulgaria)
16 Sept   (a) W 4–1 (O'Rourke 3, Martin)
30 Sept   (h) W 2–0 (Joicey, Blockley)
2nd round v Bayern Munich (West Germany)
20 Oct   (a) L 1–6 (Hunt)
 3 Nov   (h) W 2–1 (Martin, O'Rourke)

EVERTON

1962–63 FAIRS CUP
1st round v Dunfermline (Scotland)
24 Oct   (h) W 1–0 (Stevens)
31 Oct   (a) L 0–2

1963–64 EUROPEAN CUP
Preliminary round v Inter–Milan (Italy)
18 Sept   (h) D 0–0
25 Sept   (a) L 0–1

1964–65 FAIRS CUP
1st round v Valerengen (Norway)
23 Sept   (a) W 5–2 (Pickering 2, Harvey, Temple 2)
14 Oct   (h) W 4–2 (Young 2, Vernon, og)
2nd round v Kilmarnock (Scotland)
11 Nov   (a) W 2–0 (Morrissey, Temple)
23 Nov   (h) W 4–1 (Harvey, Pickering 2, Young)
3rd round v Manchester United (England)
20 Jan   (a) D 1–1 (Pickering)
 9 Feb   (h) L 1–2 (Pickering)

1965–66 FAIRS CUP
1st round v Nuremberg (West Germany)
28 Sept   (a) D 1–1 (Harris)
12 Oct   (h) W 1–0 (Gabriel)
2nd round v Ujpest Dozsa (Hungary)
 3 Nov   (a) L 0–3
16 Nov   (h) W 2–1 (Harris, og)

1966–67 European Cup Winners' Cup
1st round v Aalborg (Denmark)
28 Sept   (a) D 0–0
11 Oct   (h) W 2–1 (Morrissey, Ball)
2nd round v Real Zaragoza (Spain)
 9 Nov   (a) L 0–2
23 Nov   (h) W 1–0 (Brown)

1970–71 EUROPEAN CUP
1st round v Keflavik (Iceland)
16 Sept   (h) W 6–2 (Ball 3, Kendall, Royle 2)
30 Sept   (a) W 3–0 (Royle 2, Whittle)
2nd round v Borussia Moenchengladbach (West Germany)
21 Oct   (a) D 1–1 (Kendall)
 4 Nov   (h) D 1–1 (Morrissey)
Won 4–3 on penalties
Quarter-final v Panathinaikos (Greece)
 9 March (h) D 1–1 (Johnson)
24 March (a) D 0–0
Lost on away goals

1975–76 UEFA CUP
1st round v AC Milan (Italy)
17 Sept   (h) D 0–0
 1 Oct   (a) L 0–1

1978–79 UEFA CUP
1st round v Finn Harps (Republic of Ireland)
12 Sept   (a) W 5–0 (King 2, Thomas, Walsh, Latchford)
26 Sept   (h) W 5–0 (King, Latchford, Walsh, Ross, Dobson)
2nd round v Dukla Prague (Czechoslovakia)
18 Oct   (h) W 2–1 (Latchford, King)
 1 Nov   (a) L 0–1
Lost on away goals

1979–80 UEFA CUP
1st round v Feyenoord (Holland)
19 Sept   (a) L 0–1
 3 Oct   (h) L 0–1

1984–85 EUROPEAN CUP WINNERS' CUP
1st round v University College Dublin (Republic of Ireland)
19 Sept   (a) D 0–0
 2 Oct   (h) W 1–0 (Sharp)
2nd round v Inter Bratislava (Czechoslovakia)
24 Oct   (a) W 1–0 (Bracewell)
 7 Nov   (h) W 3–0 (Heath, Sharp, Sheedy)
Quarter-final v Fortuna Sittard (Holland)
 6 March (h) W 3–0 (Gray 3)
20 March (a) W 2–0 (Reid, Sharp)
Semi-final v Bayern Munich (West Germany)
10 April   (a) D 0–0
24 April   (h) W 3–1 (Gray, Sharp, Steven)
Final v Rapid Vienna (Austria) In Rotterdam
15 May   W 3–1 (Gray, Sheedy, Steven)

IPSWICH TOWN

1962–63 EUROPEAN CUP
Preliminary round v Floriana (Malta)
18 Sept   (a) W 4–1 (Crawford 2, Phillips 2)
25 Sept   (h) W 10–0 (Crawford 5, Moran 2, Phillips 2, Elsworthy)
1st round v AC Milan (Italy)
14 Nov   (a) L 0–3
28 Nov   (h) W 2–1 (Crawford, Blackwood)

1973–74 UEFA CUP
1st round v Real Madrid (Spain)
19 Sept (h) W 1–0 (og)
3 Oct (a) D 0–0
2nd round v Lazio (Italy)
24 Oct (h) W 4–0 (Whymark 4)
7 Nov (a) L 2–4 (Viljoen [pen], Johnson)
3rd round v Twente Enschede (Holland)
28 Nov (h) W 1–0 (Whymark)
12 Dec (a) W 2–1 (Morris, Hamilton)
Quarter-final v Lokomotiv Leipzig (E Germany)
6 March (h) W 1–0 (Beattie)
20 March (a) L 0–1
Lost on penalties

1974–75 UEFA CUP
1st round v Twente Enschede (Holland)
18 Sept (h) D 2–2 (Hamilton, Talbot)
2 Oct (a) D 1–1 (Hamilton)
Lost on away goals

1975–76 UEFA CUP
1st round v Feyenoord (Holland)
17 Sept (a) W 2–1 (Whymark, Johnson)
1 Oct (h) W 2–0 (Woods, Whymark)
2nd round v FC Bruges (Belgium)
22 Oct (h) W 3–0 (Gates, Peddelty, Austin)
5 Nov (a) L 0–4

1977–78 UEFA CUP
1st round v Landskrona (Sweden)
14 Sept (a) W 1–0 (Whymark)
28 Sept (h) W 5–0 (Whymark 4 [1 pen], Mariner)
2nd round v Las Palmas (Spain)
19 Oct (h) W 1–0 (Gates)
2 Nov (a) D 3–3 (Mariner 2, Talbot)
3rd round v Barcelona (Spain)
23 Nov (h) W 3–0 (Gates, Whymark, Talbot)
7 Dec (a) L 0–3
Lost 1–3 on penalties

1978–79 EUROPEAN CUP WINNERS' CUP
1st round v AZ 67 Alkmaar (Holland)
13 Sept (a) D 0–0
27 Sept (h) W 2–0 (Mariner, Wark [pen])
2nd round v SW Innsbruck (Austria)
18 Oct (h) W 1–0 (Wark [pen])
1 Nov (a) D 1–1 (Burley)
Quarter-final v Barcelona (Spain)
7 March (h) W 2–1 (Gates 2)
21 March (a) L 0–1
Lost on away goals

1979–80 UEFA CUP
1st round v Skeid Oslo (Norway)
19 Sept (a) W 3–1 (Mills, Turner, Mariner)
3 Oct (h) W 7–0 (Wark, Muhren 2, McCall 2, Mariner, Thijssen)
2nd round v Grasshoppers (Switzerland)
24 Oct (a) D 0–0
7 Nov (h) D 1–1 (Beattie)
Lost on away goals

1980–81 UEFA CUP
1st round v Aris Salonika (Greece)
17 Sept (h) W 5–1 (Wark 4 [3 pens], Mariner)
1 Oct (a) L 1–3 (Gates)
2nd round v Bohemians Prague (Czechoslovakia)
22 Oct (h) W 3–0 (Wark 2, Beattie)
5 Nov (a) L 0–2
3rd round v Widzew Lodz (Poland)
26 Nov (h) W 5–0 (Wark 3, Brazil, Mariner)
10 Dec (a) L 0–1
Quarter-final v St Etienne (France)
4 March (a) W 4–1 (Mariner 2, Wark, Brazil)
18 March (h) W 3–1 (Butcher, Wark [pen], Mariner)
Semi-final v Cologne (West Germany)
8 April (h) W 1–0 (Wark)
22 April (a) W 1–0 (Butcher)
Final v AZ 67 Alkmaar (Holland)
6 May (h) W 3–0 (Wark [pen], Thijssen, Mariner)
20 May (a) L 2–4 (Thijssen, Wark)

1981–82 UEFA CUP
1st round v Aberdeen (Scotland)
16 Sept (h) D 1–1 (Thijssen)
30 Sept (a) L 1–3 (Wark [pen])

1982–83 UEFA CUP
1st round v Roma (Italy)
15 Sept (a) L 0–3
29 Sept (h) W 3–1 (Gates, McCall, Butcher)

LEEDS UNITED

1965–66 FAIRS CUP
1st round v Torino (Italy)
29 Sept (h) W 2–1 (Bremner, Peacock)
6 Oct (a) D 0–0
2nd round v Lokomotiv Leipzig (East Germany)
24 Nov (a) W 2–1 (Lorimer, Bremner)
1 Dec (h) D 0–0
3rd round v Valencia (Spain)
2 Feb (h) D 1–1 (Lorimer)
16 Feb (a) W 1–0 (O'Grady)
Quarter-final v Ujpest Dozsa (Hungary)
2 March (h) W 4–1 (Cooper, Bell, Storrie, Bremner)
9 March (a) D 1–1 (Lorimer)
Semi-final v Real Zaragoza (Spain)
20 April (a) L 0–1
27 April (h) W 2–1 (Johanneson, Charlton)
11 March (n) L 1–3 (Charlton)

1966–67 FAIRS CUP
1st round bye
2nd round v DWS Amsterdam (Holland)
18 Oct (a) W 3–1 (Bremner, Johanneson, Greenhoff)
26 Oct (h) W 5–1 (Johanneson 3, Giles, Madeley)

3rd round v Valencia (Spain)
18 Jan (h) D 1–1 (Greenhoff)
8 Feb (a) W 2–0 (Giles, Lorimer)
Quarter-final v Bologna (Italy)
22 March (a) L 0–1
19 April (h) W 1–0 (Giles [pen])
Won on toss of coin
Semi-final v Kilmarnock (Scotland)
19 May (h) W 4–2 (Belfitt 3, Giles [pen])
24 May (a) D 0–0
Final v Dynamo Zagreb (Yugoslavia)
30 Aug (a) L 0–2
6 Sept (h) D 0–0

1967–68 FAIRS CUP
1st round v Spora Luxembourg (Luxembourg)
3 Oct (a) W 9–0 (Lorimer 4, Greenhoff 2, Madeley, Jones, Bremner)
17 Oct (h) W 7–0 (Johanneson 3, Greenhoff 2, Cooper, Lorimer)
2nd round v Partizan Belgrade (Yugoslavia)
29 Nov (a) W 2–1 (Lorimer, Belfitt)
6 Dec (h) D 1–1 (Lorimer)
3rd round v Hibernian (Scotland)
20 Dec (h) W 1–0 (E Gray)
10 Jan (a) D 0–0
Quarter-final v Rangers (Scotland)
26 March (a) D 0–0
9 April (h) W 2–0 (Lorimer, Giles [pen])
Semi-final v Dundee (Scotland)
1 May (a) D 1–1 (Madeley)
15 May (h) W 1–0 (E Gray)
Final v Ferencvaros (Hungary)
7 Aug (h) W 1–0 (Charlton)
11 Sept (a) D 0–0

1968–69 FAIRS CUP
1st round v Standard Liege (Belgium)
18 Sept (a) D 0–0
23 Oct (h) W 3–2 (Charlton, Lorimer, Bremner)
2nd round v Napoli (Italy)
13 Nov (h) W 2–0 (Charlton 2)
27 Nov (a) L 0–2
Won on toss of coin
3rd round v Hanover 96 (West Germany)
18 Dec (h) W 5–1 (O'Grady, Hunter, Lorimer 2, Charlton)
4 Feb (a) W 2–1 (Belfitt, Jones)
Quarter-final v Ujpest Dozsa (Hungary)
5 March (a) L 0–1
19 March (h) L 0–2

1969–70 EUROPEAN CUP
1st round v Lyn Oslo (Norway)
17 Sept (h) W 10–0 (O'Grady, Jones 3, Clarke 2, Bremner 2, Giles 2)
1 Oct (a) W 6–0 (Belfitt 2, Hibbitt 2, Jones, Lorimer)
2nd round v Ferencvaros (Hungary)
12 Nov (h) W 3–0 (Giles, Jones 2)
26 Nov (a) W 3–0 (Jones 2, Lorimer)

(Leeds United continued)

Quarter-final v Standard Liege (Belgium)
4 March   (a) W 1–0 (Lorimer)
18 March   (h) W 1–0 (Giles [pen])
Semi-final v Celtic (Scotland)
1 April   (h) L 0–1
15 April   (a) L 1–2 (Bremner)
at Hampden Park

1970–71 FAIRS CUP
1st round v Sarpsborg (Norway)
15 Sept   (a) W 1–0 (Lorimer)
29 Sept   (h) W 5–0 (Charlton 2, Bremner 2,
                      Lorimer)
2nd round v Dynamo Dresden (East Germany)
21 Oct   (h) W 1–0 (Lorimer)
4 Nov   (a) L 1–2 (Jones)
Won on away goals
3rd round v Sparta Prague (Czechoslovakia)
2 Dec   (h) W 6–0 (Clarke, og, Bremner, E
                      Gray 2, Charlton)
9 Dec   (a) W 3–2 (E Gray, Clarke, Belfitt)
Quarter-final v Vitoria Setubal (Portugal)
10 March   (h) W 2–1 (Lorimer, Giles [pen])
24 March   (a) D 1–1 (Lorimer)
Semi-final v Liverpool (England)
14 April   (a) W 1–0 (Bremner)
28 April   (h) D 0–0
Final v Juventus (Italy)
27 May   (a)   *match abandoned*
28 May   (a) D 2–2 (Madeley, Bates)
3 June   (h) D 1–1 (Clarke)
Won on away goals

1971–72 UEFA CUP
1st round v Lierse (Belgium)
15 Sept   (a) W 2–0 (Galvin, Lorimer)
29 Sept   (h) L 0–4

1972–73 EUROPEAN CUP WINNERS' CUP
1st round v Ankaragucu (Turkey)
13 Sept   (a) D 1–1 (Jordan)
28 Sept   (h) W 1–0 (Jones)
2nd round v Carl Zeiss Jena (East Germany)
25 Oct   (a) D 0–0
8 Nov   (h) W 2–0 (Cherry, Jones)
Quarter-final v Rapid Bucharest (Romania)
7 March   (h) W 5–0 (Giles, Clarke, Lorimer
                      2, Jordan)
23 March   (a) W 3–1 (Jones, Jordan, Bates)
Semi-final v Hajduk Split (Yugoslavia)
11 April   (h) W 1–0 (Clarke)
25 April   (a) D 0–0
Final v AC Milan (Italy) In Salonika
16 May   L 0–1

1973–74 UEFA CUP
1st round v Stromsgodset (Norway)
19 Sept   (a) D 1–1 (Clarke)
3 Oct   (h) W 6–1 (Clarke 2, Jones 2, F
                      Gray, Bates)
2nd round v Hibernian (Scotland)
24 Oct   (h) D 0–0
7 Nov   (a) D 0–0
Won 5–4 on penalties

3rd round v Vitoria Setubal (Portugal)
28 Nov   (h) W 1–0 (Cherry)
12 Dec   (a) L 1–3 (Liddell)

1974–75 EUROPEAN CUP
1st round v FC Zurich (Switzerland)
18 Sept   (h) W 4–1 (Clarke 2, Lorimer
                      [pen], Jordan)
2 Oct   (a) L 1–2 (Clarke)
2nd round v Ujpest Dozsa (Hungary)
23 Oct   (a) W 2–1 (Lorimer, McQueen)
6 Nov   (h) W 3–0 (McQueen, Bremner,
                      Yorath)
Quarter-final v Anderlecht (Belgium)
5 March   (h) W 3–0 (Jordan, McQueen,
                      Lorimer)
19 March   (a) W 1–0 (Bremner)
Semi-final v Barcelona (Spain)
9 April   (h) W 2–1 (Bremner, Clarke)
24 April   (a) D 1–1 (Lorimer)
Final v Bayern Munich (West Germany) In Paris
28 May   L 0–2

1979–80 UEFA CUP
1st round v Valletta (Malta)
19 Sept   (a) W 4–0 (Graham 3, Hart)
3 Oct   (h) W 3–0 (Curtis, Hankin, Hart)
2nd round v Universitea Craiova (Romania)
24 Oct   (a) L 0–2
7 Nov   (h) L 0–2

LIVERPOOL

1964–65 EUROPEAN CUP
Preliminary round v KR Reykjavik (Iceland)
17 Aug   (a) W 5–0 (Wallace 2, Hunt 2,
                      Chisnall)
14 Sept   (h) W 6–1 (Bryne, St John 2,
                      Graham, Hunt,
                      Stevenson)
1st round v Anderlecht (Belgium)
25 Nov   (h) W 3–0 (St John, Hunt, Yeats)
16 Dec   (a) W 1–0 (Hunt)
Quarter-final v FC Cologne (West Germany)
10 Feb   (a) D 0–0
17 March   (h) D 0–0
24 March   (n) D 2–2 (St John, Hunt)
in Rotterdam
Won on toss of coin
Semi-final v Inter–Milan (Italy)
4 May   (h) W 3–1 (Hunt, Callaghan,
                      St John)
12 May   (a) L 0–3

1965–66 EUROPEAN CUP WINNERS' CUP
1st round v Juventus (Italy)
29 Sept   (a) L 0–1
13 Oct   (h) W 2–0 (Lawler, Strong)
2nd round v Standard Liege (Belgium)
1 Dec   (h) W 3–1 (Lawler 2, P Thompson)
15 Dec   (a) W 2–1 (Hunt, St John)
Quarter-final v Honved (Hungary)
1 March   (a) D 0–0
8 March   (h) W 2–0 (Lawler, St John)

Semi-final v Glasgow Celtic (Scotland)
14 April   (a) L 0–1
19 April   (h) W 2–0 (Smith, Strong)
Final v Borussia Dortmund (West Germany)
in Glasgow
5 May   L 1–2 (Hunt) *after extra time*

1966–67 EUROPEAN CUP
1st round v Petrolul Ploesti (Romania)
28 Sept   (h) W 2–1 (St John, Callaghan)
12 Oct   (a) L 1–3 (Hunt)
19 Oct   (n) W 2–0 (St John, P Thompson)
in Brussels
2nd round v Ajax (Holland)
7 Dec   (a) L 1–5 (Lawler)
14 Dec   (h) D 2–2 (Hunt 2)

1967–68 FAIRS CUP
1st round v Malmo (Sweden)
19 Sept   (a) W 2–0 (Hateley 2)
4 Oct   (h) W 2–1 (Yeats, Hunt)
2nd round v Munich 1860 (West Germany)
7 Nov   (h) W 8–0 (St John, Hateley, P
                      Thompson, Smith [pen],
                      Hunt 2, Callaghan 2)
14 Nov   (a) L 1–2 (Callaghan)
3rd round v Ferencvaros (Hungary)
28 Nov   (a) L 0–1
9 Jan   (h) L 0–1

1968–69 FAIRS CUP
1st round v Athletic Bilbao (Spain)
18 Sept   (a) L 1–2 (Hunt)
2 Oct   (h) W 2–1 (Lawler, Hughes)
Lost on toss of coin

1969–70 FAIRS CUP
1st round v Dundalk (Republic of Ireland)
16 Sept   (h) W 10–0 (Evans 2, Smith 2,
                      Graham 2, Lawler,
                      Lindsay, P Thompson,
                      Callaghan)
30 Sept   (a) W 4–0 (P Thompson 2,
                      Graham, Callaghan)
2nd round v Vitoria Setubal (Portugal)
11 Nov   (a) L 0–1
26 Nov   (h) W 3–2 (Smith [pen], Evans,
                      Hunt)
Lost on away goals

1970–71 FAIRS CUP
1st round v Ferencvaros (Hungary)
15 Sept   (h) W 1–0 (Graham)
29 Sept   (a) D 1–1 (Hughes)
2nd round v Dinamo Bucharest (Romania)
21 Oct   (h) W 3–0 (Lindsay, Lawler,
                      Hughes)
4 Nov   (a) D 1–1 (Boersma)
3rd round v Hibernian (Scotland)
9 Dec   (h) W 1–0 (Toshack)
22 Dec   (h) W 2–0 (Heighway, Boersma)
Quarter-final v Bayern Munich (W Germany)
10 March   (h) W 3–0 (Evans 3)
24 March   (a) D 1–1 (Ross)
Semi-final v Leeds United
14 April   (h) L 0–1
28 April   (a) D 0–0

1971–72 EUROPEAN CUP WINNERS' CUP
1st round v Servette Geneva (Switzerland)
15 Sept   (a)   L   1–2 (Lawler)
29 Sept   (h)   W   2–0 (Hughes, Heighway)
2nd round v Bayern Munich (West Germany)
20 Oct   (h)   D   0–0
3 Nov   (a)   L   1–3 (Evans)

1972–73 UEFA CUP
1st round v Eintracht Frankfurt (W Germany)
12 Sept   (h)   W   2–0 (Keegan, Hughes)
26 Sept   (a)   D   0–0
2nd round v AEK Athens (Greece)
24 Oct   (h)   W   3–0 (Boersma, Cormack,
                Smith [pen])
2 Nov   (a)   W   3–1 (Hughes 2, Boersma)
3rd round v Dynamo Berlin (East Germany)
29 Nov   (a)   D   0–0
12 Dec   (h)   W   3–1 (Boersma, Heighway,
                Toshack)
Quarter-final v Dynamo Dresden
(East Germany)
7 March   (h)   W   2–0 (Hall, Boersma)
21 March   (a)   W   1–0 (Keegan)
Semi-final v Tottenham Hotspur (England)
10 April   (h)   W   1–0 (Lindsay)
25 April   (a)   L   1–2 (Heighway)
Won on away goals
Final v Borussia Moenchengladbach
(West Germany)
10 May   (h)   W   3–0 (Keegan 2, Lloyd)
23 May   (a)   L   0–2

1973–74 EUROPEAN CUP
1st round v Jeunesse D'Esch (Luxembourg)
19 Sept   (a)   D   1–1 (Hall)
3 Oct   (h)   W   2–0 (Toshack, og)
2nd round v Red Star Belgrade (Yugoslavia)
24 Oct   (a)   L   1–2 (Lawler)
6 Nov   (h)   L   1–2 (Lawler)

1974–75 EUROPEAN CUP WINNERS' CUP
1st round v Stromsgodset (Norway)
17 Sept   (h)   W   11–0 (Lindsay [pen], Boersma
                2, Phil Thompson 2,
                Heighway, Cormack,
                Hughes, Callaghan,
                Smith, Kennedy)
1 Oct   (a)   W   1–0 (Kennedy)
2nd round v Ferencvaros (Hungary)
23 Oct   (h)   D   1–1 (Keegan)
5 Nov   (a)   D   0–0
Lost on away goals

1975–76 UEFA CUP
1st round v Hibernian (Scotland)
17 Sept   (a)   L   0–1
30 Sept   (h)   W   3–1 (Toshack 3)
2nd round v Real Sociedad (Spain)
22 Oct   (a)   W   3–1 (Heighway, Callaghan,
                Phil Thompson)
4 Nov   (h)   W   6–0 (Toshack, Kennedy 2,
                Fairclough, Heighway,
                Neal)
3rd round v Slask Wroclaw (Poland)
26 Nov   (a)   W   2–1 (Kennedy, Toshack)
10 Dec   (h)   W   3–0 (Case 3)

Quarter-final v Dynamo Dresden (E Germany)
3 March   (a)   D   0–0
17 March   (h)   W   2–1 (Case, Keegan)
Semi-final v Barcelona (Spain)
30 March   (a)   W   1–0 (Toshack)
14 April   (h)   D   1–1 (Phil Thompson)
Final v FC Bruges (Belgium)
28 April   (h)   W   3–2 (Kennedy, Case,
                Keegan [pen])
19 May   (a)   D   1–1 (Keegan)

1976–77 EUROPEAN CUP
1st round v Crusaders (Northern Ireland)
14 Sept   (h)   W   2–0 (Neal [pen], Toshack)
28 Sept   (a)   W   5–0 (Keegan, Johnson 2,
                McDermott, Heighway)
2nd round v Trabzonspor (Turkey)
20 Oct   (a)   L   0–1
3 Nov   (h)   W   3–0 (Heighway, Johnson,
                Keegan)
Quarter-final v St Etienne (France)
2 March   (a)   L   0–1
16 March   (h)   W   3–1 (Keegan, Kennedy,
                Fairclough)
Semi-final v FC Zurich (Switzerland)
6 April   (a)   W   3–1 (Neal 2 [1 pen],
                Heighway)
20 April   (h)   W   3–0 (Case 2, Keegan)
Final v Borussia Moenchengladbach
(West Germany) in Rome
25 May   W   3–1 (McDermott, Smith,
                Neal [pen])

1977–78 EUROPEAN CUP
1st round bye
2nd round v Dynamo Dresden (East Germany)
19 Oct   (h)   W   5–1 (Hansen, Case 2, Neal
                [pen], Kennedy)
2 Nov   (a)   L   1–2 (Heighway)
Quarter-final v Benfica (Portugal)
1 March   (a)   W   2–1 (Case, Hughes)
15 March   (h)   W   4–1 (Callaghan, Dalglish,
                McDermott, Neal)
Semi-final v Borussia Moenchengladbach
(West Germany)
29 March   (a)   L   1–2 (Johnson)
12 April   (h)   W   3–0 (Kennedy, Dalglish, Case)
Final v FC Bruges (Belgium) at Wembley
10 May   W   1–0 (Dalglish)

1978–79 EUROPEAN CUP
1st round v Nottingham Forest (England)
13 Sept   (a)   L   0–2
27 Sept   (h)   D   0–0

1979–80 EUROPEAN CUP
1st round v Dynamo Tbilisi (USSR)
19 Sept   (h)   W   2–1 (Johnson, Case)
3 Oct   (a)   L   0–3

1980–81 EUROPEAN CUP
1st round v Oulun Palloseura (Finland)
17 Sept   (a)   D   1–1 (McDermott)
1 Oct   (h)   W   10–1 (Souness 3 [1 pen],
                McDermott 2, Dalglish,
                Lee, R Kennedy,
                Fairclough 2)

2nd round v Aberdeen (Scotland)
22 Oct   (a)   W   1–0 (McDermott)
5 Nov   (h)   W   4–0 (og, Neal, Dalglish,
                Hansen)
Quarter-final v CSKA Sofia (Bulgaria)
4 March   (h)   W   5–1 (Souness 3, Lee,
                McDermott)
18 March   (a)   W   1–0 (Johnson)
Semi-final v Bayern Munich (West Germany)
8 April   (h)   D   0–0
22 April   (a)   D   1–1 (R Kennedy)
Won on away goals
Final v Real Madrid (Spain) in Paris
27 May   W   1–0 (A Kennedy)

1981–82 EUROPEAN CUP
1st round v Oulun Palloseura (Finland)
16 Sept   (a)   W   1–0 (Dalglish)
30 Sept   (h)   W   7–0 (Dalglish, McDermott 2,
                R Kennedy, Johnson,
                Rush, Lawrenson)
2nd round v AZ 67 Alkmaar (Holland)
21 Oct   (a)   D   2–2 (Johnson, Lee)
4 Nov   (h)   W   3–2 (McDermott [pen],
                Rush, Hansen)
Quarter-final v CSKA Sofia (Bulgaria)
3 March   (h)   W   1–0 (Whelan)
17 March   (a)   L   0–2

1982–83 EUROPEAN CUP
1st round v Dundalk (Republic of Ireland)
14 Sept   (a)   W   4–1 (Whelan 2, Rush,
                Hodgson)
28 Sept   (h)   W   1–0 (Whelan)
2nd round v HJK Helsinki (Finland)
19 Oct   (a)   L   0–1
2 Nov   (h)   W   5–0 (Dalglish, Johnson,
                Neal, A Kennedy 2)
Quarter-final v Widzew Lodz (Poland)
2 March   (a)   L   0–2
16 March   (h)   W   3–2 (Neal [pen], Rush,
                Hodgson)

1983–84 EUROPEAN CUP
1st round v Odense BK (Denmark)
14 Sept   (a)   W   1–0 (Dalglish)
28 Sept   (h)   W   5–0 (Robinson 2, Dalglish 2,
                og)
2nd round v Athletic Bilbao (Spain)
19 Oct   (h)   D   0–0
2 Nov   (a)   W   1–0 (Rush)
Quarter-final v Benfica (Portugal)
7 March   (h)   W   1–0 (Rush)
21 March   (a)   W   4–1 (Whelan 2, Johnston,
                Rush)
Semi-final v Dinamo Bucharest (Romania)
11 April   (h)   W   1–0 (Lee)
25 April   (a)   W   2–1 (Rush 2)
Final v AS Roma (Italy) in Rome
30 May   W   1–1 (Neal)
Won 4–2 on penalties

1984–85 EUROPEAN CUP
1st round v Lech Poznan (Poland)
19 Sept   (a)   W   1–0 (Wark)
3 Oct   (h)   W   4–0 (Wark 3, Walsh)

(Liverpool continued)

2nd round v Benfica (Portugal)
24 Oct   (h) W 3–1 (Rush 3)
7 Nov   (a) L 0–1
Quarter-final v FK Austria
6 March (a) D 1–1 (Nicol)
20 March (h) W 4–1 (Walsh 2, Nicol, og)
Semi-final v Panathinaikos (Greece)
10 April   (a) W 4–0 (Wark, Rush 2, Beglin)
24 April   (a) W 1–0 (Lawrenson)
Final v Juventus (Italy) in Brussels
29 May   L 0–1

1991–92 UEFA CUP
1st round v Kuusysi Lahti (Finland)
18 Sept (h) W 6–1 (Saunders 4,
                          Houghton 2)
2 Oct   (a) L 0–1
2nd round v Auxerre (France)
23 Oct   (a) L 0–2
6 Nov   (h) W 3–0 (Molby [pen], Marsh,
                         Walters)
3rd round v Swarvoski Tirol (Austria)
27 Nov   (a) W 2–0 (Saunders 2)
11 Dec   (h) W 4–0 (Saunders 3, Venison)
Quarter-final v Genoa (Italy)
4 March (a) L 0–2
18 March (h) L 1–2 (Rush)

MANCHESTER CITY

1968–69 EUROPEAN CUP
1st round v Fenerbahce (Turkey)
18 Sept (h) D 0–0
2 Oct   (a) L 1–2 (Coleman)

1969–70 EUROPEAN CUP WINNERS' CUP
1st round v Athletic Bilbao (Spain)
17 Sept (a) D 3–3 (Young, Booth, og)
1 Oct   (h) W 3–0 (Oakes, Bell, Bowyer)
2nd round v Lierse (Belgium)
12 Nov   (a) W 3–0 (Lee 2, Bell)
26 Nov   (h) W 5–0 (Bell 2, Lee 2,
                         Summerbee)
Quarter-final v Academica Coimbra (Portugal)
4 March (a) D 0–0
18 March (h) W 1–0 (Towers)
Semi-final v Schalke 04 (West Germany)
1 April   (a) L 0–1
15 April   (h) W 5–1 (Young 2, Doyle, Lee,
                         Bell)
Final v Gornik Zabrze (Poland) in Vienna
29 April   W 2–1 (Young, Lee [pen])

1970–71 EUROPEAN CUP WINNERS' CUP
1st round v Linfield (Northern Ireland)
16 Sept (h) W 1–0 (Bell)
30 Sept (a) L 1–2 (Lee)
Won on away goals
2nd round v Honved (Hungary)
21 Oct   (a) W 1–0 (Lee)
4 Nov   (h) W 2–0 (Bell, Lee)
Quarter-final v Gornik Zabrze (Poland)
10 March (a) L 0–2
24 March (h) W 2–0 (Mellor, Doyle)

---

31 March (n) W 3–1 (Young, Booth, Lee)
in Copenhagen
Semi-final v Chelsea
14 April   (a) L 0–1
28 April   (a) L 0–1

1972–73 UEFA CUP
1st round v Valencia (Spain)
13 Sept (h) D 2–2 (Mellor, Marsh)
27 Sept (a) L 1–2 (Marsh)

1976–77 UEFA CUP
1st round v Juventus (Italy)
15 Sept (h) W 1–0 (Kidd)
29 Sept (a) L 0–2

1977–78 UEFA CUP
1st round v Widzew Lodz (Poland)
14 Sept (h) D 2–2 (Barnes, Channon)
28 Sept (a) D 0–0
Lost on away goals

1978–79 UEFA CUP
1st round v Twente Enschede (Holland)
13 Sept (a) D 1–1 (Watson)
27 Sept (h) W 3–2 (Kidd, Bell, og)
2nd round v Standard Liege (Belgium)
18 Oct   (h) W 4–0 (Hartford, Kidd 2
                       [1 pen], Palmer)
1 Nov   (a) L 0–2
3rd round v AC Milan (Italy)
23 Nov   (a) D 2–2 (Kidd, Power)
6 Dec   (h) W 3–0 (Booth, Hartford, Kidd)
Quarter-final v Borussia Moenchengladbach
(West Germany)
7 March (h) D 1–1 (Channon)
21 March (a) L 1–3 (Deyna)

MANCHESTER UNITED

1956–57 EUROPEAN CUP
Preliminary round v Anderlecht (Belgium)
12 Sept (a) W 2–0 (Viollet, T Taylor)
26 Sept (h) W 10–0 (Viollet 4, T Taylor 3,
                       Whelan 2, Berry)
1st round v Borussia Dortmund
(West Germany)
17 Oct   (h) W 3–2 (Viollet 2, Pegg)
21 Nov   (a) D 0–0
Quarter-final v Athletic Bilbao (Spain)
16 Jan   (a) L 3–5 (T Taylor, Viollet,
                       Whelan)
6 Feb   (h) W 3–0 (Viollet, T Taylor, Berry)
Semi-final v Real Madrid (Spain)
11 April   (a) L 1–3 (T Taylor)
25 April   (h) D 2–2 (T Taylor, Charlton)

1957–58 EUROPEAN CUP
Preliminary round v Shamrock Rovers
(Republic of Ireland)
25 Sept (a) W 6–0 (Whelan 2, T Taylor 2,
                       Berry, Pegg)
2 Oct   (h) W 3–2 (Viollet 2, Pegg)
1st round v Dukla Prague (Czechoslovakia)
20 Nov   (h) W 3–0 (Webster, T Taylor, Pegg)
4 Dec   (a) L 0–1

Quarter-final v Red Star Belgrade (Yugoslavia)
14 Jan   (h) W 2–1 (Charlton, Colman)
5 Feb   (a) D 3–3 (Viollet, Charlton 2)
Semi-final v AC Milan (Italy)
8 May   (h) W 2–1 (Viollet, E Taylor [pen])
14 May   (a) L 0–4

1963–64 EUROPEAN CUP WINNERS' CUP
1st round v Tilburg Willem II (Holland)
25 Sept (a) D 1–1 (Herd)
15 Oct   (h) W 6–1 (Setters, Law 3,
                      Charlton, Chisnall)
2nd round v Tottenham Hotspur
3 Dec   (a) L 0–2
10 Dec   (h) W 4–1 (Herd 2, Charlton 2)
Quarter-final v Sporting Lisbon (Portugal)
26 Feb   (h) W 4–1 (Law 3 [2 pens],
                      Charlton)
18 March (a) L 0–5

1964–65 FAIRS CUP
1st round v Djurgaarden (Sweden)
23 Sept (a) D 1–1 (Herd)
27 Oct   (h) W 6–1 (Law 3 [1 pen],
                      Charlton 2, Best)
2nd round v Borussia Dortmund
(West Germany)
11 Nov   (a) W 6–1 (Herd, Charlton 3, Best,
                      Law)
2 Dec   (h) W 4–0 (Charlton 2, Law,
                      Connelly)
3rd round v Everton
20 Jan   (h) D 1–1 (Connelly)
9 Feb   (a) W 2–1 (Connelly, Herd)
Quarter-final v Strasbourg (France)
12 May   (a) W 5–0 (Connelly, Herd, Law 2,
                      Charlton)
19 May   (h) D 0–0
Semi-final v Ferencvaros (Hungary)
31 May   (h) W 3–2 (Law [pen], Herd 2)
6 June   (a) L 0–1
16 June   (n) L 1–2 (Connelly)

1965–66 EUROPEAN CUP
Preliminary round v HJK Helsinki (Finland)
22 Sept (a) W 3–2 (Herd, Connelly, Law)
6 Oct   (h) W 6–0 (Connelly 3, Best 2,
                      Charlton)
1st round v Vorwaerts Berlin (East Germany)
17 Nov   (a) W 2–0 (Law, Connelly)
1 Dec   (h) W 3–1 (Herd 3)
Quarter-final v Benfica (Portugal)
2 Feb   (h) W 3–2 (Herd, Law, Foulkes)
9 March (a) W 5–1 (Best 2, Connelly,
                      Crerand, Charlton)
Semi-final v Partizan Belgrade (Yugoslavia)
13 April   (a) L 0–2
20 April   (h) W 1–0 (og)

1967–68 EUROPEAN CUP
1st round v Hibernians (Malta)
20 Sept (h) W 4–0 (Sadler 2, Law 2)
27 Sept (a) D 0–0
2nd round v Sarajevo (Yugoslavia)
15 Nov   (a) D 0–0
29 Nov   (h) W 2–1 (Aston, Best)

Quarter-final v Gornik Zabrze (Poland)
28 Feb   (h) W 2–0 (Kidd, og)
13 March (a) L 0–1
Semi-final v Real Madrid (Spain)
24 April (h) W 1–0 (Best)
15 May   (a) D 3–3 (Sadler, Kidd, Foulkes)
Final v Benfica (Portugal) at Wembley
29 May   W 4–1 after extra time
                    (Charlton 2, Best, Kidd)

1968–69 EUROPEAN CUP
1st round v Waterford (Republic of Ireland)
18 Sept   (a) W 3–1 (Law 3)
2 Oct   (h) W 7–1 (Stiles, Law 4, Burns,
                    Charlton)
2nd round v Anderlecht (Belgium)
13 Nov   (h) W 3–0 (Kidd, Law 2)
27 Nov   (a) L 1–3 (Sartori)
Quarter-final v Rapid Vienna (Austria)
26 Feb   (h) W 3–0 (Best 2, Morgan)
5 March   (a) D 0–0
Semi-final v AC Milan (Italy)
23 April (a) L 0–2
15 May   (h) W 1–0 (Charlton)

1976–77 UEFA CUP
1st round v Ajax (Holland)
15 Sept   (a) L 0–1
29 Sept   (h) W 2–0 (Macari, McIlroy)
2nd round v Juventus (Italy)
20 Oct   (h) W 1–0 (Hill)
3 Nov   (a) L 0–3

1977–78 EUROPEAN CUP WINNERS' CUP
1st round v St Etienne (France)
14 Sept   (a) D 1–1 (Hill)
5 Oct   (h) W 2–0 (Pearson, Coppell)
2nd round v Porto (Portugal)
19 Oct   (a) L 0–4
2 Nov   (h) W 5–2 (Coppell 2, og 2,
                    Nicholl)

1980–81 UEFA CUP
1st round v Widzew Lodz (Poland)
17 Sept   (h) D 1–1 (McIlroy)
1 Oct   (a) D 0–0
Lost on away goals

1982–83 UEFA CUP
1st round v Valencia (Spain)
15 Sept   (h) D 0–0
29 Sept   (a) L 1–2 (Robson)

1983–84 EUROPEAN CUP WINNERS' CUP
1st round v Dukla Prague (Czechoslovakia)
14 Sept   (h) D 1–1 (Wilkins)
27 Sept   (a) D 2–2 (Robson, Stapleton)
Won on away goals
2nd round v Spartak Varna (Bulgaria)
19 Oct   (a) W 2–1 (Robson, Graham)
2 Nov   (h) W 2–0 (Stapleton 2)
Quarter-final v Barcelona (Spain)
7 March   (a) L 0–2
21 March (h) W 3–0 (Robson 2, Stapleton)
Semi-final v Juventus (Italy)
11 April (h) D 1–1 (Davies)
24 April (a) L 1–2 (Whiteside)

1984–85 UEFA CUP
1st round v Raba Gyor (Hungary)
19 Sept   (h) W 3–0 (Robson, Muhren,
                    Hughes)
3 Oct   (a) D 2–2 (Brazil, Muhren)
2nd round v PSV Eindhoven (Holland)
24 Oct   (a) D 0–0
7 Nov   (h) W 1–0 (Strachan)
3rd round v Dundee United (Scotland)
28 Nov   (h) D 2–2 (Strachan, Robson)
12 Dec   (a) W 3–2 (Hughes, Muhren, og)
Quarter-final v Videoton (Hungary)
6 March   (h) W 1–0 (Stapleton)
20 March (a) L 0–1
Lost 5–4 on penalties

1990–91 EUROPEAN CUP WINNERS' CUP
1st round v Pecsi Munkas (Hungary)
19 Sept   (h) W 2–0 (Blackmore, Webb)
3 Oct   (a) W 1–0 (McClair)
2nd round v Wrexham
23 Oct   (h) W 3–0 (McClair, Bruce [pen],
                    Pallister)
7 Nov   (a) W 2–0 (Robins, Bruce)
Quarter-final v Montpellier (France)
6 March   (h) D 1–1 (McClair)
19 March (a) W 2–0 (Blackmore, Bruce [pen])
Semi-final v Legia Warsaw (Poland)
10 April (a) W 3–1 (McClair, Hughes, Bruce)
24 April (h) D 1–1 (Sharpe)
Final v Barcelona (Spain) in Rotterdam
15 May   W 2–0 (Hughes 2)

1991–92 EUROPEAN CUP WINNERS' CUP
1st round v Athinaikos (Greece)
23 Sept   (a) D 0–0
2 Oct   (h) W 2–0 *aet* (McClair, Hughes)
2nd round v Atletico Madrid (Spain)
23 Oct   (a) L 0–3
7 Nov   (h) D 1–1 (Hughes)

NOTTINGHAM FOREST

1961–62 FAIRS CUP
1st round v Valencia (Spain)
13 Sept   (a) L 0–2
4 Oct   (h) L 1–5 (Cobb)

1967–68 FAIRS CUP
1st round v Eintracht Frankfurt (W Germany)
20 Sept   (a) W 1–0 (Baker)
17 Oct   (h) W 4–0 (Baker 2, Chapman,
                    Lyons)
2nd round v Zurich (Switzerland)
31 Oct   (h) W 2–1 (Newton, Moore [pen])
14 Nov   (a) L 0–1
Lost on away goals

1978–79 EUROPEAN CUP
1st round v Liverpool
13 Sept   (h) W 2–0 (Birtles, Barrett)
27 Sept   (a) D 0–0
2nd round v AEK Athens (Greece)
18 Oct   (a) W 2–1 (McGovern, Birtles)
1 Nov   (h) W 5–1 (Needham, Woodcock,
                    Anderson, Birtles 2)

Quarter-final v Grasshoppers (Switzerland)
7 March   (h) W 4–1 (Birtles, Robertson
                    [pen], Gemmill, Lloyd)
21 March (a) D 1–1 (O'Neill)
Semi-final v Cologne (West Germany)
11 April (h) D 3–3 (Birtles, Bowyer,
                    Robertson)
25 April (a) W 1–0 (Bowyer)
Final v Malmo (Sweden) in Munich
30 May   W 1–0 (Francis)

1979–80 SUPER CUP
Final v Barcelona (Spain)
30 June   (h) W 1–0 (George)
5 Feb   (a) D 1–1 (Burns)

1979–80 EUROPEAN CUP
1st round v Oster Vaxjo (Sweden)
19 Sept   (h) W 2–0 (Bowyer, og)
3 Oct   (a) D 1–1 (Woodcock)
2nd round v Arges Pitesti (Romania)
24 Oct   (h) W 2–0 (Woodcock, Birtles)
7 Nov   (a) W 2–1 (Bowyer, Birtles)
Quarter-final v Dynamo Berlin (East Germany)
5 March   (h) L 0–1
19 March (a) W 3–1 (Francis 2, Robertson
                    [pen])
Semi-final v Ajax (Holland)
9 April   (h) W 2–0 (Francis, Robertson
                    [pen])
23 April (a) L 0–1
Final v SV Hamburg (West Germany) in Madrid
28 May   W 1–0 (Robertson)

1980–81 SUPER CUP
Final v Valencia (Spain)
25 Nov   (h) W 2–1 (Bowyer 2)
17 Dec   (a) L 1–1

1980–81 EUROPEAN CUP
1st round v CSKA Sofia (Bulgaria)
17 Sept   (a) L 0–1
1 Oct   (h) L 0–1

1983–84 UEFA CUP
1st round v Vorwaerts (East Germany)
14 Sept   (h) W 2–0 (Wallace, Hodge)
28 Sept   (a) W 1–0 (Bowyer)
2nd round v PSV Eindhoven (Holland)
19 Oct   (a) W 2–1 (Davenport, Walsh
                    [pen])
2 Nov   (h) W 1–0 (Davenport)
3rd round v Celtic (Scotland)
23 Nov   (h) D 0–0
7 Dec   (a) W 2–1 (Hodge, Walsh)
Quarter-final v Sturm Graz (Austria)
7 March   (h) W 1–0 (Hart)
21 March (a) D 1–1 (Walsh [pen])
Semi-final v Anderlecht (Belgium)
11 April (h) W 2–0 (Hodge 2)
25 April (a) L 0–3

1984–85 UEFA CUP
1st round v FC Bruges (Belgium)
19 Sept   (h) D 0–0
3 Oct   (a) L 0–1

QUEEN'S PARK RANGERS

1976–77 UEFA CUP
1st round v Brann Bergen (Norway)
15 Sept   (h) W 4–0 (Bowles 3, Masson)
29 Sept   (a) W 7–0 (Bowles 3, Givens 2,
                                  Thomas, Webb)
2nd round v Slovan Bratislava (Czechoslovakia)
20 Oct   (a) D 3–3 (Bowles 2, Givens)
3 Nov   (h) W 5–2 (Givens 3, Bowles,
                                  Clement)
3rd round v FC Cologne (West Germany)
24 Nov   (h) W 3–0 (Givens, Webb, Bowles)
7 Dec   (a) L 1–4 (Masson)
Won on away goals
Quarter-final v AEK Athens (Greece)
2 March   (h) W 3–0 (Francis 2 [pens],
                                  Bowles)
16 March   (a) L 0–3
Lost 6–7 on penalties

1984–85 UEFA CUP
1st round v KR Reykjavik (Iceland)
18 Sept   (a) W 3–0 (Stainrod 2, Bannister)
2 Oct   (h) W 4–0 (Bannister 3, Charles)
2nd round v Partizan Belgrade (Yugoslavia)
24 Oct   (h) W 6–2 (Gregory, Fereday,
                                  Stainrod, Neill,
                                  Bannister 2)
7 Nov   (a) L 0–4
Lost on away goals

SHEFFIELD WEDNESDAY

1961–62 FAIRS CUP
1st round v Lyon (France)
12 Sept   (a) L 2–4 (Ellis, Young)
4 Oct   (h) W 5–2 (Fantham 2, Griffin,
                                  McAnearney [pen],
                                  Dobson)
2nd round v AS Roma (Italy)
29 Nov   (h) W 4–0 (Fantham, Young 3)
13 Dec   (a) L 0–1
Quarter-final v Barcelona (Spain)
28 Feb   (h) W 3–2 (Fantham 2, Finney)
28 March   (a) L 0–2

1963–64 FAIRS CUP
1st round v DOS Utrecht (Holland)
25 Sept   (a) W 4–1 (Holliday, Layne, Quinn,
                                  og)
15 Oct   (h) W 4–1 (Layne 3 [1 pen],
                                  Dobson)
2nd round v FC Cologne (West Germany)
6 Nov   (a) L 2–3 (Pearson 2)
27 Nov   (h) L 1–2 (Layne)

SOUTHAMPTON

1969–70 FAIRS CUP
1st round v Rosenborg (Norway)
17 Sept   (a) L 0–1
1 Oct   (h) W 2–0 (Davies, Paine)

2nd round v Vitoria Guimaraes (Portugal)
4 Nov   (a) D 3–3 (Channon, Davies,
                                  Paine)
12 Nov   (h) W 5–1 (Gabriel, Davies 2
                                  [1 pen], Channon, og)
3rd round v Newcastle United
17 Dec   (a) D 0–0
13 Jan   (h) D 1–1 (Channon)
Lost on away goals

1971–72 UEFA CUP
1st round v Athletic Bilbao (Spain)
15 Sept   (h) W 2–1 (Jenkins, Channon
                                  [pen])
29 Sept   (a) L 0–2

1976–77 EUROPEAN CUP WINNERS' CUP
1st round v Marseille (France)
15 Sept   (h) W 4–0 (Waldron, Channon 2
                                  [1 pen], Osgood)
29 Sept   (a) L 1–2 (Peach)
2nd round v Carrick Rangers
(Northern Ireland)
20 Oct   (a) W 5–2 (Channon 2, Stokes,
                                  McCalliog, Osgood)
3 Nov   (h) W 4–1 (Williams, Hayes 2,
                                  Stokes)
Quarter-final v Anderlecht (Belgium)
2 March   (a) L 0–2
3 Nov   (h) W 2–1 (Peach [pen],
                                  MacDougall)

1981–82 UEFA CUP
1st round v Limerick (Republic of Ireland)
16 Sept   (a) W 3–0 (Moran 2, Armstrong)
29 Sept   (h) D 1–1 (Keegan)
2nd round v Sporting Lisbon (Portugal)
21 Oct   (a) L 2–4 (Keegan [pen],
                                  Channon)
4 Nov   (a) D 0–0

1982–83 UEFA CUP
1st round v Norrköping (Sweden)
15 Sept   (h) D 2–2 (Williams, Wright)
29 Sept   (a) D 0–0
Lost on away goals

1984–85 UEFA CUP
1st round v Hamburg (West Germany)
19 Sept   (h) D 0–0
3 Oct   (a) L 0–2

TOTTENHAM HOTSPUR

1961–62 EUROPEAN CUP
Preliminary round v Gornik Zabrze (Poland)
13 Sept   (a) L 2–4 (Jones, Dyson)
20 Sept   (h) W 8–1 (Blanchflower [pen],
                                  Jones 3, Smith 2,
                                  Dyson, White)
1st round v Feyenoord (Holland)
1 Nov   (a) W 3–1 (Dyson, Saul 2)
15 Nov   (h) D 1–1 (Dyson)
Quarter-final v Dukla Prague (Czechoslovakia)
14 Feb   (a) L 0–1
26 Feb   (h) W 4–1 (Smith 2, Mackay 2)

Semi-final v Benfica (Portugal)
21 March   (a) L 1–3 (Smith)
5 April   (h) W 2–1 (Smith, Blanchflower
                                  [pen])

1962–63 EUROPEAN CUP WINNERS' CUP
1st round bye
2nd round v Rangers (Scotland)
31 Oct   (h) W 5–2 (White, Greaves, Allen,
                                  Norman, og)
11 Dec   (a) W 3–2 (Greaves, Smith 2)
Quarter-final v Slovan Bratislava
(Czechoslovakia)
5 March   (a) L 0–2
14 March   (h) W 6–0 (Mackay, Smith,
                                  Greaves 2, Jones,
                                  White)
Semi-final v OFK Belgrade (Yugoslavia)
24 April   (a) W 2–1 (White, Dyson)
1 May   (h) W 3–1 (Mackay, Jones, Smith)
Final v Atletico Madrid (Spain) in Rotterdam
15 May   W 5–1 (Greaves 2, White,
                                  Dyson 2)

1963–64 EUROPEAN CUP WINNERS' CUP
1st round bye
2nd round v Manchester United
3 Dec   (h) W 2–0 (Mackay, Dyson)
10 Dec   (a) L 1–4 (Greaves)

1967–68 EUROPEAN CUP WINNERS' CUP
1st round v Hajduk Split (Yugoslavia)
20 Sept   (a) W 2–0 (Robertson, Greaves)
27 Sept   (h) W 4–3 (Robertson 2, Gilzean,
                                  Venables)
2nd round v Lyon (France)
29 Nov   (a) L 0–1
13 Dec   (h) W 4–3 (Greaves 2 [1 pen],
                                  Jones, Gilzean)
Lost on away goals

1971–72 UEFA CUP
1st round v Keflavik (Iceland)
14 Sept   (a) W 6–1 (Gilzean 3, Coates,
                                  Mullery 2)
28 Sept   (h) W 9–1 (Chivers 3, Gilzean 2,
                                  Perryman, Coates,
                                  Knowles, Holder)
2nd round v Nantes (France)
20 Oct   (a) D 0–0
2 Nov   (h) W 1–0 (Peters)
3rd round v Rapid Bucharest (Romania)
8 Dec   (h) W 3–0 (Peters, Chivers 2)
15 Dec   (a) W 2–0 (Pearce, Chivers)
Quarter-final v UT Arad (Romania)
7 March   (a) W 2–0 (Morgan, England)
21 March   (h) D 1–1 (Gilzean)
Semi-final v AC Milan (Italy)
5 April   (h) W 2–1 (Perryman 2)
19 April   (a) D 1–1 (Mullery)
Final v Wolverhampton Wanderers
3 May   (a) W 2–1 (Chivers 2)
17 May   (h) D 1–1 (Mullery)

1972–73 UEFA CUP
1st round v Lyn Oslo (Norway)
13 Sept　(a)　W　6–3　(Peters, Pratt, Gilzean 2, Chivers 2)
27 Sept　(h)　W　6–0　(Chivers 3, Pearce, Coates 2)
2nd round v Olympiakos Piraeus (Greece)
25 Oct　(h)　W　4–0　(Pearce 2, Chivers, Coates)
　8 Nov　(a)　L　0–1
3rd round v Red Star Belgrade (Yugoslavia)
29 Nov　(h)　W　2–0　(Chivers, Gilzean)
13 Dec　(a)　L　0–1
Quarter-final v Vitoria Setubal (Portugal)
　7 March　(h)　W　1–0　(Evans)
21 March　(a)　L　1–2　(Chivers)
Won on away goals
Semi-final v Liverpool
10 April　(a)　L　0–1
25 April　(h)　W　2–1　(Peters 2)
Lost on away goals

1973–74 UEFA CUP
1st round v Grasshoppers (Switzerland)
19 Sept　(a)　W　5–1　(Chivers 2, Evans, Gilzean 2)
　3 Oct　(h)　W　4–1　(og, Peters 2, England)
2nd round v Aberdeen (Scotland)
24 Oct　(a)　D　1–1　(Coates)
　7 Nov　(h)　W　4–1　(Peters, Neighbour, McGrath 2)
3rd round v Dynamo Tbilisi (USSR)
28 Nov　(a)　D　1–1　(Coates)
12 Dec　(h)　W　5–1　(McGrath, Chivers 2, Peters 2)
Quarter-final v FC Cologne (West Germany)
　6 March　(a)　W　2–1　(McGrath, Peters)
20 March　(h)　W　3–0　(Chivers, Coates, Peters)
Semi-final v Lokomotiv Leipzig (East Germany)
10 April　(a)　W　2–1　(Peters, McGrath)
24 April　(h)　W　2–0　(McGrath, Chivers)

Final v Feyenoord (Holland)
21 May　(h)　D　2–2　(England, og)
29 May　(a)　L　0–2

1981–82 EUROPEAN CUP WINNERS' CUP
1st round v Ajax (Holland)
16 Sept　(a)　W　3–1　(Falco 2, Villa)
29 Sept　(h)　W　3–0　(Galvin, Falco, Ardiles)
2nd round v Dundalk (Republic of Ireland)
21 Oct　(a)　D　1–1　(Crooks)
　4 Nov　(h)　W　1–0　(Crooks)
Quarter-final v Eintracht Frankfurt (West Germany)
　3 March　(h)　W　2–0　(Miller, Hazard)
17 March　(a)　L　1–2　(Hoddle)
Semi-final v Barcelona (Spain)
　7 April　(h)　D　1–1　(Roberts)
21 April　(a)　L　0–1

1982–83 EUROPEAN CUP WINNERS' CUP
1st round v Coleraine (Northern Ireland)
15 Sept　(a)　W　3–0　(Crooks 2, Archibald)
28 Sept　(h)　W　4–0　(Crooks, Mabbutt, Brooke, Gibson)
2nd round v Bayern Munich (West Germany)
20 Oct　(h)　D　1–1　(Archibald)
　3 Nov　(a)　L　1–4　(Hughton)

1983–84 UEFA CUP
1st round v Drogheda (Republic of Ireland)
14 Sept　(a)　W　6–0　(Falco 2, Crooks, Galvin, Mabbutt 2)
28 Sept　(h)　W　8–0　(Falco 2, Roberts 2, Brazil 2, Archibald, Hughton)
2nd round v Feyenoord (Holland)
19 Oct　(h)　W　4–2　(Archibald 2, Galvin 2)
　2 Nov　(a)　W　2–0　(Hughton, Galvin)
3rd round v Bayern Munich (West Germany)
23 Nov　(a)　L　0–1
　7 Dec　(h)　W　2–0　(Archibald, Falco)
Quarter-final v Austria Vienna (Austria)
　7 March　(h)　W　2–0　(Archibald, Brazil)
21 March　(a)　D　2–2　(Brazil, Ardiles)

Semi-final v Hajduk Split (Yugoslavia)
11 April　(a)　L　1–2　(Falco)
25 April　(h)　W　1–0　(Hazard)
Won on away goals
Final v Anderlecht (Belgium)
　9 May　(a)　D　1–1　(Miller)
23 May　(h)　D　1–1　(Roberts)
Won 4–3 on penalties

1984–85 UEFA CUP
1st round v Sporting Braga (Portugal)
19 Sept　(a)　W　3–0　(Falco 2, Galvin)
　3 Oct　(h)　W　6–0　(Stevens, Hughton, Crooks 3)
2nd round v FC Bruges (Belgium)
24 Oct　(a)　L　1–2　(Allen)
　7 Nov　(h)　W　3–0　(Hazard, Allen, Roberts)
3rd round v Bohemians Prague (Czechoslovakia)
28 Nov　(h)　W　2–0　(Stevens, og)
12 Dec　(a)　D　1–1　(Falco)
Quarter-final v Real Madrid (Spain)
　6 March　(h)　L　0–1
20 March　(a)　D　0–0

1991–92 EUROPEAN CUP WINNERS' CUP
Preliminary round v Sparkasse Stockerau (Austria)
21 Aug　(a)　W　1–0　(Durie)
　4 Sept　(h)　W　1–0　(Mabbutt)
1st round v Hajduk Split (Yugoslavia)
17 Sept　(a)　L　0–1 in Luz, Austria
　2 Oct　(h)　W　2–0　(Durie, Tuttle)
2nd round v Porto (Portugal)
23 Oct　(h)　W　3–1　(Lineker 2, Durie)
　7 Nov　(a)　D　0–0
Quarter-final v Feyenoord (Holland)
　4 March　(a)　L　0–1
18 March　(h)　D　0–0

Blackburn Rovers, Crystal Palace, Middlesbrough, Norwich City, Oldham Athletic, Sheffield United and Wimbledon have never appeared in European competitions.

FOOTBALL AND TELEVISION

by Martin Tyler

*I*n British Broadcasting there has never been a pact like the new contract between the FA Premier League and Sky Sports. It is a partnership designed very much for the future of football.

Satellite television is tailored for the specialist, whether you are a movie buff, an avid follower of world news or a football fanatic. The controllers of the terrestrial channels have to strike a balance between all the various subjects at their disposal. Sport has to fight for its share of the available air time. On Sky Sports it is there every day of the week, every week of the year. You can be sure of finding entertainment close to your heart.

Live football from the Premier League will be the prominent feature, broadcast on Sundays, and on many Mondays, from August to May. The choice of fixtures will be influenced by the requirements of the clubs and their followers. There will be live midweek action as well and an opportunity, on Sunday mornings, to catch up with the highlights of all the Saturday games.

Each club in the Premier League will have a strong television identity. It is a big challenge for our producers, directors, presenters, reporters and commentators, but one that is being met with enormous energy by a young channel.

The Premier League is of course even more fledgling. Its creation caused the biggest upheaval in the structure of the English game since clubs began to compete for points back in 1888.

Now the top twenty-two clubs have the responsibility of taking football into the twenty-first century. Financial stability is assured. It is a time for the industry to be inspirational. The rank and file spectator must be a high priority. Corporate hospitality has an accepted place in our grounds in the executive boxes, but television would soon lose interest if the rattle of knives and forks replaced the roar of the crowd. Admission prices must not outstrip the cash in the average pocket and television will help.

Collective marketing under the Premier League logo should also bring quality to offshoots of the industry. I returned from the European Championship in Sweden full of admiration for UEFA's innovation of names on the players' shirts and numbers front and back. That kind of spectator-friendly approach will, I'm sure, be high on the agenda of Premier League executives. It is a chance for the clubs to restrict their conflicts to where it matters, out on the pitch, and to combine their efforts in many other areas.

I also hope that the profits may be invested in two key areas which are so often neglected. A career in football administration should be properly rewarded, an incentive for bright minds to be attracted to the profession. Club secretaries slave all year round, often with very little back-up.

Even more important, the status of the coaches in charge of youth teams should be elevated. In the increasingly competitive world of European football, we must pep up this production line of talent. Those in charge in these formative years are very important figures and should be recognised as such.

Football and television have one similar aim – the pursuit of excellence. Both the Premier League and Sky Sports are approaching this special season with that target very much in mind.

I do hope you will join us!